Cinematic Ethics

How do movies evoke and express ethical ideas? What role does our emotional involvement play in this process? What makes the aesthetic power of cinema ethically significant? Can movies 'do ethics'?

Cinematic Ethics: Exploring Ethical Experience through Film addresses these questions by examining the idea of cinema as a medium of ethical experience with the power to provoke emotional engagement and philosophical thinking.

In a clear and engaging manner, Robert Sinnerbrink examines the key philosophical approaches to ethics in contemporary film theory and philosophy using detailed case studies of cinematic ethics across different genres, styles, and filmic traditions.

Written in a lucid and lively style that will engage both specialist and non-specialist readers, this book is ideal for use in the academic study of philosophy and film. Key features include annotated suggestions for further reading at the end of each chapter and a filmography of movies useful for teaching and researching cinematic ethics.

Robert Sinnerbrink is ARC Future Fellow and Senior Lecturer in Philosophy at Macquarie University, Australia.

Cinematic Ethics

Exploring Ethical Experience through Film

Robert Sinnerbrink

Routledge
Taylor & Francis Group

LONDON AND NEW YORK

First published 2016
by Routledge
2 Park Square, Milton Park, Abingdon, Oxon OX14 4RN

and by Routledge
711 Third Avenue, New York, NY 10017

Routledge is an imprint of the Taylor & Francis Group, an informa business

British Library Cataloguing in Publication Data
A catalogue record for this book is available from the British Library

Library of Congress Cataloging in Publication Data
Sinnerbrink, Robert.
Cinematic ethics : exploring ethical experience through film / Robert Sinnerbrink.
pages cm
Includes bibliographical references and index.
1. Motion pictures--Moral and ethical aspects. 2. Motion pictures--Philosophy. I. Title.
PN1995.5.S595 2016
791.4301--dc23
2015024903

ISBN: 978-1-138-82615-1 (hbk)
ISBN: 978-1-138-82616-8 (pbk)
ISBN: 978-1-315-66012-7 (ebk)

Typeset in Times New Roman
by Taylor & Francis Books
Printed and bound in Great Britain by
Ashford Colour Press Ltd, Gosport, Hampshire

To Louise, Eva, and Mimi – my favourite film-philosophers.

Contents

Figures

Preface

The idea for this book emerged over a number of years during which I became fascinated by the question of film as philosophy. In what ways can we understand cinema not only as an object of theoretical analysis but as a medium capable of contributing to philosophical understanding? As I tried to explain what my research was about to puzzled colleagues and curious friends, I frequently found myself having recourse to citing films that dealt with ethical or moral issues. Trying to persuade sceptical interlocutors that film could be philosophical was more successful when discussing a film dealing with existential crises, moral dilemmas, or political problems than when exploring questions of visual representation or the ontology of the image. The same was true for students in my 'Film and Philosophy' course, many of whom were more inspired by moral issues and ethico-political problems than by epistemological puzzles or metaphysical questions, even though the most philosophical films seemed to demand engagement with all of these problems in order to be appreciated. Moreover, the seeming neglect of ethics and politics in much recent philosophy of film, compared with their centrality in the days of so-called 'Grand Theory', struck me as regrettable and regressive: it signalled an unfortunate narrowing in our conception of (film) philosophy, and of the broader cultural and ethical significance of cinematic art. And this suggested the need for further reflection in order to address the cultural problem of how to reconnect philosophy (and cinema) with some of the broader cultural conversations of our times. Although 'Grand Theory' has been displaced by a number of theoretical developments – historicism, cultural materialism, cognitivism, and philosophy of film – ethical and political questions remain central to our engagement with cinema, and thus deserve to be explored more explicitly in the new philosophical film theories emerging over the last two decades.

Interestingly, this interest in ethics was apparent already in some of the major thinkers who had devoted themselves to cinema; from Stanley Cavell and Gilles Deleuze to Noël Carroll and Jacques Rancière, philosophers of film inevitably, it seems, confront the question of ethics and film as part of their investigation of the relationship between film and philosophy. Given the growing interest in 'ethics' across the humanities, the time thus seemed ripe to extend the 'film as philosophy' thesis to encompass the idea of film *as* ethics. Hence my proposal to explore what I call 'cinematic ethics': the idea of cinema as a medium of ethical experience with the power to provoke emotional understanding and philosophical thinking. This idea picks up on the more general 'ethical turn' evident within film theory, but emphasizes, perhaps more than other perspectives, cinema's aesthetic capacity to elicit experientially rich forms of affective, emotional, and critical engagement conducive to deeper ethical understanding and cultural-political reflection – but also, in the most challenging cases, to be exercises in ethical (and political) provocation with a transformative potential.

The idea that cinema can be ethical (rather than simply manipulative) is hardly new. Indeed, it was already clear to many theorists that cinema could provide detailed 'thought experiments' relevant to philosophical-moral theories of various stripes (see Wartenberg 2007). What I wanted to understand, however, was the idea that cinema also has the capacity to express and evoke ethical experience using cinematic means, an experience that invites, and can be complemented by, philosophical reflection. In this way, cinema and philosophy can meet as equal partners in an ongoing cultural conversation, one that promises to reconnect film, the great popular artform of our age, with philosophy, a venerable but marginalized intellectual practice needing to re-establish its relationship with the everyday. For there is as much, and sometimes more, 'philosophy' happening in certain movies, it seemed to me, than in many academic conferences and intellectual debates, provided one takes a broad enough view of philosophy and its cultural contribution to the search for meaning and value in everyday life. Finally, it was my experience with contemporary movies that inspired my engagement with cinematic ethics, a renewed interest in ethical and political questions abundantly evident in the exciting films appearing globally every year across different cultures and cinematic traditions.

Overview of this book

To offer the reader a brief overview, this book explores the relationship between cinema and ethics and the idea that cinema can 'do ethics'. To this end, *Cinematic Ethics* is divided into three parts, each dealing with an important aspect of the relationship between ethics and film. In Part I, 'Cinema and/as ethics', I explore some of the reasons for the recent surge of interest in the topic (and earlier neglect of it), suggesting why this is an important development for the future of film-philosophy. I then present the idea of cinema as a medium of ethical experience as a way of exploring how film might 'do ethics' rather than just serving to illustrate ethical ideas or moral theories. We can think of this as an extension of the 'film as philosophy' idea, namely, the idea of cinema as a way of evoking and expressing ethical experience or what I call 'cinematic ethics'.

In Part II, 'Philosophical approaches to cinematic ethics', I examine some of the key philosophical approaches to ethics in contemporary film theory, from Cavell's account of moral perfectionism in movies to Deleuze's existential/ life-philosophy claims that cinema can provide 'reasons to believe in this world' and his exploration of the ethico-political potential of a 'minor cinema'. This is followed by an examination of phenomenological approaches to cinematic ethics, which emphasize the importance of emotional engagement, embodied experience, and moral sympathy as ways in which cinema can engage spectators ethically. I then link this to recent cognitivist approaches to cinematic experience, which also emphasize emotional engagement, moral allegiance, and reflective questioning. These theoretical approaches enable us to explore philosophically how narrative cinema can engage us emotionally and aesthetically in ways that not only enrich but also challenge our ethical understanding. I discuss and draw on these approaches in a dialectical manner to construct a more pluralist and comprehensive perspective on cinematic ethics.

Part III elaborates these ideas by turning to detailed case studies of cinematic ethics across different genres, styles, and filmic traditions. I commence in Chapter 5 with the 'moral melodrama', offering a critical discussion of Cavell's influential reading of the maternal melodrama *Stella Dallas*, arguing that the film's ethical dimension is concerned with the question of 'class' as much as gender or moral perfectionism. In Chapter 6 I continue the exploration of melodrama but in conjunction with an examination of social realism, analysing two generically different but thematically related films, Alejandro Iñárritu's *Biutiful* (an existential-moral melodrama) and the Dardenne Brothers' *The Promise* (a social realist drama with melodramatic and documentary elements). Both films deal with domestic dramas, social exploitation, and moral responsibility, showing the crossover between these distinctive cinematic approaches and the manner in which they can be understood as engaging in cinematic ethics. Both films, however, do so in different ways, generically and aesthetically, putting the viewer through different kinds of ethical experience in relation to complex moral problems and social-political situations. The final chapter is devoted to non-fiction film, where I take as my case study the confronting documentary, *The Act of Killing* (Oppenheimer 2012). This film deals with the perpetrators of mass killings in Indonesia during the 1960s and the ongoing social and cultural effects of this history of violence. Remarkably, the perpetrators are invited to re-enact their crimes, using a variety of cinematic genres, in an extraordinary cinematic experiment that reveals the imaginary conditions of the perpetrators' acts of killing. Such a film not only explores the traumatic effects of political violence, it also intervenes in the formation and transformation of historical memory and social identity as mediated and memorialized through cinema.

I conclude with a recapitulation of the basic argument shaping this book and some reflections on the idea of philosophical cinephilia as a form of ethical experience. In sum, *Cinematic Ethics* aims to provide an overview of current theoretical debates on the ethical significance of film, and to contribute to these debates by exploring the idea of cinema as a medium of ethical experience. It also seeks to advance our contemporary cultural conversation over the ethical value of film, showing how we might rethink the idea of 'film as philosophy' from the perspective of cinematic ethics. My hope is that the idea of cinematic ethics will encourage further engagement with cinema's ethical potential, and contribute to the acknowledgment of film as a valuable partner in the philosophical investigation of ethics and politics. In this way, the book attempts to do justice to the ethical significance of philosophically valuable films, both past and present, opening up an experientially rich, aesthetically-mediated dialogue with them that promises to broaden how we understand ethical inquiry. It may even, in its own modest way, add another voice to the ongoing philosophical conversation concerning some of the pressing ethical-political challenges our world faces today.

***

A book like this, which has taken years to gestate, involves the encouragement of many people, only some of whom I can acknowledge here. I would like to thank the following, in particular, for their conversations, questions, advice, arguments, and encouragement: Mathew Abbott, Paul Alberts-Dezeeuw, Mieke Bal, Shai Biderman, Lucy Bolton, Costica Bradatan, William Brown, Diego Bubbio, Noël Carroll, John Caruana, Mark Cauchi, Danielle Celermajer, Jinhee Choi, Alan Cholodenko, Damian Cox, Louise D'Arcens, Stefan Deines, Marc De Leeuw, Ludo De Roo, Jean-Philippe Deranty, John Di Stefano, Simone

Drichel, Andrew Dunstall, Lisabeth During, Chris Falzon, Joanne Faulkner, Gregory Flaxman, Hamish Ford, Bernd Herzogenrath, Fincina Hopgood, Tanya Horeck, Berenike Jung, Tina Kendall, Jeanette Kennett, Andrew Klevan, Angelos Koutsourakis, Marguerite LaCaze, Tarja Laine, David Macarthur, Nayla Majestya, Adrian Martin, Philip Martin, David Martin-Jones, Kathryn Millard, Robert B. Pippin, Patricia Pisters, Murray Pomerance, Orna Raviv, Isabel Rocamora, Richard Rushton, Luke Russell, Libby Saxton, Philipp Schmerheim, Martin Seel, Berndt Sellheim, Matthew Sharpe, Daniel Shaw, Murray Smith, Richard Smith, David Sorfa, Jane Stadler, Omid Tofighian, Lisa Trahair, Camil Ungureanu, Dimitris Vardoulakis, Julia Vassileva, Tom Wartenberg, Catherine Wheatley, Jess Whyte, and Daniel Yacavone.

I am also grateful to my anonymous reviewers for their excellent reports on my draft manuscript; their incisive questions, critical suggestions, and constructive criticisms motivated me to revise and refine the structure and argument of the text as much as possible.

Some of the material contained in this book was previously published in a different form. A portion of Chapter 1 appeared in Robert Sinnerbrink, 'Angelopolous' Gaze: Modernism, History, Cinematic Ethics', Angelos Koutsourakis and Mark Steven (eds), *The Cinema of Theo Angelopolous* (Edinburgh: Edinburgh University Press, 2015), 80–96. Portions of Chapter 6 appeared in Robert Sinnerbrink, 'Post-Secular Ethics: The Case of Iñárritu's *Biutiful*', Costica Bradatan and Camil Ungureanu (eds), *Religion in Contemporary European Cinema: The Postsecular Constellation* (Abingdon and New York: Routledge, 2014), 166–185. Portions of Chapter 7 were published in 'Gangster Film: Cinematic Ethics in *The Act of Killing*', John Di Stefano and Mikhaela Rodwell (eds), *The Image in Question/The Sceptical Image* [Exhibition Program] (Rozelle: Sydney College of The Arts, 2014), 12–20.

I am grateful to the Australian Research Council (ARC) for their support of the research towards this book, which was funded by an ARC Future Fellowship grant on the topic of cinematic ethics. My editors at Routledge, Emma Joyes, Rebecca Shillabeer, and Lucy Vallance, are owed warm thanks for their enthusiasm and professionalism. My colleagues in the Department of Philosophy at Macquarie University, including my undergraduate and postgraduate students, have been a great source of ideas, inspiration, and encouragement. I am grateful for the stimulating and supportive environment that they have provided for me, and look forward to continuing this wonderfully collegial form of philosophical friendship.

I am especially grateful to my wife Louise, whose loving encouragement, brilliant conversations, and practical can-do attitude did more to help me than I could have imagined. All of the people mentioned here have contributed, in different ways, to the intellectual (and ethical) formation of this book. I hope that *Cinematic Ethics* can do some justice to all of these remarkable individuals, and to the extraordinary films that are responsible for its inception.

Part I

CINEMA AND/AS ETHICS

1 Cinematic ethics

Film as a medium of ethical experience

> Because cinema has its centre in the gesture and not in the image, it belongs essentially to the realm of ethics and politics (and not simply to that of aesthetics).
>
> Giorgio Agamben (1992/2000, 55)

Giorgio Agamben, a philosopher only occasionally mentioned in contemporary film-philosophy, offers here an acute observation about cinema's ethical (and political) significance. Although at one level film clearly belongs to aesthetics or the philosophy of art, the more challenging thesis he proposes is that it belongs essentially to the realms of ethics and politics, a thesis explored by many thinkers and filmmakers over the last century or so. For cinema, as Agamben suggests, is not simply an audio-visual medium centred on the capture, composition, and projection of moving images; it is a medium concerned with exploring what he calls the 'gesture': that expressive, non-linguistic, corporeal aspect of human action which remains irreducible to our intentional aims, instrumental goals, or attempts at defining through language. If cinema is concerned with gestures, in all their performative ambiguity and disruption of meaning, as well as with images, actions, emotions, and experience, then aesthetics must join forces with ethics (and politics) in order for us to understand the medium's philosophical as well as cultural-historical significance. Taking a step beyond the aesthetics of cinema, in short, we can explore the idea of cinema as ethics (and politics): its potential to evoke ethical experience and invite philosophical reflection. That is the purpose and aim of this book, and the contribution I hope it can make to contemporary film theory.

Two perspectives on cinema and ethics

In Giuseppe Tornatore's nostalgic memory picture *Cinema Paradiso* (1988), Salvatore, the film's filmmaker protagonist, recalls the excitement he experienced discovering the movies as a child. He becomes fascinated, even obsessed with them, helping the village projectionist Alfredo [Philippe Noiret] work his projector at the local cinema. The young Salvatore [Salvatore Cascio] witnesses the village priest's ham-fisted acts of censorship, watching with glee as Father

Adelfio [Leopoldo Trieste] scrutinizes each new film in private, ringing a bell when he finds 'immoral' love scenes that Alfredo will later have to cut. Salvatore is transported by these images, especially the love scenes, and remains fascinated by the mysterious mechanics and magic of the cinema. He develops a lifelong passion for film, learning to use a 16mm camera, and develops a friendship with Alfredo that leads to his leaving the village to pursue a career as a filmmaker. In the final scene, the now adult Salvatore [Jacques Perrin], a successful movie director who has returned to the village for Alfredo's funeral, watches a montage of excised love scenes and screen kisses, a parting gift from the old projectionist, and is transported by this nostalgic vision. In addition to nostalgia, the viewer has the pleasure of a communal cinephilia, acknowledging the power of cinema as a shared form of cultural experience. This nostalgic recollection of Salvatore's life story suggests how a communal experience of cinema – shared by the village filmgoers, a raucous, demonstrative audience crossing barriers of age and class – expresses a moral-cultural good in danger of being lost, with Salvatore's beloved 'Nuovo Cinema Paradiso' due to be demolished to make way for a car park.

Contrast this uplifting film fable with Alex [Malcolm McDowell], the violent gang leader and charismatic narrator of Stanley Kubrick's *A Clockwork Orange* (1971). Alex's story is a cautionary moral and political tale, exploring the limits of moral autonomy, political authority, and what to do when individual freedom clashes with societal expectations (see Andersen 2014). He explains how his aesthetic passion for Beethoven, his cinematic immersion in the 'feelies', and bouts of random ultraviolence, were 'cured' through forced exposure to images of sex and violence coupled with electroshock therapy – a visual, visceral, and moral re-education that robs Alex of the capacity to 'enjoy' his former sociopathic and aesthetic pursuits. Far from being a source of communal cinephilia, shared cultural memory, or moral-ethical value, cinematic images, in Alex's perverse and violent world, are both the cause and cure of a socially-sanctioned violence and anti-social perversity. At the same time, we are invited to watch and respond to Alex's narration – and Kubrick's depiction – of his rebellious, anti-social activities, as well as the state's brutal and cynical attempts to harness, 'cure', and exploit Alex for its own political purposes. That Kubrick presents this confronting moral-political fable in the form of a compelling work of cinema only underlines our complicity as spectators of such a film and the ambiguity of its engagement with the philosophical and moral-political questions it raises.

These films present two extremes in the way the cinema can be figured in relation to ethics: as an 'innocent' form of communal storytelling, sensory-imaginative experience, and shared cultural memory; and as a 'corrupting' moral and political force, whose audiovisual powers can desensitize viewers, even incline them to violence.[1] They reflect opposing views concerning the morally corrupting *and* ethically educative potential of cinema, views that find their correlates in the history of film theory. On the one hand, there is the persistent cultural concern with the psychologically damaging, morally corrupting, or ideologically manipulative effects of cinema, and on the other, a utopian vision of cinema's psychological, cultural, even politically transformative power to question social reality and empower us to experience and see the world anew. How do these two opposing views of cinema relate to each other? How should we conceptualize cinema's power not only to reflect social, cultural, and moral values but to exercise our moral imaginations and deepen our ethical experience? How might film contribute to philosophy, indeed to ethical understanding, via cinematic means? This book seeks to address these questions and to explore a conception of cinema as a medium of *ethical experience*, one with the capacity not only to enhance our grasp of philosophical approaches to ethics, and to exercise our capacity for moral perception and ethical understanding, but to provoke philosophical thinking through experiential, which is to say aesthetic and cinematic, means.

Despite the flourishing of philosophy of film in recent decades (see Elsaesser and Hagener 2009, 185–187), there have been few explicit theoretical investigations of the relationship between ethics and cinema (see Choi and Frey 2014, Jones and Vice 2011, Sinnerbrink 2014, Tersman 2009). That film has an ethical potential – for exploring moral issues, ethically-charged situations, or moral 'thought experiments' – is clear, however, from the way in which philosophical film theorists have explored cinema from a variety of philosophical perspectives (Flory 2008, Mulhall 2008, Shaw 2012, Wartenberg 2007). More recently, theorists have begun to explore the ways in which cinema can be read alongside philosophical approaches to ethics, or how certain filmmakers can be understood as engaging in ethics through film (Cooper 2006, Downing and Saxton 2010, Stadler 2008, Wheatley 2009). Indeed, film theory, philosophy of film, and film-philosophy,[2] have not only begun to explore the question of ethics, but could be described as undergoing an 'ethical turn' – along with other areas of the humanities – in reflecting upon cinema as a distinctive way of thinking through ethical concerns (see Choi and Frey 2014).

This is an important development that will enable the tradition of film theory concerned with politics and ideology to be revived and re-appropriated in new ways. It will also broaden the reach of philosophical engagement with film beyond abstract questions of ontology and metaphysics as well as more technical and formal questions concerning epistemology and film aesthetics (while recognizing the intimate relations that obtain between these different aspects of the philosophy of film). Beyond sophisticated questions of ontology, aesthetics, or spectatorship, one could say that 'film ethics' describes the more culturally familiar sense in which moviegoers might think of cinema as having philosophical significance. When non-academic film viewers describe a film as 'philosophical' they generally mean it deals with moral or ethical rather than metaphysical or aesthetic themes. Yet philosophers, on the whole, have given the question of ethics and film scant attention, even within aesthetics, philosophy of film, and film theory. Indeed, we still need to analyse philosophically the ways in which cinema can be related to ethics, map conceptually the film-ethics relationship, and explain how particular films might both express and evoke moral reflection. This kind of inquiry into cinema and ethics, as I argue in this book, opens up the possibility that cinema can be understood as a medium of ethical experience: a 'cinematic ethics' that brings film and philosophy together in order to cultivate an experiential approach to ethical understanding and philosophical reflection. It can even expose us to morally confronting, ethically estranging, and emotionally challenging forms of experience that demand some kind of philosophical response on our part: an effort of thinking to which we might otherwise remain oblivious or that we might otherwise prefer to ignore.

The idea of 'cinematic ethics'

Cinema and philosophy have always enjoyed a close, if sometimes fraught, relationship. From early film theorists such as Hugo Münsterberg, classical theorists such as Bazin and Kracauer, semiotic and psychoanalytic theorists such as Baudry and Metz, to contemporary philosophers of film such as Stanley Cavell, Gilles Deleuze, and Noël Carroll, the exploration of the relationship between philosophy and film inevitably broaches the question of ethics (and politics), the possibility that cinema might have an important ethical dimension. Nonetheless, it is striking how few philosophers have explicitly addressed the question of film and ethics, despite widespread acknowledgement of cinema's philosophical as well as ethico-political potential.

So how are film and philosophy related? French philosopher Alain Badiou (2013, 208–211) provides a helpful conceptual map by identifying five ways in which philosophy – or philosophically-oriented film theory – has approached thinking through cinema. As Badiou observes, the first way of thinking through the film-philosophy relationship is to commence with a theoretical inquiry into the moving image; hence this approach is defined by questions of ontology (the ontology of cinematic images, reflections on representation in cinema, the problem of realism, and so on). Bazin's theoretical and aesthetic reflections on cinema (1967, 1971), focusing on the ontology of the cinemato-graphic image and the problem of moral and aesthetic realism, are exemplary cases of this way of thinking. The second concerns the problem of time (and of movement) raised by the cinematographic image: moving images are temporal phenomena that provide a novel means of capturing and exploring time in a manner that both emulates and goes beyond ordinary temporal, perceptual experience. Phenomenological approaches to cinema have become important representatives of this kind of theoretical perspective on the moving image (see Sobchack 1992).

The third approach, prevalent in early film theory, was to theorize cinema in relation to the other arts (painting, theatre, photography, drama, literature, music, and so on), exploring questions such as whether the 'seventh art' was indeed a new kind of art form, what relations it bore to earlier arts, whether it could be understood as synthesizing elements from previous art forms, and so on (Badiou 2013, 210). Here one thinks of early and classical film theorists such as Hugo Münsterberg (2002 [1916]), Rudolf Arnheim (1957), and Bazin (1967, 1971) but continuing today in philosophical debates, for example, on the relationship between photography and cinema and the related question of the ontological 'transparency' of moving images (see Cavell 1979, Scruton 1981). The fourth approach concerns the complex relationship between art and non-art that is introduced by the cinema (Badiou 2013, 210–211), which has always been a 'hybrid' art form combining elements of popular entertainment (circus, burlesque, sideshows, photography) with elements borrowed from 'higher' culture (painting, drama, literature, opera, music) (see Rancière 2006). Given cinema's character as the technological, mechanized, industrialized art form *par excellence* (especially with the shift to digital media), we can see this trend appearing in those important strands of film and media theory that explore the relationships between technology, aesthetic experience, and cultural-historical meaning.

Finally, the fifth way of conceptualizing the relationship between film and philosophy, according to Badiou, is by way of its ethical significance (2013, 211). Drawing on both mythic and literary narratives, cinema has always been an art form concerned with the human figure in action, the individual in relation to the community, the human being against nature, or the interpersonal world of psychological and emotional conflict.[3] As Badiou remarks, with the development of narrative cinema, this ethical and moral dynamic was readily translated into the great film genres: '[t]he major genres of cinema, the most coded ones, such as the melodrama and the western, are in fact ethical genres, genres that are addressed to humanity so as to offer it a moral mythology' (2013, 211). In this respect, the movies are heir to the moral and cultural functions of the theatre, taking over its role as an open, 'democratic' sphere of the artistic, even mythological, exploration of ethical, socio-cultural, and ideological themes. At the same time, cinema develops its own forms of narration and myth-making, creating genres that can challenge and question, but also justify and confirm, all sorts of significant cultural values, ideological beliefs, and ethical forms of meaning.

Badiou's characterization of the five ways of conceptualizing the film-philosophy relationship is illuminating and helps makes sense of the often confusing accounts of how film can be understood as philosophical. It is also to our purpose that he identifies ethics as one of the fundamental ways to think about the relationship between film and philosophy: to explore how the distinctive features of cinema – the powerful syntheses of images, of appearances and reality, time and memory, perception and experience, individual and community, that it makes possible – open up new ways of thinking that invite further philosophical reflection and ethical engagement. Nonetheless, one might query Badiou's account of cinema's 'ethical' dimension for its exclusive focus on the 'heroic' aspect of classical narrative film, its focus on 'the great figures of humanity in action', its presentation of the world as 'a kind of universal stage of action and its confrontation with common values' (Badiou 2013, 239). In short, one can question here Badiou's rather narrow focus on the narrative, representational, and dramatic elements of popular narrative film as distinct from its more aesthetic, specifically cinematic dimensions.

To be sure, it is not hard to see how cinema retains this popular emphasis on heroes in a post-heroic age, its dramatization of common values in conflict – 'the great American battle between Good and Evil' (Badiou 2013, 239–240) – its valorization of the actions of heroic individuals over the power of thought or the virtues of contemplation. At the same time, however, even popular genres and forms of narrative cinema have explored aesthetic dimensions of cinematic presentation that can intensify, undermine, question, or ironize the narrative 'content' and thematic emphasis on values that Badiou identifies: one thinks, for example, of *film noir*, certain kinds of Western and crime drama (Ford, Mann, Hawks), melodrama (Minnelli, Sirk), even comedy and romantic comedy (Chaplin, Keaton, Sturges, Cukor) as genres whose 'formal' aesthetic features can stand in tension with or even ironize their ostensible narrative content. Certain kinds of cinema, moreover, have questioned this 'heroic' form of narrative, and sought to present reality, including nature, society, and history, from multiple, ambiguous, often conflicting perspectives, showing us different, alternative, even inarticulable aspects of our experience of the world rather than directing us towards certain kinds of action or definite forms of belief. Indeed, we can find in cinema another potential, one more subtle than the spectacular staging of clashing values, of heroic action, or of moral codes in tragic conflict. This is a conception of cinema as providing new ways of evoking and expressing *ethical experience*: not only emotional *engagement* facilitating moral sympathy and empathy but also emotional *estrangement* through which conflicting, clashing, or incompatible ideas, commitments, or beliefs can be revealed.[4] It chimes with the influential idea of film as philosophy, that is, of film-philosophy as providing new 'paths for thinking' that have ethical significance, that create new 'syntheses' of thought and image with the power to provoke our moral imaginations, expand our ethical horizons, but also to provoke philosophical thinking (see Andersen 2014, Mulhall 2008, Pippin 2010, 2012, Rushton 2013, Sinnerbrink 2011, Wartenberg 2007). Analysing cinema can also be a way of exploring ethical experience, of enhancing moral imagination, and of developing our capacity to engage in ethical reflection and thus deepening our moral-political understanding. Indeed, the idea of 'cinematic ethics' I elaborate in this book is an extension of the idea that film can contribute to, but in some instances also challenge, our philosophical thinking.

Until recently, however, most of the work in the philosophy of film has been concerned with the question of whether films might reflect philosophical arguments, stage philosophical thought experiments, or be understood in relation to particular philosophies of cinema, be they Deleuzian, Cavellian, phenomenological, or cognitivist (see, for example, Read and Goodenough 2005, Wartenberg 2007, Livingston 2009, Martin-Jones 2011, Mullarkey 2009, Pisters 2012). Although many philosophers of film will invoke moral theories (utilitarianism, Kantian universalism, Aristotelian virtue ethics, or moral perfectionism) or ethical problems (moral responsibility, ethical obligation, friendship, moral virtues and vices, moral and political freedom) few have delved further into the question of how cinema might be understood as ethical, or indeed how it might contribute to our ethical experience. Rather, philosophies of film have focused on ontological, epistemological, aesthetic, and phenomenological aspects of cinema rather than on ethical questions or the relationship between film and ethics as such (Carroll 2008, Gaut 2010). To borrow a distinction from classical phenomenology, ethics and moral thinking have been *operative* in philosophies of cinema (assumed and used in various ways) without being *thematic* (explicitly theorized or conceptualized). As remarked above, if one were to ask ordinary spectators whether movies can be philosophical, I suspect most would mention films exploring ethical issues, political themes, or moral-existential situations; but this of course does not mean that we therefore can claim to know or understand or appreciate the complexities and potentialities of the cinema-ethics relationship. To paraphrase Metz, we might say that film as ethics is difficult to explain because it is easy to understand.

Ethics in cinema (and cinema as ethics) represent much more than a minor branch of the philosophy of film. This is arguably the most culturally significant way in which cinema can be understood philosophically. It not only makes a contribution to our philosophical understanding of the world but enhances our ability to engage with complex forms of moral experience. Exploring cinematic ethics also provides a rich way of inheriting and renewing the legacy of film theory, especially with regard to cinema's ideological and political dimensions. A focus on the ethical potential of cinema is one way of ensuring that film-philosophy does not neglect this important legacy of twentieth-century film theory.

My claim in this book is that we need a philosophy of film that concerns itself not only with the 'ethics of film' but with the idea of film as a medium that can express and evoke ethical experience – the idea of 'film as ethics' or what I am calling 'cinematic ethics'. I use this term to distinguish an experiential approach to thinking through ethics, one that proceeds via the aesthetic experience, emotional engagement, and cognitive understanding that cinema so richly provides. Cinema's power of perceptual fascination, emotional engagement, and cognitive understanding give it a remarkable capacity to evoke ethically significant experience with the power to provoke philosophical thinking. Although film can be used for moral pedagogy (or, alternatively, for political propaganda), it can also prompt us to question our moral assumptions, dogmatic beliefs, and ideological convictions. Cinema can question and explore social, cultural, and political situations in ways that force viewers to rethink what they regard as morally significant; it can also prompt us to see our world – or multiple worlds – in a more psychologically nuanced, socially complex, ethically revealing light. It can reveal obscured or ignored background elements of a fictional world, or the emotional and existential complexities of a character's social situation, in ways that might otherwise have escaped our notice. It can even challenge our ways of thinking through exposing us to confronting forms of ethical experience, showing us the importance, or in some cases the dangers, of certain ways of being, thinking, and feeling, provoking us towards a more philosophical engagement with the world, and perhaps a richer, more complex ethical attitude towards others.

This book maps out some of the ways in which we might conceptualize the relationship between ethics and cinema but also explores the idea of a cinematic ethics or of film as a medium of ethical experience. And it does so by way of close critical engagement with a number of important films, bringing philosophical and ethical reflection into dialogue with film analysis and aesthetic evaluation. It seeks to open up a path towards a different kind of ethical understanding, a cinematically-mediated ethical engagement that has the potential to be more experientially rich and emotionally challenging than traditional modes of ethical inquiry. Cinematic ethics offers 'thick' descriptions of complex forms of ethical experience that might otherwise be difficult to comprehend, hard to imagine, difficult to accept, or escape theoretical notice. From this point of view, philosophy not only provides a path for thinking about cinema and ethics, cinema provides an experientially rich way of extending, enhancing, even transforming ethical inquiry.

Cinematic ethics: mapping an encounter

To explore the idea of cinematic ethics, let us begin by mapping some of the ways in which cinema and ethics have been related. We can describe ethical approaches to cinema as tending to focus on one of three aspects of the relationship between film, spectator, and context: 1) ethics *in* cinema (focusing on narrative content including dramatic scenarios involving morally charged situations, conflicts, decisions, or actions); 2) the ethics (politics) *of* cinematic representation (focusing on the ethical issues raised by elements of film production and/or audience reception, for example, ongoing debates over the effects of screen violence); and 3) the ethics of cinema *as* a cultural medium expressing moral beliefs, social values, or ideology (such as feminist film analysis of gender or Marxist analyses of ideology). Each of these three aspects of the film-spectator-context relationship has spawned a distinctive approach to the question of cinema and ethics (see Choi and Frey 2014, Downing and Saxton 2010, Jones and Vice 2011, Shaw 2012, Stadler 2008, Wheatley 2009), though few theorists have attempted to articulate the relationships between these aspects with a view toward their ethical significance and theoretical implications.

A common approach in much recent philosophy of film is 1) to focus on ethics *within* cinematic representation (morally relevant themes, problems, and scenarios within the narrative or approaching film as a moral 'thought experiment'). To cite an example to which I shall return in Chapter 5, think of Stanley Cavell's 'moral perfectionist' reading of the melodrama *Stella Dallas* (Cavell 1996), according to which brassy Stella comes to a greater understanding of herself and makes an ethical decision to give her daughter Laurel a chance at marital and social happiness by deliberately withdrawing herself from her daughter's life. Or consider the Dardenne Brothers' film *The Promise* [*La promesse*] (1996) (which I discuss further in Chapter 6), where teenage Igor [Jérémie Renier] decides to defy his father and assist illegal immigrant widow Assita in escaping exploitation, honouring his promise to the woman's dying husband that he will look after Assita and her baby son. Or take Alejandro Amenábar's *The Sea Inside* [*Mar adrento*] (2004), based on the true story of Ramón Sampredo [Javier Bardem], who became a quadriplegic at the age of 28 and campaigned for the rest of his life in support of euthanasia and the right to die with dignity – a film notable for Bardem's performance and for its innovative cinematic composition to provide a powerful ethical experience for the viewer as a kind of cinematic 'argument' for assisted euthanasia.

Film theorists have often focused on 2) the ethics *of* cinematic representation, whether from the filmmaker perspective (production) or from the spectator perspective (reception). Consider, for example, debates over objectivity and truth in documentary representation, or whether a filmmaker can use elements of fiction in the presentation of what purports to be fact (Michael Moore's creative reorganization of dates and events in his documentary *Roger and Me* (1989)). Or we might ponder the ethics of how a filmmaker treats cast and crew (Werner Herzog's filming of the epic *Fitzcarraldo* (1982) in the jungles of Peru or the cat-poisoning scene in Béla Tarr's *Sátántango* (1994)). Or we might be drawn to debates over how spectators respond to images of sex and violence (depictions of rape in 'new French extremity' cinema (see Horeck and Kendall 2011), for example, or the use of non-simulated sex scenes in von Trier's *Antichrist* (2009) and *Nymphomaniac* (2014) (see Frey 2014)). The ethics of cinematic spectatorship is one of the central concerns in recent film theory, an approach that attracts much attention in research on the relationship between film and ethics (see Choi and Frey 2014, Stadler 2008, Wheatley 2009).

Film theory, however, has also been long concerned with the broader social, cultural, and political implications of cinema. Since the 1970s it has emphasized 3) the ethics (and politics) of cinema as a medium symptomatic of broader cultural-historical or ideological perspectives (such as feminist analyses of gender and Marxist analyses of ideology). Among many possible examples, let us take Kathryn Bigelow's two films on the Iraq war, *The Hurt Locker* (2008) and *Zero Dark Thirty* (2012). These films were both celebrated for their cinematic accomplishment as powerful and suspenseful action/war movies, but also criticized for offering ideologically slanted depictions of

American soldiers fighting an 'irrational' enemy in Iraq. *Zero Dark Thirty*, for example, implies that the 'heightened interrogation techniques' deployed by the CIA ultimately led to the capture of Osama bin Laden. It thus offered a dubious utilitarian 'moral' justification (the 'ticking bomb' scenario) for the use of torture in prosecuting the so-called 'War on Terror' (see Westwell 2014). At the same time, Bigelow's focalizing of the narrative through female CIA operative Maya [Jessica Chastain], who doggedly pursues bin Laden when her male peers have given up, lends this film an interestingly 'feminist' slant that complicates – generically and dramatically – the straightforward 'ideological' critique of the film as an apologia for American militarism.

It is clear that all three aspects of the cinema-ethics relationship are important, but the challenge is to think them together. All three aspects contribute to our understanding of the ethico-political dimensions of film. We can see this quite explicitly in a classic action-thriller like Steven Spielberg's *Jaws* (1975). At a narrative level, 1) it is clear that the film dramatizes a utilitarian moral question concerning how to maximize the 'happiness' or beneficial utility (which could be preferences, or norms of action) of the most people: whether the risk of a shark attack means that the Island's beaches should be closed for the annual Fourth of July holiday weekend (police chief [Roy Scheider] and marine scientist's [Richard Dreyfuss] position) versus the economic harm that this decision would bring to the community thanks to the number of local businesses who rely on the holiday trade (the Mayor's [Murray Hamilton's] position). 2) At an extra-filmic level, one could examine the ethical implications for filmmakers and the viewing public of depicting sharks as irrational killing machines posing a natural environmental threat to vulnerable human beings, a threat that can only be neutralized by destroying them (cf. the worldwide panic that followed the release of the film, which prompted over-zealous culling of sharks in many countries). Although based on a 'true story' (the 1916 Jersey Shore attacks on the US East Coast), one might object to the movie's distorted depiction of sharks as a deadly threat to humans, exploiting our irrational fear of sharks (relative to the threat they actually pose), rather than using a fictitious creature to embody the terrifying 'monster' in the movie.

From a more 'symptomatic' critical theory perspective (see Heath 1985), one could argue 3) that the film presents an ideological parallel between the American use of the atomic bomb to stop Japan's military aggression during WWII, and the final act of the film that results in the killer shark being blown to smithereens by an exploding gas tank.[5] The Melville-esque hunt for the great white shark led by old seafarer Mr Quint [Robert Shaw] is framed by his gripping tale of having been a sailor on the USS *Indianapolis* when on its secret mission to deliver parts for the atomic bomb dropped on Hiroshima. The *Indianapolis* was torpedoed by the Japanese and sank within nine minutes, killing over 300 men, with most of the survivors eventually eaten by marauding sharks. Having survived the sharks after the sinking of the *Indianapolis*, and successfully hunting down the shark off Amity Island, Mr Quint is finally taken by the terrifying Leviathan, leaving it to Police Chief Brody to blow up the shark and restore peace to the community. Quint and Brody both have recourse to 'bombs' to blow up a deadly, implacable threat, Quint surviving the one only to perish thanks to the other. The ideological parallel is clear: that the use of violence is sometimes necessary to preserve the American way of life from implicit existential threats, be they military or marine.

It is clear that all three dimensions are at play in a popular narrative drama like *Jaws*, and that film theorists can readily thematise one or other aspect in particular critical readings of the film. All three are important for under-standing how the film works and should be treated both separately and in relation to each other in order to understand how the film is capable of evoking varieties of ethical experience, albeit in this case of a fairly conven-tional, not especially thought-provoking, character. It would be a mistake, however, to claim that one or other aspect is more true or important than the others, for example that the symptomatic-ideological reading of the film neu-tralises or overrides the narrative content or contextual (production-reception) approaches. Indeed, it makes more sense to claim that it is because of Spielberg's skill in eliciting and orchestrating emotional involvement, conflicting moral allegiances, feelings of suspense, anxiety, or dread, as well as broader cultural-ideological resonances that *Jaws* became such a popular, controversial, and influential blockbuster movie and continues – like many other recent thoughtful popular films – to provide a rich source of ethico-political, as well as philo-sophical, reflection. What I would underline is that all three aspects of the film's 'ethical' significance rely on the use of particular cinematic devices and aesthetic strategies in order to provide the kind of affectively rich, emotionally intense, immersive experience that characterize the film. Aesthetic experience, in this sense, is inseparable from the kinds of ethical meaning and critical response that the film can evoke.

The important point I wish to draw from this discussion is the need to distinguish, on the one hand, between these different levels or aspects of ethics in film, but also to be mindful, on the other, of the manner in which they relate to each other and indeed work together in evoking cinematic-ethical experience. Although it is possible to thematise in theory one or other aspect of a film's ethical significance – its narrative content, questions of production or reception, spectator response, or its symptomatic ideological meaning – all of these aspects contribute to the diverse forms of ethical experience that cinema can afford; and it is these dimensions, in their complex relationships, which film-philosophers and engaged spectators alike are invited, or provoked, to acknowledge, imagine, emotionally respond to, question, reflect upon, analyse or conceptualize in partnership with the film. We might call this the continuation of the film's aesthetic invitation to ethical engagement, an invitation which can then be elaborated and comprehended by philosophical means.

As I show throughout this book, the idea of cinema as a medium of ethical experience offers a way of bringing these three dimensions together, linking style and content, creation and reception, context and interpretation in ways that enable us to explore cinema's ethical potential and to enhance and extend what we understand by ethical inquiry. This is not to deny the important critical work done over the last century theorizing cinema and its ideological effects. My aim, rather, is to offer a new perspective on how film can contribute to philosophy: the idea of cinema as a medium of ethical experience.

Cinematic ethics: key approaches

What are the dominant approaches to cinematic ethics in philosophical film theory? I use the latter term to name a plurality of ways of theorizing on film that are concerned with philosophical aspects of cinema, focussing on philosophical problems like the ontology, aesthetics, epistemology, or ethics of cinema, or that draw on different traditions of philosophy in order to respond to central problems in film theory. Philosophical film theory overlaps with the philosophy of film, though the latter often tends to mark itself as 'independent' of film theory, whereas the former is more openly interdisciplinary in character. Not all film theory is philosophical (for example, historical film studies), and not all philosophy of film deals with film theory (for example, within analytic aesthetics). Philosophical film theory, in short, is inherently interdisciplinary.

Within this theoretical matrix I would also distinguish film-philosophy as a particular manner of practising philosophical film theory, one that does not simply apply given philosophical theories to films but stages an encounter between film and philosophy. We can define 'film-philosophy' as 'a way of thinking at the intersection between film and philosophy, linking the two in a shared enterprise that seeks to illuminate the one by means of the other' (Sinnerbrink 2014, 207). Inspired by the work of Stanley Cavell and Gilles Deleuze, film philosophers claim that film and philosophy are intimately related, sharing problems to which they respond in distinctive ways, opening up an encounter between images and concepts with the potential to suggest new paths of thought. Film-philosophy is a style or 'genre' of philosophical film theory that seeks to explore the relationship between philosophy and film in a non-reductive, mutually productive manner, and thus overlaps with, but is not reducible to, more traditional philosophy of film (Sinnerbrink 2014, 207). That said, more traditional philosophy of film – which inquires into the nature of cinema, examining ontological issues concerning moving images, aesthetic issues concerning the medium, and theorizing different aspects of our perception and understanding of movies – remains closely related to film-philosophy. One of the claims often made by film-philosophers, however, is that cinema can contribute to broadening our philosophical understanding by cinematic means (so film is not simply an object of theoretical analysis). This is a claim I would like to extend to ethics: to show how cinema can contribute to broadening our understanding of ethics by cinematic means, or how film has the potential to evoke ethically transformative experience that invites further philosophical reflection.

What are the dominant ways in which cinema and ethics are being explored today? I would identify the following approaches, which will be the focus of the chapters that follow: 1) the *Cavellian* approach (cinema as exploring scepticism, philosophy and the everyday, and moral perfectionism); 2) the *Deleuzian* perspective (cinema as exploring immanent 'modes of existence', as communicating thought, or giving us 'reasons to believe in this world'); 3) *phenomenological and post-phenomenological film theory* (focusing on subjective and intersubjective experiences of affect, perception, emotion, embodiment, and how these relate to moral-ethical experience in cinema; a related strand concerns the Levinasian ethics of responsibility towards the 'alterity' of the Other as applied to our experience of cinema); 4) *cognitivist film theory* ('naturalistic' theories of cognition exploring all aspects of cinematic experience, but in particular our affective and emotional response to film, along with more reflective, higher-order cognition, which taken together provide an account of moral allegiance with character and broader ethical evaluation in response to narrative cinema).

All of these approaches offer valuable theoretical insights for understanding cinema and ethics. All sorts of 'crossovers', moreover, are possible between these approaches – for example, Cavellian-Deleuzian, phenomenological-cognitivist, Deleuzian-phenomenological, Deleuzian-cognitivist approaches, and so on (see Brown 2013, Rushton 2011, Sinnerbrink 2011, Stadler 2008). At the same time, each approach foregrounds a different aspect of the film/screen/spectator/context relationship, sometimes emphasizing thematic concerns within the narrative, sometimes the spectator's response, sometimes a conceptual framework applied to the film, sometimes the significance of our affective or emotional engagement with it. What is less common is finding a more comprehensive way of thinking through the different but related dimensions of ethics in cinema, which is what I propose to do via a brief discussion of the idea of cinema as a medium of ethical experience, and to develop in more depth throughout the course of this book.

Cinema as medium of ethical experience

What is the significance of the 'ethical turn' in recent film theory? One response is to point out that cinema has always been concerned with ethics, or that moral concerns have always been brought to the study of cinema. These ethical concerns were largely displaced by political and ideological agendas during the 1960s and 70s, a tendency apparent in the rise of Lacanian-Althusserian 'psycho-semiotic' and feminist film theory. With the historical collapse of communism and decline of Marxism as a theoretical paradigm during the 1990s, a renewed focus on ethics – on questions of human rights, democracy, concern for the Other, and our responsibilities towards nature and the environment – became the distinctive feature of many forms of social, cultural, and political discourse. Within the academy, the reigning paradigm of film theory came under attack during the 1980s and 90s, being subjected, as Rodowick remarks, to 'a triple displacement – by history, science, and finally by philosophy' (2015, 6). At the same time, however, ethical questions concerning cinema became more prominent and continued to reverberate with the emergence of film-philosophy, most notably in the work of Cavell and Deleuze (see Sinnerbrink 2011, Rodowick 2015).

It is hardly surprising that such a shift could also be discerned in contemporary cinema across the globe, which is rife with films dealing with ethical issues, moral problems, or cultural-political concerns. Indeed, contemporary cinema is where many socially-charged ethical problems and cultural-moral debates today are most creatively explored. Cinema is where cultures across the globe can find imaginative narrative ways to address, reflect upon, question, and explore some of the most important moral-ethical and cultural-political issues of our times.

The recent attention to ethics and cinema has thus opened up a new space of engagement between film and philosophy. It provides a way for philosophy to engage with other humanities disciplines, and to articulate its concerns in critical dialogue with the most culturally significant art form of our age. And it provides cinema with inspiration and orientation through some of the most challenging problems faced today by individuals and communities. In short, thinking through cinema and ethics, or the idea of cinematic ethics, is one way that philosophy (of film) can contribute to understanding ourselves and our world, as well as fostering, in a modest way, the cultivation of a democratic ethos.

The approach I wish to develop in what follows is to explore the idea of cinema as a medium of ethical experience with a transformative potential to sharpen our moral perception, challenge our beliefs through experiential means, and thus enhance our understanding of moral-social complexity. It can also, in some cases, provoke philosophical thinking through morally confronting or provocative forms of ethical experience conveyed and evoked through film. The idea of cinematic ethics can bring together the three important aspects of the cinema-ethics relationship: ethical content in narrative cinema; the ethics of cinematic representation (from filmmaker and spectator perspectives); and the ethics of cinema as symptomatic of broader cultural, social, and ideological concerns.

To these three dimensions we can add a fourth: the *aesthetic dimension* of cinema – in particular the role of aesthetic form in intensifying our experience, refining and focusing our attention, and thus of conveying complexity of meaning through manifold means – as a way of *evoking ethical experience* and thereby inviting further ethical-critical reflection. The relationship between aesthetics and ethics in cinema, from this point of view, is recognized as an intimate, internal, and expressive one. In other words, the question of

ethics in cinema, or of cinema as ethical, is not exhausted by narrative explorations of ethics, or questions of production and consumption, or by the ethics of
spectatorship, or by the ideological-political dimensions of cinema. Rather, it
is important to understand how aesthetics and ethics are intimately and
expressively related: how the particular aesthetic elements and features of a
film are articulated with each other, and how these together serve to communicate ethical meaning via aesthetic means, ever mindful that we may only be
able to focus on particular aspects or elements in particular contexts or cases
on any given hermeneutic occasion.

The concept of cinema as a medium of ethical experience is one way of
trying to articulate these elements – from the singular to the universal; from
the embodied spectator to the cultural-historical world – so as to open up new
ways of thinking and thus of realizing cinema's ethical (and political) potential.
It is a concept that links creation and reception, context and interpretation,
image and world, so as to realize cinema's ethical potential. For cinema is a
medium with the power to project and disclose virtual worlds; to engage our
emotions, exercise our moral imaginations, and question our beliefs. It is a
medium with the potential to evoke forms of ethical experience that might
prompt a transformation of our horizons of meaning and value. As the technological art form par excellence, cinema offers the creative possibility of engaging
ethically with our technologically-mediated world, but also of recognizing and
responding to the ethical challenges that such a world poses, indeed via the
very medium of cinema itself. At the same time, it enables an experientially
'thick' exploration of subjectivity, memory, and historical experience, all of
which contribute to the kind of integration of ethical responsiveness and
philosophical reflection that characterize what I am calling cinematic ethics.

Ulysses' Gaze: the Blue Ship

By way of a brief example let us turn to a film exploring the nexus between
history, memory, cinema, and ethics. The Prologue to the late Theo Angelopolous's remarkable film, *Ulysses' Gaze* (1995), a four-minute sequence immediately after the credits, is a powerful example of how cinema can serve as an
ethical medium, in this case through a film dedicated to exploring historical
memory (see Sinnerbrink 2015).[6] The film begins with a personal dedication
and a philosophical quotation from Plato's *Alcibiades* – 'And, if the soul is to
know itself, it must gaze into the soul' – an indication that the film itself will
explore the possibility of how cinema itself might be a means of critical self-
examination, of contemplating historical experience and shared social memory.
The opening images are from the Manakis brothers' two minute silent film, *The
Weavers* (1905), which features the brothers' 114 year-old grandmother weaving
at her loom while glancing furtively towards the camera. As we watch this
historical time capsule, the sound of a film projector can be heard in the
background. Philosophical contemplation and historical recollection clearly

frame this cinematic odyssey. A voiceover, by the filmmaker A. [Harvey Keitel], comments on the footage, in quasi-documentary mode: 'Weavers, in Avdella, a Greek village, 1905. The first film made by the brothers Miltos and Yannakis Manakis. The first film ever made in Greece and the Balkans. But is that a fact? Is it the first film? The first gaze?'

The silent footage dissolves to a greyish black-and-white image of the sea and horizon, merging in the distance. The camera pulls back to reveal an old man operating a photographic camera, as a man's voice narrates, in Greek, how back in 1954, when he was Manakis's camera assistant, Manakis [Thanos Grammenos], wanted to photograph a beautiful blue ship, here in the port of Thessaloniki. The image slowly turns from black and white to colour as we see the narrator, Manakis's assistant, in modern dress, and the old man, in older costume, manipulating the camera as the ship sails by in the distance. Suddenly, the old man reels backwards, struck by a heart attack, and slumps back onto his chair. The assistant tends to the dead man, settles him in his chair, then walks slowly back towards the right of screen, the camera following him in long shot. The assistant, an old man himself, narrates how Manakis had kept 'rambling on about three undeveloped reels', a film from the turn of the century. The filmmaker A. now comes into view, also in contemporary dress; it becomes clear that the Assistant has been telling A. the anecdote about Manakis as they both stand together by the port of Thessaloniki. Forty years ago, on this very spot, he was with Manakis before his death; and now, forty years later, he is with the filmmaker A., explaining how Manakis died after attempting to photograph the mysterious blue ship.

The camera then pans slowly back to the left, following A as he walks back to the spot where we saw the old man die moments before. These camera

Figure 1.1 Still from *Ulysses' Gaze*, Dir. Theodoros Angelopoulos (1995)

movements, from left to right and back again, are also temporal movements, from the present to the past, and from the past to the present, which coexist within the one extended sequence-shot. As A. walks, moving across time and entering an inner world of cultural memory, we hear his thoughts, in voiceover, confirming his commitment to a cinematic quest: 'The three reels; the three reels; the journey…' As A. approaches the same spot where we saw the old Manakis collapse, where there is nothing now to be seen, a musical theme begins to play, a leitmotif that will recur throughout the film. A. pauses and gazes off into the distance, the camera perched behind his shoulder, from which point the ship can be seen sailing serenely from right to left, continuing its mythic journey through time and memory. As the camera zooms slowly towards the ship, its soft blue sails and hull gradually filling the frame, the music swells, expressing a contemplative mood anticipating the journey to come. The simultaneously 'Odyssean' and romantic image of the blue ship sailing slowly out of frame, accompanied by Eleni Karaindrou's melancholy score, holds long enough for the vessel to disappear from view. A.'s historical-ethical quest has been defined: to retrieve this cinematic memorialization of historical experience in the hope that this 'first gaze' will shed light on the tragedies of twentieth-century history and the ongoing conflicts defining a contemporary Europe in crisis.

This sequence from *Ulysses' Gaze* foregrounds the role of cultural and historical memory in the formation of personal and social identity through historical-memorial images that evoke the traumatic suffering of the past and render it intelligible through time, memory, and affect. More broadly, within the context of the film as a whole, they also evoke the situation of marginalized subjects (minorities, wanderers, refugees, those 'without a place' in the new social orders) through a cinema of temporal duration, cultural memory, and ethical contemplation. One could thus describe Angelopolos's sequence not only as an attempt at memorializing the history of the present but as a mode of enacting a cinematic ethics: creating cinematic works that depict historical memory as a collective experience, and which thereby retrieve the fragile possibility of an ethical cinema capable of transforming our horizons of meaning. Cinematic ethics, in this context, means showing, rather than telling, what ethical experience means, exploring what such experience reveals about the complexity of a character's historical world, where this historical world is disclosed through cinematic composition and dramatic action. It examines how cinema can attune our aesthetic and moral sensibilities to the experience of historical memory, and brings us to a deeper understanding of the cultural and historical background that shapes these characters' worlds – and, by extension, reveals the historical and ethical meaning of our own.

***

As I elaborate further in what follows, the idea of cinema as a medium of ethical experience has three interrelated aspects: 1) the depiction of ethical experience undergone by characters within a film narrative, typically in the form of decisions, choices, and actions within morally-charged dramatic situations; 2) the reflexive presentation of ethical experience in the filmmaking process or that distance the spectator from what they are viewing or challenge his or her assumptions or expectations (for example, the devices of reflexive documentary); and 3) the intentional effort to evoke the ethical responses of the spectator (ethical spectatorship) via a variety of cinematic devices and aesthetic strategies in film. All three aspects of this relationship are related: the depiction of ethical experience within narrative film is aimed at eliciting an ethical response from the viewer, but also raises questions about the filmmaking process or about both filmmakers' and viewers' relationships with the image. All three aspects, it is important to note, are elicited or expressed by aesthetic means: ethical experience in the cinema does not generally involve an intellectual or abstract reflection on moral problems or ethical dilemmas but unfolds, rather, through a situated, emotionally engaged, aesthetically receptive response to images that work on us in a multimodal manner, engaging our senses, emotions, and powers of reasoning. It involves cinema's power of stimulating sensation, affective response, emotional engagement and cognitive understanding, all of which work together to elicit ethical experience via aesthetic means.

What do I mean by 'ethical experience' in the cinema? There are three strands to this idea: 1) the shared cinematic experience of engaging with the perspectives, responses, actions, or experiences of others (fictional characters) depicted in complex interpersonal, social, or political situations or ethically challenging cinematic worlds; 2) responses to the cinema where viewers are moved to reflect ethically on what they are viewing, through their experience of emotional engagement, moral sympathy, or critical reflection; and 3) responses to cinematic experience that are brought about by aesthetic means and that aim at broadening our ethical horizons of meaning or challenging our ideological prejudices or convictions (even if this involves questioning, confronting, or confounding the viewer's opinions, beliefs, or attitudes). From this point of view, the most common form of ethical responsiveness in cinematic experience is via the elicitation of moral sympathy or ethically significant forms of empathy. As I discuss further in later chapters, cinema allows for an experientially rich 'simulation' of morally significant experience involving emotional responsiveness as well as higher-order cognitive reflection. On the other hand, there are also films that evoke what we might call 'ethical' forms of emotional or intellectual estrangement: confronting us with worlds in which morally ambiguous, ethically intolerable, or politically extreme situations prompt conflicting forms of affective, emotional, and critical responses in viewers, which in turn demand some kind of philosophical engagement. Such experience, whether affirmative or negative, operates across our sensory and cognitive modalities at the same time, combining complex aesthetic responses to images with psychologically grounded, culturally contextualized, and historically situated forms of individual and communal engagement with movies.

Cinema can thus harness the aesthetic possibilities of the medium in the service of either an enlightening ethical responsiveness or an unethical ideological manipulation. The latter has received far more attention in the history of film theory than the former, even though the potential for cinema to evoke ethically significant experience has been assumed since the early days of the medium. Indeed, the politically emancipatory potential of the cinema, as envisaged by Eisenstein (1949/1977) or Benjamin (2006 [1938–39]), for example, is difficult to conceive without it. Yet philosophical film theory has tended to ignore this potential in favour of a critical focus on cinema's manipulative power; or it has focused on questions of ontology, epistemology, and formal aesthetics at the expense of inquiring into moral perception, emotional evaluation, moral psychology, and ethical experience more generally.

As I argue in this book, philosophy can work together with film to describe, analyze and conceptualize the kind of ethical experience that cinema can afford. Cinematic ethics, the capacity of cinema to evoke ethically significant experience, can be complemented, comprehended, and completed by philosophical reflection. In this way, cinema contributes to ethical understanding, while philosophy can be extended, even transformed, by its engagement with 'non-philosophical' (aesthetic) modes of ethical experience. Cinematic ethics, from this perspective, involves an education of our senses and exercise of our moral imaginations that requires not only an acknowledgement of, or responsiveness to, ethical concerns but careful attention to aesthetic composition and sensitivity to cinematic technique. It incorporates a form of collaborative ethical inquiry that proceeds by the careful description and interpretation of ethical experience in the cinema elicited by aesthetic means. Cinema can provide 'thick' descriptions of complex moral situations or forms of ethical experience that might otherwise escape our notice or be prone to misrecognition or that require philosophical reflection in order to be understood (or that, in some cases, resist such philosophical reflection and moral understanding and thereby provoke a distinctively cinematic kind of ethical responsiveness). In this way, we might think of cinematic ethics as making a contribution to restoring the attenuated or damaged link between philosophy and the everyday. Philosophy, after all, is more than an isolated academic speciality cut off from everyday life and shared social-cultural experience; cinema should no longer be dismissed (especially by philosophy) as a manipulative or trivial form of mass entertainment but acknowledged, rather, as an artistic medium capable of evoking ethical experience. Film and philosophy, I suggest, can thus meet, communicate, and interact to the benefit of both thanks to the concept of ethical experience.

Such claims, of course, can only be defended and elaborated through a combination of sustained philosophical reflection on the ethical potential of cinema and via close critical engagement with the ethical aspects of particular films. In the chapters that follow, I undertake this task by exploring some of the dominant philosophical approaches to ethics in cinema within recent philosophical film theory. All of these approaches – Cavellian, Deleuzian, phenomenological, and cognitivist – can be brought together under the concept of ethical experience. For cinema is a Janus-faced medium with the capacity to be ethically transformative as well as ideologically manipulative. It not only depicts morally complex 'thought experiments' but has the aesthetic power to 'educate' our senses, to develop our ethical receptivity, and to enhance our moral understanding through the presentation of virtual cinematic worlds, which themselves can be ethical or unethical in varying degrees. Cinema, in other words, is a medium capable of evoking transformative ethical experience, experimenting with philosophical situations in order to reveal forms of moral meaning that we might otherwise fail to see.

Notes

1 As I shall discuss in relation to other films, however, there is also a powerful ethical dimension to *A Clockwork Orange* that involves the provocation of ethical experience through affective and emotional estrangement, confronting and provoking the viewer with images that, however disturbing, demand a philosophical response.
2 I discuss the distinctions and relations between these terms below.
3 This raises the question of the relationship between cinema and literature/drama in respect of its potential to evoke ethical experience. I address this issue in Chapter 4, which explores phenomenological and cognitivist approaches to cinematic experience.
4 I explore both of these dimensions – moral-ethical empathy/sympathy as well as estrangement – in the cinematic case studies comprising the final three chapters of this book.
5 Žižek comments extensively on *Jaws* in the recent Sophie Fiennes philosophical documentary *The Pervert's Guide to the Cinema* (2013).
6 The sequence in question can be viewed on YouTube (with subtitles): www.youtube.com/watch?v=St4Okk4OeQ4

Bibliography

Agamben, Giorgio. 'Notes on Gesture' (1992). In G. Agamben, *Means Without End: Notes on Politics*. Trans. V. Binetti and C. Casarino. Minneapolis and London: University of Minnesota Press, 2000.

Andersen, Nathan. *Shadow Philosophy: Plato's Cave and Cinema*. London: Routledge, 2014.

Arnheim, Rudolf. *Film as Art*. Berkeley/Los Angeles/London: University of California Press, 1957.

Badiou, Alain. *Cinema*. Trans. Susan Spritzer. Cambridge and Malden, MA: Polity Press, 2013 [2010].

Bazin, André. *What is Cinema? Volume I*. Trans. Hugh Gray. Berkeley/Los Angeles/London: University of California Press, 1967.

Bazin, André. *What is Cinema? Volume II*. Trans. Hugh Gray. Berkeley/Los Angeles/London: University of California Press, 1971.

Benjamin, Walter. 'The Work of Art in the Age of its Technical Reproducibility, Third Version'. In Howard Eiland and Michael W. Jennings (eds), *Walter Benjamin, Selected Writings Volume 4: 1938–1940*. Cambridge, MA and London: Belknap Press, 2006 [1938–1939].

Brown, William. *Supercinema: Film-Philosophy for the Digital Age*. New York and London: Berghahn Books, 2013.

Carroll, Noël. *The Philosophy of Motion Pictures.* Malden, MA and Oxford: Blackwell Publishing, 2008.

Cavell, Stanley. *The World Viewed: Reflections on the Ontology of Film.* Enlarged Edition. Cambridge, MA and London: Harvard University Press, 1979.

Cavell, Stanley. *Contesting Tears: The Hollywood Melodrama of the Unknown Woman.* Chicago and London: University of Chicago Press, 1996.

Choi, Jinhee and Frey, Mattias (eds). *Cine-Ethics: Ethical Dimensions of Film Theory, Practice, and Spectatorship.* Abingdon and New York: Routledge, 2014.

Cooper, Sarah. *Selfless Cinema? Ethics and French Documentary.* London: Legenda, 2006.

Downing, Lisa and Saxton, Libby. *Film and Ethics: Foreclosed Encounters.* Abingdon and New York: Routledge, 2010.

Eisenstein, Sergei. *Film Form: Essays on Film Theory.* Trans. Jay Leyda (ed.). Orlando: Harcourt and Brace, 1949/1977.

Elsaesser, Thomas and Hagener, Malte. *Film Theory: An Introduction through the Senses.* Abingdon and New York: Routledge, 2009.

Flory, Dan. *Philosophy, Black Film, Film Noir.* University Park, PA: Penn State University Press, 2008.

Frey, Mattias. 'The Ethics of Extreme Cinema'. In Jinhee Choi and Mattias Frey (eds), *Cine-Ethics: Ethical Dimensions of Film Theory, Practice, and Spectatorship*, 145-162. Abingdon and New York: Routledge, 2014.

Gaut, Berys. *A Philosophy of Cinematic Art.* Cambridge: Cambridge University Press, 2010.

Heath, Stephen. 'Jaws, Ideology, and Film Theory'. In Bill Nichols (ed.), *Movies and Methods, Volume II*, 509-514. Berkeley: University of California Press, 1985.

Horeck, Tanya and Kendall, Tina. *The New Extremism. From France to Europe.* Edinburgh: Edinburgh University Press, 2011.

Jameson, Fredric. 'Reification and Utopia in Mass Culture', *Social Text*, 1 (Winter 1979): 130–148.

Jones, Ward E. and Vice, Samantha. *Ethics at the Cinema.* Oxford: Oxford University Press, 2011.

Laine, Tarja. *Feeling Cinema: Emotional Dynamics in Film Studies.* New York and London: Continuum, 2011.

Livingston, Paisley. *Cinema, Philosophy, Bergman: On Film as Philosophy.* Oxford: Oxford University Press, 2009.

Marks, Laura U. *The Skin of the Film: Intercultural Cinema, Embodiment, and the Senses.* Durham: Duke University Press, 2000.

Marks, Laura U. *Touch: Sensuous Theory and Multisensory Media.* Minneapolis: University of Minnesota Press, 2002.

Martin-Jones, David. *Deleuze and World Cinemas.* London and New York: Continuum, 2011.

Mulhall, Stephen. *On Film.* 2nd Edition. Abingdon and New York: Routledge, 2008.

Mullarkey, John. *Refractions of Reality: Philosophy and the Moving Image.* Basingstoke: Palgrave Macmillan, 2009.

Münsterberg, Hugo. *The Photoplay: A Psychological* Study [1916]. In Allen Langdale (ed.), *Hugo Münsterberg on Film.* New York and London: Routledge, 2002.

Pippin, Robert B. *Hollywood Westerns and American Myth: The Importance of Howard Hawks and John Ford for Political Philosophy.* New Haven and London: Yale University Press, 2010.

Pippin, Robert B. *Fatalism in American Film Noir: Some Cinematic Philosophy.* Charlottesville: University of Virginia Press, 2012.

Pisters, Patricia. *The Neuro-Image: A Deleuzian Film-Philosophy of Digital Screen Culture.* Stanford: Stanford University Press, 2012.

Rancière, Jacques. *Film Fables*. Trans. Emiliano Battista. Oxford and New York: Berg Books, 2006.

Read, Rupert and Goodenough, Jerry (eds). *Film as Philosophy: Essays on Cinema After Wittgenstein and Cavell*. Basingstoke: Palgrave Macmillan, 2005.

Rodowick, D. N. *Philosophy's Artful Conversation*. Cambridge, MA and London: Harvard University Press, 2015.

Rushton, Richard. *The Reality of Film: Theories of Filmic Reality*. Manchester and New York: University of Manchester Press, 2011.

Rushton, Richard. *The Politics of Hollywood Cinema: Popular Film and Contemporary Political Theory*. Basingstoke: Palgrave Macmillan, 2013.

Scruton, Roger. 'Photography and Representation', *Critical Inquiry*, 7.3 (1981): 577–601.

Shaw, Dan. *Morality and the Movies: Reading Ethics through Film*. London and New York: Continuum, 2012.

Sinnerbrink, Robert. *New Philosophies of Film: Thinking Images*. London and New York: Continuum, 2011.

Sinnerbrink, Robert. 'Film-Philosophy'. In Edward Branigan and Warren Buckland (eds), *The Routledge Encyclopedia of Film Theory*, 207–213. Abingdon and New York: Routledge, 2014.

Sinnerbrink, Robert. 'Angelopolous' Gaze: Modernism, History, Cinematic Ethics'. In Angelos Koutsourakis and Mark Steven (eds), *The Cinema of Theo Angelopolous*, 80–96. Edinburgh: Edinburgh University Press, 2015.

Sobchack, Vivian. *The Address of the Eye: A Phenomenology of Film Experience*. Princeton: Princeton University Press, 1992.

Stadler, Jane. *Pulling Focus: Intersubjective Experience, Narrative Film, and Ethics*. New York and London: Continuum, 2008.

Tersman, Folke. 'Ethics'. In Paisley Livingston and Carl Plantinga (eds), *The Routledge Companion to Philosophy and Film*, 111–120. Abingdon and New York: Routledge, 2009.

Walton, Kendall L. 'Transparent Pictures: On the Nature of Photographic Realism', *Critical Inquiry*, 11.2 (1984): 246–277.

Wartenberg, Thomas. *Thinking on Screen: Film as Philosophy*. Abingdon and New York: Routledge, 2007.

Westwell, Guy. *Parallel Lines: Post-9/11 American Cinema*. London: Wallflower Press, 2014.

Wheatley, Catherine. *Michael Haneke's Cinema: The Ethic of the Image*. New York and Oxford: Berghahn Books, 2009.

Žižek, Slavoj. In *The Pervert's Guide to the Cinema* (dir. Sophie Fiennes, 2013).

Filmography

A Clockwork Orange. Dir. Stanley Kubrick (UK/USA, 1971)

The Act of Killing [*Jagal*]. Dir. Joshua Oppenheimer, Christine Cynn, and Anonymous (Denmark/Norway/UK, 2012)

Biutiful. Dir. Alejandro González Iñárritu (Spain, 2005)

Cinema Paradiso [*Nuovo Cinema Paradiso*]. Dir. Giuseppe Tornatore (Italy/France, 1988)

The Promise [*La promesse*]. Dir. Jean-Pierre and Luc Dardenne (Belgium, 1996)

Stella Dallas. Dir. King Vidor (USA, 1937)

Talk to Her [*Hable con ella*]. Dir. Pedro Almodóvar (Spain, 2002)

Ulysses' Gaze [*To vlemma tou Odyssea*]. Dir. Theo Angelopolous. (Greece/France/Italy/Germany/UK/Federal Republic of Yugoslavia/Bosnia and Herzegovina/Albania/Romania, 1995)

Part II

PHILOSOPHICAL APPROACHES TO CINEMATIC ETHICS

2 From scepticism to moral perfectionism (Cavell)

> The laboratory of film is one in which the elitism of [moral] perfectionism is tested.
>
> Cavell (2005a, 339)

The work of Stanley Cavell has opened up the field of film-philosophy in ways that are only now being appreciated. Indeed, prior to Cavell there were no Anglophone philosophers of comparable stature who dedicated a major part of their work to the study of film, not least because it took cinema so long to be recognized as a legitimate topic of philosophical inquiry. As Cavell often remarks, the marriage between film and philosophy remains a provocation and an inspiration for both partners in this (thinking) dialogue. Cavell even claims that the invention of film 'was as if meant for philosophy', for it prompts us to reflect on the relationship between appearance and reality, the problem of representation, and the value of art and aesthetic experience. It reorients, he continues, 'everything philosophy has said about reality and its representation, about art and imitation, about greatness and conventionality, about judgment and pleasure, about scepticism and transcendence, about language and expression' (Cavell 1996, xii). The last two issues – scepticism and transcendence, language and expression – have a particular bearing on the relationship between cinema and ethics. As D. N. Rodowick observes, Cavell is 'undoubtedly the contemporary philosopher most centrally concerned with the problem of ethics in film and philosophy, above all through his characterization of an Emersonian moral perfectionism' (Rodowick, n.d., 1–2). This ethical orientation is shared, as Rodowick also notes, with Gilles Deleuze's cinematic philosophy, which explores, following its Nietzschean and Bergsonian inspiration, the thinking of movement and of time in cinema as related to 'the expression of belief in the world and its powers of transformation' (Rodowick n.d., 2). Although I agree with Rodowick's observations concerning the kinship between Cavell and Deleuze, in this chapter and the next I also wish to explore the ways in which they also diverge on cinematic ethics and its relationship to scepticism and belief, self-transformation and politics. Also central to their concerns is the manner in which the ontology of moving images – what is distinctive to their presentation of movement and time, perception, action, and subjectivity, nature and history – shapes our aesthetic experience of cinema, its ethical potential, and cultural-political significance.

In the chapter that follows, I consider Cavell's 'ethical' contribution to film-philosophy: his claim that (Emersonian) moral perfectionism, as enacted in particular cinematic genres, offers a response to (cultural and moral) scepticism via its emphasis on creative self-transformation. The ethical significance of cinema as a response to scepticism, most vividly portrayed in the genres of remarriage comedy and melodrama of the unknown woman, will be explored as a philosophical-cinematic engagement with the problem of modernity. My central concern will be to show how it is not only the path of moral perfectionism that marks the ethical contribution of these films, but the thwarting, breakdown, or impossibility of realizing this path. The latter, moreover, not only finds expression in melodrama's well-known aesthetic of 'excess' but it also serves as a provocation to critical reflection. The limits of Cavell's cinematic ethics – namely, making explicit the relation and transition between ethics and politics, thereby doing justice to the ethico-political concerns of these films – will be the focus of my conclusion and prepare the way for Chapter 3 on Deleuze's cinematic ethics.

Film as a 'moving image of scepticism'

A philosophical engagement with cinema and ethics cannot be divorced from questions of ontology, metaphysics, epistemology, and, of course, aesthetics. This is presumably what makes the relationship between cinema and ethics such a challenging proposition, even with regard to the 'negative' ethical dimensions of cinematic experience. Nonetheless, despite the evident concern with the 'unethical' aspects of cinema throughout the history of film theory, it is striking how few theorists have attempted to explore the positive ethical potential of the medium (see Rodowick, n.d., 2007).[1] As remarked, Cavell is one of the few prominent Anglophone philosophers who has explored, in a sustained and thoughtful manner, cinema's philosophical and ethical potential. Commencing with his path-breaking work, *The World Viewed: Reflections on the Ontology of Film* (1979),[2] Cavell has placed the problem of scepticism – our loss of belief or conviction in our capacity to know the world, to understand oneself, and to acknowledge others – at the centre of his philosophical engagement with cinema. Scepticism, typically articulated as an epistemological problem concerning the foundations of knowledge or the relationship between belief, knowledge, and certainty, is also intimately related to moral scepticism: it is not only a paradigmatic modern concern with the problem of knowledge and the desire for certainty concerning the world, but more profoundly a concern with our capacity – or otherwise – to know others, to understand their singular perspectives, and to have conviction in the normative values that guide our intersubjective relations. As we shall see, these are some of the key ethical issues that inform Cavell's philosophical engagement with the remarriage comedy and melodrama of the unknown woman.

Film, for Cavell, both stages and reframes the sceptical situation of a world that remains independent of us: a world that is present to us but where we are not present to it; a world that is known insofar as it can be represented and viewed as an image, but is also thereby reduced to what Heidegger called a 'world-picture' [*Weltbild*] – a defining feature of our historical experience of modernity (Heidegger 1977, Sinnerbrink 2014). If all we know of the world, however, are our representations of it, if the most significant mode of representation of reality and subjective experience in modernity turns out to be through images (and indeed moving images), then it appears that a sceptical chasm opens before us if we ask after the foundations of our knowledge, the source of our conviction in the meaningfulness of the world, the veracity of our understanding of others, or the grounding for the moral-ethical norms that structure our shared forms of life. This is not just a philosophical problem, but a moral-ethical, cultural-historical one. For it is not only philosophy, according to Cavell, but the arts – especially literature, theatre, and, more recently, movies – that respond to the condition of scepticism and its philosophical, moral, and cultural-historical implications. Indeed, for Cavell, cinema is the most pervasive expression of, and productive means of working through, the philosophical, moral, and cultural aspects of scepticism in the modern world; hence the cultural importance of film, and its close kinship, despite apparent differences, with modern philosophy (especially since Heidegger and Wittgenstein).[3]

How so? The rise of modern science, with its methodology involving the empirical observation and mathematical modelling of nature, coupled with the questioning of traditional religious certainties, lead to a questioning of the foundations of our knowledge of the world. Empirical knowledge of nature was growing apace, even though the foundations of such knowledge remained unsecured. With the loosening of traditional bonds and questioning of tradition, the individual's (social and moral) relationships with others became more autonomous and independent but also more detached and uncertain (see Taylor 1989 and Pippin 1999). Philosophically, this disappointment at not being able to know the world with certainty was famously articulated in Descartes' attempt to rationally reconstruct our knowledge from the indubitable foundation of *ego cogito, ergo sum* ('I think therefore I am'). Culturally, it was expressed in the dramas of Shakespeare and in the literature of romanticism, which sought a way back from metaphysical isolation via the aesthetic valorization of individual subjectivity (Cavell 1979, 22). The modern sceptical predicament, whether expressed in philosophy or in art, centres on the metaphysically isolated individual desirous of certainty about the world, the self, and others; an ego that remains confined within its own subjectivity while also doubting their rational capacity to overcome this epistemic isolation with its debilitating sense of metaphysical and moral uncertainty.

How does film respond to this scenario culturally and philosophically? Cinema is the most accomplished expression of modernity's technologically-mediated culture; it is the global art form that takes the visual rendering of the world through images to its apogee. It is both the highest exemplar of Heidegger's 'age of the world-picture', the reduction of the world to an image-world, and the medium that explores all the possibilities of scepticism – of disconnection, disengagement, or isolation from the world – via the mediation of moving images. By projecting a virtual world of images – one which is present to us, yet for which we are absent; one that thus presents a world of images independent of us, yet which is also meaningful for us, thereby rejuvenating our attenuated sense of reality; one that reconnects and reconciles us with a more ambiguous, uncertain, contingent sense of the world and of others – cinema both enacts and overcomes the modern experience of scepticism.

To make sense of this claim we should recall the underlying realism informing Cavell's ontology of film. Following Panofsky and Bazin, for Cavell the photographic basis of moving images means that they are fundamentally images of a world ('of reality or nature') (Cavell 1979, 16): images of things that are not present, yet that have a certain presence through the image, images which are composed, projected and screened as a meaningful whole (a cinematic 'world') that is both a part of our world and in important ways distinct from it. Moreover, the 'automatism' of the moving image, its mechanical basis as a 'manufactured' artefact (Cavell 1979, 20) dependent on the relationship between an object, light, and the camera, is a defining element of its ontology and of the medium's ambiguous claims to realism, whether understood subjectively or objectively (capturing images emulating our conscious experience but also views of the world, selected and stylized aspects of reality independent of us). What photography and cinema reveal is that, although the world exists independently of us, we nonetheless maintain a connection with it; that reality remains present to us even if we are not present to it; that we can maintain our 'presentness to the world' by accepting our absence from it; and that the world the cinema shows us, a world presented to me but one to which I am not present, is experienced as a world 'past' (Cavell 1979, 23). This inherent ambiguity of the cinematic image, both in the present and of the past, showing what is absent as present, and what is present as also absent, as projecting and revealing a world ('of reality or nature') but also immersing us in a cinematic reality distinct from that world, lies at the basis of Cavell's claims concerning cinema, scepticism, and philosophy. The lesson of cinema is that scepticism is an ineliminable possibility of our (always partial) experience and one that can be 'worked through' only by acknowledging the finitude of our knowledge.

It is in these cultural and philosophical senses that Cavell will describe film as 'a moving image of scepticism' (1979, 188): a world of moving images that both presents and dissolves scepticism. The philosophical experience of cinema, we might say, is one that both distances us from and re-engages us with the world; an experience that makes manifest the recognition of scepticism as a condition from which we can never fully be delivered, only learn to acknowledge, accept, and live with ethically in a manner that is enabling rather than destructive. From this perspective, film becomes philosophical in showing us how we can retrieve a sense of the ordinary, now transfigured and revealed in its richness, ambiguity, and contingency, reconnecting us with the world via the very medium of images that might otherwise facilitate or exacerbate our alienation from it.

From a philosophical perspective, such scepticism has traditionally been viewed as an epistemological threat: the problem of grounding our knowledge of the world in certainty, of ensuring that our representations match up with external reality, is typically construed as an epistemological problem related to the theory of knowledge. It is also, however, a problem with moral and ethical dimensions, which plays out differently within Anglophone and 'Continental' philosophical traditions (see Critchley 2001 and Glendinning 2006). Within Anglophone philosophy, it has been largely confined within the epistemological problematic of 'other minds' (how do I know that others have minds, representations, beliefs, attitudes, intentions, and responses, the same as I do?). Within so-called 'Continental' European philosophy (in Hegelian dialectics, phenomenology, or poststructuralist thought), it has taken the more ethically-slanted form of the problem of 'the Other' (how the other subject, human being, or consciousness is related to me, what implications my relations with others have for my self-identity, what the ethical significance of my relations with the 'otherness' of the other person might be). At the same time, both philosophical traditions have acknowledged the more confronting problem of moral scepticism, the view that morality, norms, and values may not only lack certainty but any objective foundation, thus leading to relativism and nihilism, whether on an individual or cultural-historical scale. Ethically speaking, the acknowledgment of scepticism extends, in sum, to our knowledge of others, our capacity to understand and respond to their otherness, and to the possibility of scepticism concerning the foundations of morality and the validity of shared ethical norms.

Although they remain related, Cavell is more concerned, in his work on film, with the moral-ethical aspects of scepticism and the manner in which cinema, like the other arts, can respond to it as a pervasive cultural condition. Interestingly, however, these moral-ethical dimensions only find their full expression in Cavell's work when he considers the manner in which movies can enact and explore the possibilities of (Emersonian) *moral perfectionism*. This philosophical background, however, remains vital for understanding why Cavell turns to moral perfectionism in movies as a way of exploring culturally significant responses to scepticism. As with epistemology and metaphysics, we need to rethink ethics and morality in order to respond to the spectre of scepticism, to experience how it might be acknowledged without expecting it to be dissolved, and thus find new ways, culturally and philosophically, of being no longer beholden to it. We need to 'get over' scepticism (rather than overcome it theoretically), which is where the experience of cinema has something important, both philosophically and ethically, to offer.

Film and moral perfectionism

In his more recent work elaborating cinematic responses to scepticism, Cavell (2004) approaches the two Hollywood genres he has studied most – remarriage comedy and the melodrama of the unknown woman – via the ethical perspective of moral perfectionism: a post-foundational, non-teleological conception of ethics that foregrounds the creative ethical task of individuals shaping their conduct and composing their lives as open-ended projects. Drawing on the thought of Ralph Waldo Emerson (whom we might call the American Nietzsche), Cavell suggests that narrative cinema is ideally suited for exploring characters embarking on a quest for self-knowledge or experience of creative self-transformation; the ethical process, as Nietzsche described, of 'becoming who one is' (2007 [1888]), independent of canonical moral rules or abstract theoretical reflection. What is distinctive about moral perfectionism, from a philosophical perspective, is its eschewal of universalist moral principles, a utilitarian calculus of consequences, or the cultivation of culturally-valorised moral virtues, in favour of an individualist, experimental, 'existential' commitment to freedom and autonomous self-transformation. Moral perfectionism's creative response to ethics in the absence of metaphysical foundations, rationalistic calculation, or rigid moral principles, makes it an ideal ethical response to scepticism on the moral-cultural plane.

So what is moral perfectionism? For Cavell (2004, 12–13), it is not a distinct moral theory but rather a dimension of moral thinking or 'register of moral life' that can be found in a variety of philosophical texts and traditions (from Plato's *Republic*, Emerson's essays and Nietzsche's aphorisms, to Heidegger's *Being and Time* and Wittgenstein's *Philosophical Investigations*). We can describe moral perfectionism as an 'anti-foundationalist' way of conceptualizing ethical experience, one that has a practical, 'existential' emphasis on the importance of making oneself intelligible to others, of transforming oneself throughout one's life, and of practising 'philosophy as a way of life' (Cavell 2004, 13; Hadot 2005, 1995). In this respect, moral perfectionist thinking can be found not only in certain philosophical texts but also in poetry, literature, drama, and, of course, in movies. Perhaps because of its broader cultural significance, however, moral perfectionism remains a neglected way of thinking ethics within academic philosophy compared with the dominant theories of morality: Kantian universalism, utilitarianism, and Aristotelian virtue ethics. Indeed, it hearkens back to traditions of ancient Greek thought, but also resonates with modern strands of romantic-existentialist thinking. In this respect it stands in stark contrast with the major traditions of moral philosophy and more academic forms of moral inquiry.

Although there explorations of Kantian, utilitarian, and Aristotelian virtue ethics in relation to film (Litch 2010, Kowalski 2012, Kupfer 1999, Shaw 2012), these dominant moral theories do not exhaust the conceptual possibilities for thinking about ethics. Consider, for example, existentialist and phenomenological approaches to ethics, which have become increasingly influential (see Cooper 2006, Downing and Saxton 2010, Boljkovac 2013, Girgus 2010). The dominant Kantian, utilitarian, and Aristotelian approaches neglect these alternative traditions of ethical inquiry, which are nonetheless important reference points for contemporary cinema (existentialist film, for example, is a subgenre on its own account). It soon becomes clear, however, why philosophy of film has been reluctant to explore ethics: if one assumes that Kantian universalism, utilitarianism, or virtue theory exhaust the philosophical options for approaching ethics, it becomes difficult to see how narrative cinema could be regarded as philosophically relevant. At best, one can show how ethical problems or moral situations depicted in film are amenable to critical analysis using the standard moral theories, thus treating individual films as illustrative examples of moral problems better analysed by philosophy proper.

This view, however, is open to objection. It assumes that these predominant moral theories exhaust how we can conceptualize ethics in film, and thus rules out the possibility that movies might explore ethical experience in other ways. It also assumes that there is but one way of 'arguing' in philosophy, namely by adopting the methods typically used in contemporary academic philosophy publications. How well, then, does the moral perfectionist task of transforming oneself fit with the three dominant models of moral philosophy? It is not a universalist rule-based form of morality (we cannot demand that all rational agents *must* do so in accordance with their moral duty); it is not a life-choice amenable to a rationalist calculation of utility (it may involve 'disutility' at various levels, or be incompatible with a rationalist calculation of consequences); it may not cohere with the Aristotelian account of ethically desirable virtues (since it may involve rejecting or transforming culturally received virtues (and vices) given one's context or circumstances). Consequently, if we assume that 'ethics' refers either to universalizable rules of conduct, the rational calculation of utility, or the cultivation of received moral virtues, then we miss the ethical significance of many important 'philosophical' films that fall outside these three categories – films better described, Cavell claims, as exploring moral perfectionism.

Of all three ethical perspectives, virtue ethics is perhaps closest to Cavell's version of moral perfectionism (despite Aristotelian ethics remaining tied to a teleological or goal-oriented conception of the good life). What they share is a focus on the singularity of moral situations and the importance of developing an ethical character as a way of being responsive to the variegated demands of the moral life. As Martha Nussbaum (1992) has argued, an important domain of ethical experience concerns our responsiveness to the singularity and complexity of moral situations; being an ethical individual requires skill in the exercise of imaginative sympathy and use of ethical understanding in response to this moral complexity. Indeed, not all morally relevant actions, decisions, or responses, are amenable to abstract reflection or rationalistic calculation. As Nussbaum and Cavell suggest, the experience of moral sympathy, which requires emotional responsiveness to the needs of others, is better cultivated by imaginative engagement with fiction than by purely abstract reflection. Although they have yet to be explored fully, such insights have important implications for cinematic ethics (see Stadler 2008, Rodowick n.d.). This is one significant contribution that Cavell's cinematic ethics can make to contemporary film-philosophy.

Cavell's starting point is the observation that, unlike ancient thought, modern philosophy is defined by a sense of disappointment with our knowledge of the world, or with the world in which we find ourselves (see also Critchley 1997). The Kantian division between our sensuous world of appearances and the supersensible world of thought is a powerful expression of this division defining modern philosophy; but so are the Hegelian, Nietzschean, or 'existentialist' conceptions of the self as divided against itself, searching for ways in which to create itself, reconcile with, or discover the world anew (see Pippin 1999, Taylor 1989). This sense of disappointment with our limits generates a desire to transcend them, either by transforming ourselves, or the world in which we exist, in light of higher ideals. Philosophical criticism presents a vantage point from which the present state of the world can be judged and a new world envisaged in the future; or it can offer a way of evaluating our current world as preferable to the alternatives that might be proffered in the future:

> The very conception of a divided self and a doubled world, providing a perspective of judgment on the world as it is, measured against the world as it may be, tends to express disappointment with the world as it is, as the scene of human activity and prospects, and perhaps to lodge the demand or desire for a reform or transfiguration of the world.
>
> (Cavell 2004, 2)

This moral-existential alienation, leading to a dialectic of disappointment with the world coupled with a desire for its transformation, is the primary motivation for the development of moral perfectionism: a 'register of moral life' that precedes, intervenes in, or accompanies, the more familiar forms of moral theory (Cavell 2004, 2). The moral calling of philosophy may begin with disappointment in the world, but it offers the prospect of transforming ourselves and our relationship with it. This 'therapeutic' dimension of modern philosophy is something Cavell finds in Wittgenstein and Heidegger, but also in Emerson and Nietzsche – thinkers who claim that philosophy is less about knowledge than about transforming our way of experiencing and being in the world. From this point of view, philosophy is about acknowledging our *finitude* as human beings and knowing subjects; it is about renewing our sense of being limited, mortal beings in a meaningful world, and overcoming the desire to transcend this world in favour of pure theoretical knowledge or an ideal metaphysical reality. This is Cavell's 'pragmatic' version of the perfectionist path to renewing our common being-in-the-world or to creating a meaningful form of human life.

Cavell's account of moral perfectionism thus offers an alternative perspective on prevailing moral theories, one centred on achieving self-understanding and ethical self-transformation. It advocates a creative shaping of one's own existence without recourse to pre-given moral principles, social conventions, or universal duties. In this sense it could be understood as a response to the spectre of moral scepticism, cultivating a non-foundationalist way of finding meaning and value in creative and an open-ended process of self-transformation that strives to remain independent of any dogmatic reliance on rigid universalist moral principles, the utilitarian calculation of consequences, or the cultivation of culturally-approved moral virtues. At the same time, it does not deny the possibility of scepticism but in responding to it strives to avoid overly speculative metaphysical commitments that dog other forms of moral thinking and ethical practice (and which in turn tend to collapse into scepticism or even nihilism). Unlike Plato's conception of perfectionism (a teleological account of striving to attain a transcendent ideal), and recalling romanticist and existentialist conceptions of ethical choice (without over-dramatizing the empty and ungrounded significance of 'freedom'), Cavell's 'non-teleological' moral perfectionism involves an autonomous, practical, immanent 'existential' quest to become what one is, to approach, as Emerson put it, one's 'unattained but attainable self':

> In Emerson and Thoreau's sense of human existence, there is no question of reaching a final state of the soul but only and endlessly taking the next step to what Emerson calls 'an unattained but attainable self' – a self that is always and never ours – a step that turns us not from bad to good, or wrong to right, but from confusion and constriction toward self-knowledge and sociability.
>
> (Cavell 2004, 13)

For Cavell, moral perfectionism is not only a viable alternative tradition of modern moral thinking and ethical practice, but the mode of thinking that best defines the moral-ethical significance of the two genres of Hollywood film that he studies in *Pursuits of Happiness* (1981) and *Contesting Tears* (1996): the remarriage comedy and the melodrama of the unknown woman. These films focus on couples seeking acknowledgement and self-education as to their desire, transforming themselves in a manner that can be either comic or tragic; they are films that remain related to earlier dramatic and literary traditions (Shakespearean comedy, nineteenth-century social-domestic drama) but that do not fit readily in any of the three major categories of academic moral philosophy (Kantian universalism, utilitarianism, or virtue ethics). They are films that explore the question of critical self-transformation, the characters' desire to reinvent themselves, and to explore the possibility of a transfigured world in which new ways of being with one another might be possible. In this regard, they remain closely related to Emersonian perfectionism, which does not strive for a utopian ideal, nor dismiss the existing world as inherently meaningless. Rather, in calling these films 'Emersonian', Cavell suggests that they participate in the perfectionist quest for self-transformation within a world that could be itself transformed, however partially, by reinventing our relations with others within a democratic community.

Cavell explores these possibilities of transformation most comprehensively in his book *Cities of Words* (2004). Based on his Harvard lecture course in moral reasoning, Cavell reveals this enduring strain of moral perfectionist thought by pairing philosophical texts by Emerson, Locke, Mill, Kant, Rawls, Nietzsche, Plato, and Aristotle with Hollywood films such as *The Philadelphia Story, Adam's Rib, Gaslight, It Happened One Night, Stella Dallas*, and *The Awful Truth*. He explores the ways in which these films and texts speak to each other about the possibilities of moral perfectionism as a way of engaging in ethical reflection in a manner that is imaginative and dramatic, even comic and tragic. These films explore ethical situations via narrative so as to broaden our conception of moral reasoning, attuning us to more subtle and complex registers of ethical life, thus enhancing and extending the kind of moral-aesthetic experience we can have with cinema. These are films less concerned with traditional theories of morality than with the manner in which particular characters in singular situations can transform themselves through mutual acknowledgement (or show how such transformation can be thwarted by the failure of acknowledgement). They are concerned with existential questions at the level of the ordinary, rather than the metaphysical; they explore what kind of person one is to become, rather than what the concept of a person means. As Cavell remarks:

> The issues the principal pair in these films confront each other with are for-mulated less well by questions concerning what they ought to do, what it would be best or right for them to do, than by the question of how they shall live their lives, what kind of persons they aspire to be. This aspect or moment of morality – in which a crisis forces an examination of one's life that calls for a transformation or reorienting of it – is the province of what I emphasize as moral perfectionism.
>
> (Cavell 2004, 11)

From this point of view, moral perfectionism is an alternative perspective on the major ethical theories in modern culture. It does not displace universalism or utilitarianism (both Kant and J.S. Mill, according to Cavell, have 'deep perfectionist strains in their views' (2004, 11)), but emphasizes the therapeutic aspect of moral experience which concerns what we might otherwise call authenticity, self-knowledge, or the 'care of the self' (Foucault). It links up with the romanticist and existentialist ethics of authenticity, while maintaining a concern with the relationship between individuals and the everyday world in which they find themselves, exploring how the task of self-transformation might be achieved within a democratic form of community. It is not in philosophy, however, but in modern literature and film that moral perfectionism has found a cultural home, a fact that reflects the dispiriting isolation of academic philosophy from the broader moral conversation in our culture. Indeed, academic philosophers have tended to dismiss it as 'elitist' and incompatible with an egalitarian democratic ethos: a charge Cavell challenges in relation to Nietzsche and Emerson, whose moral perfectionism, he argues, does not entail a pre-modern, hierarchical form of society predicated on social inequality (2004, 90–91, 218–226).

So how does moral perfectionism relate to film? We can identify at least three strands: 1) through cinema's egalitarian capacity to thematise and reveal the ordinary in all its rich texture of meaning; 2) through the development of narrative film and of specific genres in which the themes of self-transformation, acknowledging others, and either reconciling with or transforming the world can be explored; and 3) through film's capacity to transfigure human figures as depicted on screen, to capture and convey emotional expression and psychological complexity through gesture and performance. All three aspects are at play in the genres of remarriage comedy and the melodrama of the unknown woman. Indeed, it is through these films' cinematic presentation of singular characters confronting the ordinary moral challenges of love and friendship, freedom and fulfilment, recognition and reinvention, that an ethical experience of moral perfectionism becomes vividly manifest.

Cavell explores the cinematic parallels with some of the key philosophical concerns evident in these canonical texts; but he also highlights the ways in which these films both stage and subvert dominant philosophical accounts of morality and ethics. They are films that serve to teach viewers how they are to be read, rather than being dependent upon philosophy instructing us on what such films are about. They reconnect philosophy with the everyday, showing how abstract theoretical discussions of morality connect with aesthetic presentations of ethical experience. As Cavell remarks:

> These films are rather to be thought of as differently configuring intellectual and emotional avenues that philosophy is already in exploration of, but which, perhaps, it has cause sometimes to turn from prematurely, particularly in its forms since its professionalization, or academization. [...] The implied claim is that film, the latest of the great arts, shows philosophy to be the often invisible accompaniment of the ordinary lives that film is so apt to capture.
>
> (Cavell 2004, 6)

As we shall see with Deleuze, for Cavell, too, cinema reflects on problems that philosophy has traditionally addressed but tended to eschew in its 'professionalized' guise. Academic philosophers today often dismiss existential questions of value and meaning as either speculative or naïve; yet these questions animate much contemporary cinema, suggesting that cinema and its shadow (philosophy) are, at least potentially, ethical partners in retrieving the ordinary from metaphysical oblivion. Cinema and philosophy meet here on the same ground: recovering the meaningfulness of the everyday as a response to scepticism, and finding ways to make oneself intelligible to others through mutual acknowledgment – cinematic philosophy as a path to ethical self-transformation.

This Emersonian aspect of Cavell's vision of moral perfectionism demands further reflection. Cavell identifies a number of themes explored in his readings of comedy and melodrama. Emersonian moral perfectionism is defined by the desire for self-knowledge: the quest for authentic self-identity through cultivation and education, the individual's striving for continuous self-transformation as a life-defining project. It interprets moral reasoning as the practice of making oneself morally intelligible, so has an intimate connection with the idea of morality as a practice of communication with others ('moral confrontation as one soul's examination of another' (2004, 49)). Hence its preferred communicative form is the dialogue or conversation rather than the treatise or argument. This emphasis on conversation is directed towards the Friend, the one who will assist me in my quest, perhaps question my sincerity, acknowledge my identity, and facilitate my self-transformation. In this respect Emersonian moral perfectionism casts itself in counterpoint with the philosophical tradition, challenging the manner in which philosophy is traditionally written, reasserting its kinship with literature, and availing itself of idioms and genres that venture outside standard argumentation. This leads to moral perfectionism's concern with moral paradoxes, its stress on the ambiguity of moral relations, the importance of careful reading, and the ideals of authenticity and ethical freedom beyond a rigid universalism, narrow utilitarianism, or dogmatic moralism (Cavell 2004, 27–34). These Emersonian themes will resonate strongly with the particular movies Cavell studies as exemplars of the remarriage comedy and melodrama of the unknown woman.

Moral perfectionism and remarriage comedy

As remarked, Cavell's two major philosophical works on film, *Pursuits of Happiness* and *Contesting Tears*, identify and explore two related genres of Hollywood film, the remarriage comedy and the melodrama of the unknown woman. These two genres transform the theme of marriage, either as a utopian possibility of mutual acknowledgment in the comedies, or as a block to the woman's quest for self-knowledge in the melodramas. In these earlier books, however, Cavell does not explicitly link either genre with Emersonian moral perfectionism, although Emerson's thought remains, as ever, a constant reference point. Rather, he draws attention to the manner in which such films thematize their condition as visual media, their inheritance of literary and dramatic traditions, their relationships with other films and constitution of a genre, and their reflection on morally relevant themes, including the Emersonian critique of conformity, and the possibility of an egalitarian relationship between the sexes. It is only in *Cities of Words* (2004) that Cavell explicitly recasts both genres as participating in the philosophical discourse of moral perfectionism present in modern culture since Shakespeare and Milton, Ibsen and Eliot, Emerson and Nietzsche.

To be precise, Cavell focuses on a particular subgenre of the romantic comedy, a small selection of 'seven talkies made in Hollywood between 1934 and 1949' (2005b, 136): *It Happened One Night* (1934), *The Awful Truth* (1937), *Bringing Up Baby* (1938), *His Girl Friday* (1940), *The Philadelphia Story* (1940), *The Lady Eve* (1941), and *Adam's Rib* (1949). Although they share many features with other romantic comedies, these 'remarriage comedies' are also distantly related to Shakespearean romances like *The Winter's Tale* and *The Tempest*. Unlike classical comedy and romance, where a young couple is shown 'overcoming obstacles to their love and at the end achieving marriage,' remarriage comedies commence with a mature couple, getting or threatening to get their divorce, so that 'the drive of the narrative is to get the original pair together *again*' (Cavell 2004, 4). They are distinguished from other versions of romantic comedy (related to what Northrop Frye called 'new comedy') in which a male character pursues his beloved and battles familial and social barriers to their desired marriage. Resonating with Frye's account of 'old comedy', in the remarriage comedies it is the woman who is the focus of the narrative, except that now she embarks on a 'sentimental journey' to educate herself as to her desire, deciding whether the man in question is a suitable partner for her project of self-transformation. These are films that explore the concept of conversation, the ethical idea of marriage as a 'meet and happy conversation' (as Milton put it in his famous tract on divorce). They explore forms of social and personal exchange in which each partner is acknowledged in his or her uniqueness, yet where each provides the other with an educative perspective as to his or her self-identity. This raises the question whether the relationship of equality between the sexes envisaged by the couple is realizable within the social, cultural, and ethical norms of the community in which the couple find themselves. The utopian aspect of these comedies thus lies not only in their exploration of a mutually transformative relationship between the sexes, but also in imagining a form of democratic community in which self-reliance and interpersonal intimacy can be mediated with social freedom and political equality.

The remarriage motif, as Cavell remarks, is prompted by the changed situation of marriage, which is 'no longer assured or legitimized by church or state or sexual compatibility or children' but rather by the 'willingness for remarriage, a way of continuing to affirm the happiness of one's initial leap'

(2005b, 137). Marriage, in other words, is at once a romantic and an ethical relationship sustained by an existential will to repeat one's commitment to seek happiness through mutual acknowledgement with an equal. The focus is not only on the question of marriage but how the latter is linked with the self-education of the woman. Through this experience she learns the true nature of her desire, seeking to establish her self-identity, and openness towards the future, through a process of mutual acknowledgement between her and her partner. The couple's trials are carried comically thanks to virtuoso dialogue and artful performance; their mutual adventures take them from the city to the country (the Shakespearean 'green world'), where the obstacles to self-realization through acknowledgment, hence to remarriage, are overcome. What the couple discover, finally, is that they are indeed 'made for each other', but only after having committed themselves, through 'happy and meet conversation', to educating themselves, and thus transforming and reinventing themselves, in felicitous partnership with one another.

By contrast, melodramas of the unknown woman, such as Ophüls' *Letter from an Unknown Woman* (1948), Cukor's *Gaslight* (1944), Rapper's *Now, Voyager* (1942), and King Vidor's *Stella Dallas* (1937), appear to negate key elements of the remarriage comedy, notably the negation of marriage itself. Within these films, the idea of marriage as a route to self-creation is 'transcended and perhaps reconceived' (Cavell 2004, 6). Indeed, the route to self-creation is not through marriage but involves, rather, a 'metamorphosis': a radical, 'melodramatic' change in the identity of the woman that takes place independently of any conversation or marital commerce with the man, and which draws its nourishment from the otherwise marginalized 'world of women' (Cavell 2004, 6). It is the woman's education towards self-reliance, and her subsequent rejection of marriage, that contrasts with the remarriage comedy, both genres nonetheless sharing an underlying commitment to (Emersonian) moral perfectionism, namely, 'working out the problematic of self-reliance and conformity, or of hope and despair' (Cavell 1996, 9). Indeed, Cavell insists that the contrasts between the comedies and the melodramas can be accommodated within the moral perfectionist frame. Whereas the remarriage comedies 'envisage a relation of equality between human beings' that Emerson described as 'a relation of rightful attraction, of expressiveness, and of joy,' the melodramas of the unknown woman envision 'the phase of the problematic of self-reliance that demands this expressiveness and joy first in relation to oneself' – a kind of excessive or 'melodramatic' doubt, or passage through scepticism, that leads the woman beyond sceptical despair and towards a fragile recovery of herself and the world (Cavell 1996, 9). Both subgenres allegorize these questions of scepticism and its overcoming in relation to the problem of marriage. Both traverse the standing possibility of sceptical doubt over our relationship to the world, our capacity for self-knowledge, our ability to know and understand one another, through comic and tragic explorations of romantic relationships, understood as expressions of the potential for acknowledgment within the everyday and the domestic. These are some of the reasons behind Cavell's otherwise surprising claim that, contrary to appearances, scepticism, understood here as 'the threat to the ordinary' that philosophy both identifies and exacerbates, should show up in fiction's favourite threats to forms of marriage, namely in forms of melodrama and of tragedy (1996, 10).

As I shall discuss further in Chapter 5, this is one of the more questionable aspects of Cavell's reading of the melodramas (counterintuitive in a way that differs from his more plausible reading of remarriage comedies). Indeed, one is tempted to modify Cavell's claim and assert that, if melodrama is the negation of remarriage comedy, then within melodrama the moral perfectionist path is blocked or thwarted (the possibility of finding and following such an ethical path is put into question). The world within which the woman's quest for self-transformation is compromised itself becomes the object of a critical reflection; the constraints and conflicts to which she is subject generate the hyperbolic emotionalism and aesthetic excess for which the genre is famous.[4] It thus remains to be seen, however, whether Cavell's account of this genre can do justice to the ethical and political significance of scepticism in the lives of melodrama's 'women on the verge' (Almodóvar), women whose plight transcends the personal and shows up the limitations of our inherited conceptions of gender, equality, power, and democracy.

Why should the remarriage comedy be regarded as philosophically significant? Beyond the question of ethical relations with others, marriage becomes philosophical, Cavell claims, as an allegory of what philosophers since Aristotle 'have thought about under the title of friendship' (2004, 15). It takes on a modern cast, moreover, once friendship moves from being conceived as a practice of homosocial relationships among free Athenian males to being linked with the freely chosen romantic relationship between the sexes.[5] This raises not only the feminist question of sexual equality but that of the broader relationship between the individual and society, what we might call the question of the basis and legitimacy of modern (social and liberal) democracy, a question examined philosophically in social contract theories from Locke and Rousseau to Kant and Rawls. At the same time, however, it is important to recognize that remarriage comedies are not simply illustrations of pre-given philosophical theories. They explore, rather, the ethical relations between individuals where recognition and responsiveness define how these individuals achieve self-knowledge and a changed identity within a community of equals – the dialectic between individualism, social institutions, and ethical (and political) life within a modern democratic community.

It is worth pausing here to note how Cavell's way of doing film-philosophy prompts one to reconsider what the relationship between film and philosophy can be. Moral perfectionism provides a way of understanding what remarriage comedies and melodramas of the unknown woman are about, while these genres prompt us to reconsider how ethical experience can be elicited and communicated. Film and philosophy enter into a mutually productive dialogue, with the film-philosopher as mediator or go-between, opening new paths for thinking and expanding our horizons of ethical experience. Instead of movies being subjected to philosophical translation in order to 'purify' their conceptual content of aesthetic ornament, movies themselves express and invite a philosophical response that might alter our sense of the ethical significance of movies as well as our conception of philosophy. To see how this works, let us consider Cavell's moral perfectionist readings of some exemplary remarriage comedies. For it is in the close critical engagement with singular films that Cavell's claims concerning moral perfectionism, its viability as a cinematically-mediated moral experience appropriate to modernity, will stand or fall.

The Philadelphia Story, His Girl Friday, and Adam's Rib

George Cukor's *The Philadelphia Story* (1940) and *Adam's Rib* (1949) are in many ways paradigmatic of the genre – understood as an artistic use of the medium rather than a strict cycle of narratives – of remarriage comedy. Indeed, such films, Cavell claims, do not deal so much with 'front-page' moral issues – for example, abortion, euthanasia, scapegoating, rape, spousal abuse, child neglect, capital punishment, and the like (although *His Girl Friday*, to some extent, does do so) – as they are concerned with the question of marriage, or rather re-marriage. They focus on a performative or lived sense of ethics: how to act in situations in which 'it is a question whether a moral issue is to be raised' (2004, 39). We might call this an ethics of the care of the self, which also incorporates, given the emphasis on romance and friendship, one's ethical relationships with others.

The central characters, usually privileged in accordance with their social class, are engaged with the task of deciding 'on what kinds of lives they wish to live and whether they wish to live them together, to consent to each other, to say yes to their lives and their life together' (Cavell 2004, 39). It is not a matter of ethical virtue in the Aristotelian sense, that is, of judging what the appropriate form of conduct is in a given situation, drawing on moral character traits or a refined sense of practical judgment. The very question of how one is to act, what to say, how to respond, remains in question, whether or not a given situation or decision is a moral or ethical one. Marriage is figured here, we should note, as comprising the romantic relationship between the sexes, and as a figure for a more egalitarian, ethical relationship of mutual acknowledgment between loving partners (the idea of a marriage as a synthesis of romantic and ethical union, a form of romantic friendship).

There are two questions that arise in studying Cavell's readings of remarriage comedies. First, does this focus on the individual's quest for happiness, mutual acknowledgment, and self-transformation leave these films open to the charge of being elitist, bourgeois, or apolitical? This question is linked to Cavell's concern to defend moral perfectionism from the criticism – made by John

Rawls (1971, 25, 535 fn.), for example – that it is an elitist form of ethics incompatible with democracy. Secondly, are we to regard remarriage comedies as having a feminist dimension in their 'battle of the sexes' dramas, and if so, do Cavell's readings of these films do justice to this aspect of their ethical (and political) significance?

In *The Philadelphia Story*, for example, Cavell emphasizes the philosophical self-reflexivity of these films, what we might call their 'modernist' aspect (2004, 41): the manner in which such films reflect upon their relationships with other films, or their status as belonging to, or being related to, a particular genre. Indeed, Cavell comments on the manner in which 'the film calls attention to, and questions, the condition of its existence as a film – namely in its two closing images' (2004, 41), which not only thematize marriage, and images of marriage, but also cinema's relationship with photography and its propensity to capture the everyday: 'life passing itself by'.[6] Although these aspects of the film also occupy centre stage in Cavell's earlier reading of the film (in *Pursuits of Happiness*), in *Cities of Words* it is the film's ethical significance as a study in moral perfectionism that is the focus of his discussion. Once again, this ethical dimension of the film is not reducible to a utilitarian calculus or to Kantian universality, but like any form of moral reasoning it requires that reasons be given for one's attitude, convictions, or conduct. It concerns the rationality of acting on one's desire (or the irrationality of failing to do so), and of finding the right words to communicate one's reasons for acting thus (or failing to do so). Hence it involves conversation between individuals who mutually recognize each other, yet who remain open to moral persuasion or mutual engagement precisely through conversation with each other.

This is the aim of moral reasoning within the perfectionist perspective: not to calculate consequences or universalize principles but to acknowledge the need to make one's reasons for acting intelligible to others as well as to oneself (Cavell 2004, 42). It is a perspective that is sensitive to the fact that many moral situations arise 'not from an ignorance of your duties or a conflict of duties, but from a confusion over your desires, your attractions and aversions'; a remark that well describes the situations faced by the characters in *The Philadelphia Story*, for example, whether one should get remarried, face the 'sense of failure' in another divorce, whether Tracy Lord's desire 'to be useful in the world' arises from fear, vanity (Cavell 2004, 42) – or, one could add, whether she is feeling unrecognized in being defined principally as a wife, or a future mother, and as little else besides.

Such ethical challenges are not necessarily resolved by the moral agent exercising his or her reason in splendid isolation. They require, rather, open conversation between equals and, more specifically, the perspective of a friend – an intimate who enjoys a favoured moral standing – who might understand but also test one's sense of personal integrity. It is this sense of ethical friendship that proves essential to the possibility, authenticity, and longevity of romantic relationships. This aspect of remarriage comedy Cavell identifies as a need to 'educate the woman': to respond to her sense of lacking an education as to the moral intelligibility of her identity, and thus to facilitate the task of ethical self-transformation. This education, however, also raises the questions I mentioned above (concerning the limits of moral perfectionism as a way of entertaining broader social and political concerns, and whether it can acknowledge and engage with a feminist perspective on such concerns).

For his part, Cavell emphasizes the 'gendered' nature of the quest for self-knowledge: the woman desires an education (concerning her desire and recovery of her sense of identity) and so must find the most suitable partner to facilitate that education. In *The Philadelphia Story*, it is Tracy Lord's [Katharine Hepburn] 'desire to be useful in the world' that shapes her feeling and reasoning with respect to her three suitors: would-be husband George, who fails to take her desire seriously and in fact wants to prevent her from being 'useful in the world'; Dexter [Cary Grant], who criticizes Tracy for having been a scold (in relation to his drinking); and writer/journalist Connor ('Mike') [James Stewart], who seems to have touched her heart in an episode of romantic intimacy, only to find that their midnight swim reawakens her memory and desire for Dexter (Cavell 2004, 43–44). To underline the claim, Cavell notes the Shakespearean resonances of Tracy's choice between three suitors (like Portia in *The Merchant of Venice*), and her allusion to a line from a Browning poem concerning death and resurrection (2004, 44–45). Although Mike has reawakened her desire, showing that she has 'feet of clay', he is still immature and not yet ready for marriage, as Tracy remarks, adding that it would not please Liz, his photographer-partner (Cavell 2004, 46–47). Rather, it is Dexter who shows himself to be ready for re-marriage, to affirm her feeling that she is now, as he puts it, a 'first-class human being' rather than an abstract ideal; someone capable of making serious moral demands upon him- or herself, that is, of caring for one's self, as Cavell suggests, in an ethical sense (2004, 48).

In Cavell's reading of the film, however, it remains the woman who stands in need of 'an education', one to be delivered or directed by the man, whose own desire does not appear to be, or be perceived, as lacking in self-knowledge to the same degree.[7] Dexter's drinking and other flaws, for example, do not appear to be subject to the same critical scrutiny or self-examination as Tracy's 'scolding' and her inflexible desire for 'perfection' (rather than 'perfectionism'). Tracy's decision to divorce Dexter because of his drinking is not viewed as a valid response to marital discord but as evidence of her lack of sympathy, her perfectionistic streak, her intolerance or lack of understanding. As Cynthia Willett remarks, referring to Cavell's gloss on the divorce, 'this slip on Cavell's part alerts us to be on the lookout for ways in which he tilts the reading of the genre in favour of a male perspective' (2008, 101). This 'tilting' extends to the three-way relationship between Tracy, Mike and Dexter: Mike and Dexter both catalyse and complete Tracy's desire, contributing to her education, but they are not transformed significantly in the process. And this desire, moreover, is confined to that between the romantic couple; there is little sense in which their relationship reflects broader cultural impediments to mutual equality between the sexes or how these impediments might be overcome. The ironic 'feminist' sensibility that subtly suffuses these films is given short shrift in Cavell's moral perfectionist reading of *The Philadelphia Story*. This is not to fault the latter, but to point out important ethical (and political) issues that arise in remarriage comedy, like inequality in gender relations, which may be underplayed within a moral-perfectionist perspective.

These ethical-political issues are explored more explicitly in some of the other remarriage comedies Cavell considers, notably *His Girl Friday* and *Adam's Rib*. Both of these 1940s films involve career women (Rosalind Russell as a journalist and Katharine Hepburn as a lawyer) in 'battle of the sexes' comedies that combine the remarriage scenario with broader social-cultural explorations – strikingly progressive for their time – of how relations between the sexes might be conducted in a more egalitarian ethical spirit. This 'everyday' theme, however, also links, for Cavell, through a series of steps, with the problem of social community, even the basis of political consent within democratic societies, which Cavell examines through the dual lenses of Rawlsian social contract theory and Capra's *Mr. Deeds Goes to Town* (1936) (2004, 164–207). Cavell asks, for example, why so many remarriage comedies involve newspapers, newspapers stories, and newspaper men (or women). *The Philadelphia Story* embeds the newspaper theme within the plot (Mike Connor is sent, with photographer Linda, to cover the 'society' wedding between Katharine and her unprepossessing groom, George); *Adam's Rib* includes the press as part of the publicity machine surrounding the sensational domestic court case being fought out between rival lawyers (and spouses) Adam and Amanda Bonner [Spencer Tracy and Katharine Hepburn]; *His Girl Friday* is set largely in a newspaper room with the romance in question to be settled between 'newspapermen' Hildy Johnson [Rosalind Russell] and Walter Burns [Cary Grant]. Cavell's answer is to suggest that the press serves to mediate between these 'society' marriages (or breakdown of marriages) and the broader social community. The presence of the press shows how the ordinary can 'become news', a social ratification of the personal opening out 'beyond the privacy of privilege'; it also serves to ratify the society within which the characters exist as 'a locale in which happiness and liberty can be pursued' – offering, in short, an allegory of the free consent required for democratic community (Cavell 2004, 75).

This is a provocative way of reading the philosophical significance of marriage within the broader context of a consensual form of democratic community. And Cavell goes to considerable lengths to show these themes can be articulated within a philosophical perspective that combines not only (Emersonian) moral perfectionism but broader political reflections on consent and governance in the social contract tradition of democratic theory (from Locke to Rawls).[8] At the same time, precisely this link between the personal and the political, or the domestic and the social, raises the questions I canvassed earlier: whether the moral perfectionist approach can address adequately the broader societal and political concerns that frame relations between the sexes, especially in regard to marriage, and whether Cavell's moral perfectionist reading does justice to these films' feminist ethical and political concerns with gender inequality.

Cavell's reading of *Adam's Rib*, for example, focuses on the theme of remarriage, exploring its ethical validity, and taking it allegorically as a relationship that 'is meant to epitomize the fate of the democratic social bond' (1981, 193). As the reader no doubt recalls, married attorneys Adam and Amanda Bonner find themselves defending another couple caught up in a domestic drama: Amanda is defending estranged wife Mrs Attinger [Judy Holliday], who is charged with the attempted shooting murder of her philandering husband Mr Attinger [Tom Ewell] (whom Adam is defending), after she discovers him with his provocative mistress Beryl Caighn [Jean Hagen] in a seedy apartment. Amanda takes on the case with enthusiasm, despite Adam's objections that she should respect their marital privacy by declining it (the case has been assigned to him, against his will). Amanda, however, sides with the accused wife in the case, who, as a wronged, abused spouse, has 'natural justice' on her side. Moreover, she regards the case as a symbolic example of widespread female disenfranchisement, and thus defies Adam by accepting the case as a public examination of the inequality that still afflicts all 'modern' marriages (including their own). The trial of the hapless couple thereby becomes a trial of the contemporary social institution of marriage and of the sexual inequality and moral hypocrisy that still underpins it.

At the same time, Cavell interprets the courtroom battle of the sexes between married attorneys as Amanda's attempt to expose her own marriage to public scrutiny; to 'confront her marriage and its world with one another', and in so doing, 'to let them rebuke one another (like America and American law)' (2004, 197). Her aim, Cavell claims, is not to launch a feminist campaign so much as to contest her husband's masculinist delusions about women, delusions that Adam shares, it seems, with accused husband Mr Attinger. In short, it is to teach him a moral-practical lesson concerning mutual acknowledgement and genuine equality between the sexes (although Adam will also teach Amanda a lesson in taking seriously the relationship between morality and law, between natural justice and institutional legality, as evident in the famous mock 'shooting' scene with the liquorice gun). In this way, according to Cavell (1981, 197), it is not the attempted murder trial that puts the institution of marriage on trial; rather, it is the way in which this trial serves to expose to public scrutiny what we might call Amanda and Adam's private marital 'struggle for recognition'. In short, the Attinger case, for Cavell, is a pretext, rather than a 'cause', to explore the interpersonal dynamic between Adam and Amanda: the 'battle of the sexes'-style confrontation between their professed beliefs and the practical reality of their commitments to marital equality, mutual acknowledgment, and public justice.[9] In this manner, Cavell will draw a parallel between the Bonner's marital conflict, their dramatic performance of the dialectic between private and public, and the democratic struggle for recognition that strives for social equality through public conversation and collective political deliberation.

This enfolding of ethico-political reflection within the remarriage comedy is also evident in Cavell's reading of Hawks' *His Girl Friday* (1981, 163 ff.) He foregrounds again its kinship with Shakespearean romantic comedy (as well as Jonsonian satire), while emphasizing the film's acknowledgement of its own status and its relationship with other films within the remarriage comedy sub-genre. Like *Adam's Rib*, it too nests the feminist question of sexual equality within the humorous banter and byplay between savvy newspaper editor Walter Burns [Cary Grant] and his former wife and star reporter Hildy Johnson [Rosalind Russell]. The film opens with Hildy paying her old newspaper office one last visit before marrying bland but dependable Bruce Baldwin [Ralph Bellamy], apparently to remind the dashing but disreputable Walter to stop calling her now that she is going to be married. Thanks to Grant's snappy charm and clever machinations, however, she is talked into covering one last story, that of confused everyman Earl Williams [John Qualen], serving time on death row for killing a black police officer. Despite the narrative framing of the remarriage 'battle of the sexes' comedy, the bulk of the film centres on Hildy's ethical commitment as a journalist to write Williams' death-row story from a sympathetic perspective, critical of the death penalty, and her clever efforts to outwit corrupt Mayor [Clarence Kolb] and his compliant police commissioner, who seek to orchestrate Williams' speedy execution in order to boost the Governor's political ambitions (to secure the black vote in an upcoming election). It would be difficult to produce a better example of how popular Hollywood cinema can also engage in the critical exploration of complex ethical situations and political issues (see Rushton 2013).

According to Cavell, the inclusion of this dark underbelly of crime, prison, capital punishment, racism, and political manipulation threatens to undermine *His Girl Friday*'s claim as belonging to the genre of the remarriage comedy. Curiously, this 'black world', as Cavell calls it, should be viewed, rather, as compensating for the absence of an idyllic 'Green world' (typically a country retreat set in Connecticut) otherwise explicitly present in the other remarriage comedies. The political subtext, in other words, should be seen as supplementing a generic lack rather than making an independent contribution to the film's ethico-political meaning. Cavell's marginalizing of a central feature of the film here in favour of a reading that emphasizes its belonging to a particular genre (or subgenre) is an example, I would argue, of the inadequacy of the moral-perfectionist perspective when confronted by ethico-political concerns. Indeed, the presence of this 'black world' of crime, punishment, and political corruption in *His Girl Friday* is central, I suggest, to the ethical and political significance of the film as a whole. Hildy's tough but principled perspective, her clever yet justifiable stratagems, are on full display in this part of the film, during which time the 'remarriage' theme is very much relegated to the background. *His Girl Friday* thus reframes the remarriage comedy within a broader, more ambiguous public milieu, one in which the question of sexual inequality opens out to broader questions of social inequality, political corruption, media manipulation of the public sphere, exploring the various dangers these pose to the flourishing of a democratic community.

Both *Adam's Rib* and *His Girl Friday* incorporate these broader ethico-political and social issues within the generic framework of the remarriage comedy. And far from using these themes as a narrative pretext to get the couple back together, the reunion of the couple is framed, rather, by the broader ethical and political struggles for recognition within the democratic community of which they are a part (struggles between the sexes, between classes, but also encompassing the complex relationships between the media, the law, and institutional politics). Both films are critical of the pernicious manipulation of emotion and sentiment that scandalous 'personal' but politically-driven stories can have thanks to a sensationalist mass media. Both films also make understated but explicit feminist claims: *Adam's Rib* stresses the social constraints on achieving equality that afflict both uneducated, socially disenfranchised as well as educated, professional women, while *His Girl Friday* evokes the 'private' institutional dynamics – including the politicized use of sexual scandal and ideological prejudices about women and sexual morality – that shape the legal administration of punishment in order to satisfy communal fears or public demands for retributive satisfaction. These more explicitly ethical and political themes are carefully integrated into the comedic 'battle of the sexes' dramas that provide the narrative drive as well as the ethical import of the remarriage comedy as a genre.

Again, this is not to deny the significance, but to draw attention to some of the limitations, of Cavell's moral-perfectionist approach. Because of its focus on the individual, interpersonal relations, moral friendship, and eschewal of collective action, Emersonian moral perfectionism tends to overlook the relationship between ethics and politics. It offers an oblique, attenuated perspective on the manner in which the ethical question of self-transformation is enabled, but also constrained, by the social institutions and cultural norms of the larger political community to which individuals belong. For it is always in the context of, in response to, and being enabled (or disabled) by, the norms, practices, and material conditions of one's social-cultural community that the quest for a moral perfectionist form of ethical education and self-transformation can at all take place. In short, remarriage comedies are not just centred on the moral perfectionist quest for moral intelligibility, the creative pursuit of an ethical ideal of marriage as mutual acknowledgement between the sexes. Rather, they are also feminist-slanted social critiques of the persisting inequalities in the observation of sexual and gender norms that can hinder the exercise of women's agency and the fulfilment of their desire for self-transformation with modern liberal democratic communities. Such films are not just moral perfectionist parables but ethico-political forms of cinematic critique: a romantic, comedic, but also critical engagement with the everyday world (of work, interpersonal and social relations, but also of the media, the law, and the political institutions of democracy) that is both mediated and reflexively staged by and through film.

The question that arises here in respect of Cavell's moral perfectionist approach is how to navigate this difficult but necessary passage from ethics to politics (or from 'the personal to the political') within contemporary cinema. For the ethical experience is also one that reveals the broader social, cultural, historical, and political dimensions of one's world, showing, in an experientially rich manner, how the latter profoundly can both shape and constrain, both motivate and stymie, personal as well as collective forms of self-transformation. How can film-philosophy capture more effectively the dialectic between individual and community while also integrating broader social-cultural and political dimensions into a more individualist narrative framework? How does aesthetic engagement with film enable us to apprehend our world more ethically, to find meaning in a world afflicted by (moral and cultural) scepticism? Is contemporary cinema up to this task? To address these questions, I turn to Deleuze's cinematic philosophy, setting it in critical dialogue with Cavell's, in order to explore a complementary but contrasting view of cinematic ethics and its dialectical relationship with aesthetics and politics.

Notes

1　One of the few recent texts that does so is D. N. Rodowick's 'Ethics in film philosophy (Cavell, Deleuze, Levinas)' (n.d), an unpublished text of a rejected entry from the *Routledge Encyclopedia of Philosophy and Film*.

2　The first edition of *The World Viewed* was published in 1971.

3　The two key texts, for Cavell, are Heidegger's *Being and Time* (1927) and Wittgenstein's *Philosophical Investigations* (1953), which have profoundly shaped the course of twentieth century European ('Continental') and Anglophone ('analytic') philosophy.

4　In Chapter 5 I discuss this question in relation to Cavell's reading of *Stella Dallas*.

5　There is no reason to assume that this would exclude gay marriage, despite the heterosexual focus of traditional remarriage comedies.

6　The latter refer to the two concluding shots of the heroine [Katharine Hepburn] and her two suitors, former husband C.K. Dexter Haven [Cary Grant] and writer and would-be groom Macaulay Connor [James Stewart], followed by a 'posed' shot of bride Tracy Lord and groom C.K. Dexter Haven kissing for the camera, taken by the chief of *Spy* Magazine, for whom Connor has been covering the wedding only to become swept up in a brief romance with Lord. Given that one of the central dramatic tensions in the film is between the false publicity of the press and the authentic coupling of private and public performed by the couple, Cavell is moved to question what the purpose of ending the film with these ambiguous images might be, suggesting that they serve to prompt the viewer to 'reframe' all that he or she has seen in the movie as a whole.

7　One thinks here of Lone Scherfig's *An Education* (2009), whose teenage protagonist Jenny Mellor [Carey Mulligan] undergoes a sentimental and emotional education, with a feminist slant, in her encounter with older, worldlier, sophisticate David Goldman [Peter Sarsgaard], against the background of the nascent sexual and cultural revolution in 1960s England.

8　See the chapters on Locke (Cavell 2004, 49–69) and *Adam's Rib* (70–81), along with Rawls (164–189) and *Mr. Deeds Goes to Town* (190–207) that Cavell reads in parallel as cinematic and philosophical treatments of the same issues. The difficulties that arise with Cavell's tendency towards 'allegorical' readings (the marriage bond as allegorical of the social contract, for example) are addressed presently.

9 Cavell comments that he is 'trying to find a cause of Amanda's actions that I can believe in' (1981, 197), suggesting that she does not really take the condition of women in post-war America to be akin to a kind of enslavement, hence that the overtly feminist motivation of her defence of Mrs Attinger is not plausible. Rather, it is her desire to expose the private domain of her marriage to public scrutiny and thereby teach her well-meaning but inadvertently sexist husband a lesson that provides a more plausible scenario. Although these two dimensions of *Adam's Rib* are clearly linked, I suggest that Cavell does not take the feminist motivation as seriously as the film does: for it stages the trial as one that does seek to 'put marriage on trial' in a cultural context in which marriage remains predicated on a denial of sexual equality to women and thus a lack of mutual acknowledgement between men and women, despite claims to democratic equality, which includes relations between the sexes. Katharine Hepburn's own 'authorship' of this film (she financed and helped produce it based on a script written for Hepburn and Spencer by their friends, married couple Garson Kanin and Ruth Gordon) should be taken into account here, for it supports the idea that the film uses the marital 'battle of the sexes' theme as a pretext to launch a feminist-inspired social critique, rather than the reverse.

Bibliography

Boljkovac, Nadine. *Untimely Affects: Gilles Deleuze and an Ethics of Cinema*. Edinburgh: Edinburgh University Press, 2013.

Cavell, Stanley. *The World Viewed: Reflections on the Ontology of Film*. Enlarged Edition. Cambridge, MA and London: Harvard University Press, 1979.

Cavell, Stanley. *Pursuits of Happiness: The Hollywood Comedy of Remarriage*. Cambridge, MA and London: Harvard University Press, 1981.

Cavell, Stanley. *Contesting Tears: The Hollywood Melodrama of the Unknown Woman*. Chicago and London: University of Chicago Press, 1996.

Cavell, Stanley. *Cities of Words: Pedagogical Letters on a Register of Moral Life*. Cambridge, MA and London: Belknap Press of Harvard University Press, 2004.

Cavell, Stanley. 'The Good of Film'. In William Rothman (ed.), *Cavell on Film*, 333–348. Albany: State University of New York Press, 2005a.

Cavell, Stanley. 'A Capra Moment'. In William Rothman (ed.), *Cavell on Film*, 135–143. Albany: State University of New York Press, 2005b.

Cooper, Sarah. *Selfless Cinema? Ethics and French Documentary*. London: Legenda, 2006.

Critchley, Simon. *Very Little…Almost Nothing: Death, Philosophy, Literature*, Revised Edition. London and New York: Routledge, 1997.

Critchley, Simon. *Continental Philosophy: A Very Short Introduction*. Oxford: Oxford University Press, 2001.

Downing, Lisa and Saxton, Libby. *Film and Ethics: Foreclosed Encounters*. Abingdon and London: Routledge, 2010.

Girgus, Sam B. *Levinas and the Cinema of Redemption: Time, Ethics, and the Feminine*. New York: Columbia University Press, 2010.

Glendinning, Simon. *The Idea of Continental Philosophy*. Edinburgh: Edinburgh University Press, 2006.

Hadot, Pierre. *Philosophy as a Way of Life: Spiritual Exercises from Socrates to Foucault*. Trans. Michael Chase; ed. Arnold Davidson. Oxford: Basil Blackwell, 1995.

Hadot, Pierre. 'There are Nowadays Professors of Philosophy but no Philosophers'. Trans. J. Aaron Simmons. *Journal of Speculative Realism*, 19.3 (2005): 229–237.

Heidegger, Martin. *Being and Time: A Translation of Sein und Zeit*. Trans. Joan Stambaugh. Albany: State University of New York Press, 1996 [1927].

Heidegger, Martin. 'The Age of the World-Picture'. In *The Question Concerning Technology*, 115–154. Trans. W. Lovitt. New York: Harper and Row, 1977.

Kowalski, Dean. A. *Moral Theory at the Movies: An Introduction to Ethics*. Lanham: Rowman and Littlefield Publishers, 2012.

Kupfer, Joseph H. *Visions of Virtue in Popular Film*. Boulder: Westview Press, 1999.

Litch, Mary M. *Philosophy through Film*. 2nd Edition. Abingdon and New York: Routledge, 2010.

Nietzsche, Friedrich. *Ecce Homo: How to Become What You Are* (Oxford World's Classics). Trans. Duncan Large. Oxford: Oxford University Press, 2007 [1888].

Nussbaum, Martha. *Love's Knowledge: Essays on Philosophy and Literature*. Oxford: Oxford University Press, 1992.

Pippin, Robert B. *Modernism as a Philosophical Problem: On the Dissatisfactions of European Higher Culture*. 2nd edition. Oxford: Basil Blackwell, 1999.

Rawls, John. *A Theory of Justice*. Harvard: Harvard University Press, 1971.

Rodowick, D. N. *The Virtual Life of Film*. Cambridge, MA and London: Harvard University Press, 2007.

Rodowick, D. N. (n.d.). 'Ethics in Film Philosophy (Cavell, Deleuze, Levinas)' (unpublished text). Available online at: http://isites.harvard.edu/fs/docs/icb.topic242308.files/Rodowick ETHICSweb.pdf

Rushton, Richard. *The Politics of Hollywood Cinema: Popular Film and Contemporary Political Theory*. Basingstoke: Palgrave Macmillan, 2013.

Shaw, Dan. *Morality and the Movies: Reading Ethics through Film*. London and New York: Continuum, 2012.

Sinnerbrink, Robert. 2014. 'Techne and Poesis: On Heidegger and Film Theory'. In Annie van den Oever (ed.), *Techne/Technology: Researching Cinema and Media Technologies – Their Development, Use, and Impact*, 65–80. Amsterdam: University of Amsterdam Press, 2014.

Stadler, Jane. *Pulling Focus: Intersubjective Experience, Narrative Film, and Ethics*. New York and London: Continuum, 2008.

Taylor, Charles. *Sources of the Self: The Making of Modern Identity*. Cambridge: Cambridge University Press, 1989.

Wartenberg, Thomas. *Thinking on Screen: Film as Philosophy*. Abingdon and New York: Routledge, 2007.

Wheatley, Catherine. *Michael Haneke's Cinema: The Ethic of the Image*. New York and Oxford: Berghahn Books, 2009.

Willett, Cynthia. *Irony in the Age of Empire: Comic Perspectives on Democracy and Freedom*. Bloomington: Indiana University Press, 2008.

Wittgenstein, Ludwig. *Philosophical Investigations*. London: Routledge, 1953.

Filmography

Adam's Rib. Dir. George Cukor (USA, 1949)
An Education. Dir. Lone Scherfig (UK/USA, 2009)
The Awful Truth. Dir. Leo McCarey (USA, 1937)
Gaslight. Dir. George Cukor (USA, 1944)
His Girl Friday. Dir. Howard Hawks (USA, 1940)
It Happened One Night. Dir. Frank Capra (USA, 1934)
Mr. Deeds Goes to Town. Dir. Frank Capra (USA, 1936)
Now, Voyager. Dir. Irving Rapper (USA, 1942)
The Philadelphia Story. Dir. George Cukor (USA, 1940)
Stella Dallas. Dir. King Vidor (USA, 1937)

3 From cinematic belief to ethics and politics (Deleuze)

> The question is no longer: does cinema give us the illusion of the world? But: how does cinema restore our belief in the world?
>
> Deleuze (1989 [1985], 181–182)

With the publication of two remarkable volumes during the 1980s, *Cinema 1: The Movement-Image* and *Cinema 2: The Time-Image*, Gilles Deleuze emerged as the most significant 'Continental' philosopher to have engaged seriously with film. Along with Cavell, Deleuze has decisively influenced the 'philosophical turn' in film theory during the last two decades, to the extent that we can now describe 'Deleuzian film-philosophy' as a distinctive school of contemporary thought. Rather than developing a more conventional or traditional 'philosophy of film', however, Deleuze questions the value of theorizing cinema as just another object of philosophical interest or as a novel field for the application of philosophical theories. Rather, he argues that both film and philosophy are *ways of thinking* – the one with images, the other with concepts – whose kinship rests on their shared approach to problems: film explores problems in its own domain – concerning movement, time, memory, and belief, for example – that are of direct relevance to philosophy with its vocation of conceptual invention (see Deleuze and Guattari 1994). Indeed, in Deleuze's approach, there is a productive parallel to be explored between cinema and philosophy, an idea that also resonates strongly with Cavell. Indeed, in this regard, both Deleuze and Cavell practise film-philosophy as a distinctive approach to thinking philosophically about cinema (see Sinnerbrink 2014).

Their work articulates two complementary directions in which film-philosophy can be developed: the creative construction of concepts specific to cinema that respond to problems shared by both film and philosophy (Deleuze); and a reflective elaboration of the film-philosophy relationship via the close reading of films, where philosophy responds to the problems that film raises as a medium, and individual films explore philosophical issues by cinematic means (Cavell). Ideally, film-philosophers can develop their work so as to encompass both aspects; the main difference between them is methodological and stylistic. Deleuze's philosophy of cinema is driven by a classificatory impetus, an analysis of the signs and concepts belonging to cinema and an analysis of different varieties of image-regime, with films expressing thought in ways that invite conceptual creation by philosophy. Cavell's film-philosophy, by contrast, is driven by the desire to engage in philosophical film criticism that takes the measure of exemplary cinematic works, exploring genres and forms of cinematic presentation for their philosophical significance by way of close readings of individual films. Both perspectives are vital, I contend, for the exploration of cinematic ethics.

Like Cavell, Deleuze is a philosopher for whom the possibility of an encounter between film and philosophy seemed destined to happen. As Deleuze remarks, it is no surprise that he discovered cinema, given his concerns with making thought move, and his conviction, like Cavell, that film and philosophy share a secret affinity as complementary, yet distinct, ways of thinking: 'How could I not discover cinema, which introduces 'real' movement into the image? I wasn't trying to *apply* philosophy to cinema, but I went straight from philosophy to cinema. The reverse was also true, one went right from cinema to philosophy' (Deleuze 2000, 366). The point, for Deleuze, is neither to apply to film a readymade philosophical theory, with its predetermined problems, concepts, and arguments, nor is it to reflect upon film as a theoretical object, translating the 'problems' to which it gives rise into philosophically recognizable arguments or debates. The encounter between film and philosophy, moreover, is not exhausted by reflection, whether theoretical reflection on the part of philosophy or self-reflection on the part of the film or filmmaker. It happens, rather, 'when one discipline realizes that it has to resolve, for itself and by its own means, a problem similar to one confronted by the other' (Deleuze 2000, 367). Philosophy and film, in Deleuze's hands, become related endeavours or practices of thought, the one creating concepts that belong to the other, but which do not reduce the other to merely illustrating the former. The point of the encounter between them, rather, is to find new ways of thinking philosophically and new ways of experiencing film. It is about creating or constructing concepts of the cinema, without thereby reducing film to philosophy, or making philosophy a mere tool for the analysis of film. For film responds in its own ways to problems that have a bearing on philosophy, which for its part constructs concepts that can transform how we understand films. The relationship between philosophy and cinema should thus be understood as one of mutually transforming encounter: philosophy constructing the concepts of cinema, and film thinking cinematically in a non-conceptual manner (that is, aesthetically) in response to shared philosophical, ethical, and cultural concerns. In short, film and philosophy are complementary ways of thinking and experiencing the world and ourselves.

Deleuzian cinematic ethics

For all the scholarly work that has been done on the two *Cinema* books, one area that has only recently attracted attention is the relationship between cinema and ethics in Deleuze's work (see Bogue 2010, Boljkovac 2013, and Rodowick 2010). For the most part, critical attention has been focussed on Deleuze's Bergsonian theses on the immanent relationship between movement, image, and time, and his historico-philosophical arguments concerning the post-war emergence of a 'time-image' cinema (see Flaxman 2000 and Rodowick 1997). Many recent studies have sought to extend Deleuze's theses with reference to various genres, styles, and individual films as well as linking Deleuzian cine-philosophy with contemporary theoretical developments in film theory (cognitivism, neuroscience, and so on) (see del Rio 2012, Kennedy 2002, Martin-Jones 2006, 2011, Pisters 2012, and Powell 2005). Some theorists are taking Deleuze's thought (and that of Deleuze and Guattari) as enacting an ethics of cinema that unfolds through affect, becoming-other, and encountering 'the new' (Boljkovac 2013). Indeed, as Alisdair King observes, it is becoming clear that 'one of the most significant arguments forwarded by Deleuze in his complex film-philosophical taxonomy of Western cinema concerns the delineation of a "cinematic ethics"' (King 2014, 57). In this spirit, Deleuze's contribution to cinematic ethics will be the focus of the following chapter. What Deleuze adds to Cavell's cinematic ethics, I suggest, is a diagnosis of cinema's response to a shared cultural-philosophical crisis of meaning (what Nietzsche called *nihilism*), and what I shall call here an 'ethico-existential imperative': to affirm the idea that cinema's powers of perceptual and cognitive engagement allow it to explore new modes of existence, to summon a 'people to come', or to give us 'reasons to believe in this world' – all of which are responses to the experience of nihilism (another way of describing the cultural problem of scepticism).

Once again, there are striking parallels here with Cavell's response to scepticism. Where Deleuze and Cavell differ, I suggest, is in their perspectives on 'the everyday': for Cavell, it needs to be rescued from metaphysical abstraction and aesthetic disenchantment; for Deleuze, it is the locus of 'the intolerable', that which prompts the shift from movement and action to time and thought. Whereas Cavell finds Hollywood genres capable of redeeming the everyday, responding creatively to (moral-cultural) scepticism, Deleuze sees it as driving the transition from an organic model of movement-image (action-driven) narrative to a 'crystalline' model of time-image narrative, which provides a shock to thought and to common opinion alike. In a word, Cavell seeks to retrieve, Deleuze to transform, the everyday, both cinematically and philosophically.

Nonetheless, as D. N. Rodowick remarks, the striking parallels between Deleuze and Cavell on cinema and ethics invite further philosophical reflection (2015, 197 ff.).[1] Although they may seem poles apart, both philosophers claim that cinema can confront our *cultural, historical, and philosophical disorientation* in a context where inherited paradigms of perception, representation, and action are in crisis (see Cavell 1979, 16–41, 60–73; and Deleuze 1986, 1–12, 58–72, 201–219). This is the heart of their concern with cinema and ethics: to explore how cinema responds to a 'crisis of belief' in inherited frameworks of value and meaning, ethical conduct and collective action. Echoing Cavell's concern with scepticism, for Deleuze cinema is the art form most able to respond to what Nietzsche (1968, 9 ff.) called the problem of *nihilism*: our collective loss of belief in the world, in inherited forms of representation, in metaphysical frameworks of value and meaning, in an age that no longer believes art can transform our experience. Cinematic ethics, for both Deleuze and Cavell, thus concerns the relationship between *cinema and belief*: how do moving images express or elicit conviction for us? What can cinema do when paradigms of representation (what Deleuze calls sensory-motor action schemas) begin to break down? Can cinema restore a sense of belief in the world understood as an assemblage of images in which we no longer quite believe? These questions, evoking a Nietzschean affirmation of art in response to pervasive forms of historical-cultural nihilism, lie at the heart of Deleuze's cinematic ethics.

Crisis of the action-image

Although it is clearly one of the most recognized theoretical claims in both *Cinema* volumes, Deleuze offers not one but rather *three* related aspects of the 'crisis of the action-image' and its philosophical and ethico-political implications. The first account can be found in the final chapter of *Cinema 1*, the conclusion to the overall analysis of the varieties of movement-image set out in the first volume (1986, 197 ff.). Interestingly, Deleuze sets out this crisis principally as an aesthetic, rather than cultural-political, problem. The chapter commences with a discussion of C. S. Peirce's concept of 'thirdness', which refers, in this context, to images depicting mental relations. Indeed, Deleuze suggests that the 'classical' narrative cinema, based on the sensory-motor action schema of perception, evoking affection, and leading to action, culminates in a cinematic exploration of mental relations, notably in Hitchcock's films (1986, 200ff.). Not only does Hitchcock introduce the 'mental image into the cinema' (Deleuze 1986, 203), taking mental relations as the object of cinematic presentation (inference, deduction, abduction, and so on), he is one of the first to fully implicate the spectator in the film (Deleuze 1986, 205), while turning characters into 'viewers' or spectators (like 'Jeff' [James Stewart] in *Rear Window*). At the same time, however, Hitchcock's 'completion' of classical narrative or action-image cinema in 'mental-images' opens up the exploration of time and thought beyond the action-image by precipitating a fully-fledged 'crisis of the traditional image of cinema' (Deleuze 1986, 205).

I. The Crisis of Belief and Image-Clichés

Despite the emphasis placed on the change in European cinema during and after WWII, the 'crisis of the action-image', as Deleuze remarks (1986, 205) has always accompanied the cinema, from the early days of pre-narrative cinema to the 'purest action films' of today. Indeed, for Deleuze, the two key aspects of this 'crisis' – the presentation of an *open totality*, which breaks open the sensory-motor action circuit, and *capturing the event* 'in the course of happening', which opens up a sense of duration – are integral to cinematic art, and 'part of the profound Bergsonianism of the cinema in general' (Deleuze 1986, 206). From this point of view, time-images, and non-standard ('crystalline') forms of narrative, are a part of cinema, even though they have played a secondary role in relation to dominant forms of imagery and narrative composition.

Nonetheless, Deleuze claims that there is a specific sense of crisis emerging in the wake of World War II with profound effects on European cinema and Hollywood. Here the emphasis shifts to the historical, cultural, and social factors that have contributed to the crisis in inherited forms of cinematic narration. As Deleuze describes:

> We might mention, in no particular order, the war and its consequences, the unsteadiness of the 'American Dream' in all its aspects, the new consciousness of minorities, the rise and inflation of images both in the external world and in people's minds, the influence on the cinema of the new modes of narrative with which literature had experimented, the crisis of Hollywood and the old genres.
>
> (Deleuze 1986, 206)

The aftermath of WWII, the post-war shifts in social, cultural, and political attitudes, as well as aesthetic shifts in classical cinema, contribute to the crisis of the action-image: an 'undoing' of the 'system of actions, perceptions, and affections on which cinema had fed up to that point', a caesura in the history of film which opened up 'the soul of cinema' to new forms of thought (Deleuze 1986, 206). Deleuze summarizes this polyvalent crisis as one in which the link between perception, affection, and action becomes attenuated, a profound development which begins to loosen, in a broader cultural sense, our meaningful links with the world. From this point of view, the 'crisis of the action-image' is both a cultural-historical and aesthetic-psychological condition. Deleuze remarks:

> We hardly believe any longer that a global situation can give rise to an action which is capable of modifying it – no more than we believe that an action can force a situation to disclose itself, even partially.
>
> (1986, 206)

As Deleuze will explain in *Cinema 2*, it is this generalized *crisis of belief* in narration and representation – the attenuation of links between situation and action, in short, a weakening of 'the sensory-motor links which produced the action-image' (1986, 206) – that underlies the shift from movement-image to time-image cinema. It is, however, also a productive 'crisis' that signals the emergence of new cinematic signs, including the new kinds of image and narrative styles that would appear in post-war cinema.

There are a number of elements that Deleuze identifies as characterizing the crisis of the action-image (1986, 207–210). First, there is the shift from globalizing or synthetic to dispersive or elliptical situations with multiple characters, weak interferences, no single principal character or defining narrative arc (Deleuze 1986, 207). Second, there is a loosening of the causal thread linking actions and events within a given spatio-temporal milieu. Situations are presented as elliptical, reality itself as dispersive; relations or connections between people, actions, and events are weak, random, or contingent; protagonists are seemingly disconnected from the events that happen to them (Deleuze 1986, 207). Third, the action-driven sensory-motor schema is replaced by meandering, episodic forms of narration that Deleuze describes as the 'voyage' or 'stroll' [*ballad*] form. Journeys feature strongly, devoid of definite destinations, and occur in an indeterminate, nondescript, generic space: the 'any-space-whatever, such as the marshalling yard, disused warehouse, the undifferentiated fabric of the city' (Deleuze 1986, 208). Fourth, this dispersed and contingent world, lacking 'totality or linkage', is held together by 'floating images, … anonymous clichés' (Deleuze 1986, 208): that is, 'sensory-motor images' of a thing, or habituated audio-visual schemata that add a semblance of instrumental meaning to objects in the world. This romanticist, sceptical critique of the banality of modern life is a constant temptation, one for which Deleuze criticizes various auteurs (mostly American), who contribute to the nihilism they would seek to critique (1986, 209). Finally, an alternative way of securing meaning appears via the theme of conspiracy, a hidden order of causality behind appearances that gives the world its fragile or ambiguous meaning (Deleuze 1986, 210). This is another trope in the romantic pessimism that Deleuze criticizes in American independent cinema, which receives short shrift compared with Deleuze's more considered discussions of post-war European cinema (Italian neo-realism, the French *nouvelle vague*, and New German cinema).

This is not merely an aesthetic judgment, however, but a critical diagnosis of the 'crisis of the American dream'. Deleuze's five characteristics of the 'new image' – 'the dispersive situation, the deliberately weak links, the voyage form, the consciousness of clichés, the condemnation of the plot' (Deleuze 1986, 210) – reflect both a crisis in the action-image and a crisis in post-war American culture. It is not entirely clear, however, whether this dual sense of cinematic and cultural-historical crises is to be understood as cinema reflecting certain underlying historical-ideological processes or cinema as an independent expression of these, one that remains irreducible to them. In any event, the relationship between cinema and politics, as elsewhere in *Cinema 2*, is an intimate and involved one. The sceptical questioning of the sensory-motor action schema in cinema, but also in American culture and politics, reveals the possibility of an alternative order of images; but one that would require a meaningful narrative framework and accompanying form of practice – 'an aesthetic and political project capable of constituting a positive enterprise' (Deleuze 1986, 201) – in order to be fully realized or culturally expressed.

Lacking such a positive project, the result is sceptical irony, romantic pessimism, or 'postmodern cynicism', which marks, for Deleuze, the limits of both American cinema and of the 'American dream' more broadly (1986, 210).

In a narrative familiar from discussions of postmodernism in the 1980s, Deleuze points to the exhaustion of the devices of classical narrative cinema and the problem of cinematic cliché. Indeed, in keeping with critiques that one can find in Jameson (1991) and others (Foster 1985), Deleuze criticizes American auteurs such as Altman and Scorsese for their nihilistic repetition of clichés, loss of conviction in artistic possibilities, and their romanticist indulgence in an ironic pessimism that remains unable to constitute new forms of (cinematic and cultural-political) creativity. One can certainly dispute Deleuze's sweeping dismissal of new American cinema as well as American cultural-political creativity, relying as it does on a slender selection of cinematic examples and a vague parallel with the waning of American/Western 'grand narratives' since the 1970s. Nonetheless, the key point is that Deleuze's diagnosis of the 'crisis of the action-image' is as much about a condition of cultural nihilism as it is about the history of cinematic art.

2. Beyond the movement-image (Italian neo-realism)

The 'great crisis of the action-image', Deleuze claims, took place in Italy immediately after World War II (1986, 211), namely with the appearance of Rossellini's great post-war trilogy, *Rome, Open City* (1945), *Paisan* (1946), and *Germany Year Zero* (1948), followed by his 1950s trilogy, *Stromboli* (1950), *Europa '51* (1952), and *Journey to Italy* (1954). In addition to the war, Deleuze alludes to various cultural and historical factors explaining why Italy became the flashpoint for the development of neo-realism (the experience of defeat, the occupation by Germany, widespread urban destruction, poverty, and corruption, a cinema industry and institutions that had managed to survive fascism, and 'a resistance and popular life underlying oppression, although one without illusion' (Deleuze 1986, 211)). This unprecedented cultural-historical situation required new images and stories that could communicate 'the elliptical and unorganised' experience of the post-war world (Deleuze 1986, 211). A new cinema was needed, one not only capable of capturing this ambiguous and uncertain reality but of 'questioning afresh all the accepted facts of the American tradition' (Deleuze 1986, 212).

The result was Italian neo-realism, which articulated the aforementioned five characteristics of the shift beyond the movement-image. Rossellini's *Rome, Open City* and *Paisan*, for example, 'discovered a dispersive and lacunary reality ... a series of fragmentary, chopped up encounters' (Deleuze 1986, 212), which could no longer be accommodated within the sensory-motor schemata of the action image (what Deleuze calls the SAS or Situation$_1$ – Action – Situation$_2$ form of action movie genres such as the Western or the War movie). De Sica's films, on the other hand, shattered the 'ASA form' (the

Action$_1$ – Situation – Action$_2$ schema found in genres such as melodrama or comedy, where a small action discloses a partially hidden or concealed situation, leading to further actions). They showed how events lose their co-ordinated causal links with each other within an attenuated, loosely unified world-context, how events are governed now more by contingency and chance than social or historical necessity: 'there is no longer a vector or line of the universe which extends and links up the events of the *Bicycle Thief*' (Deleuze 1986, 212). Insignificant events, which no longer cohere within a meaningful whole, take on significance for themselves, as in de Sica's *Umberto D.* (1952), with its microdramas of the pregnant maid Maria [Maria Pia Casilio] or the melancholy, everyday struggles of Umberto D. [Carlo Battisti] to maintain his room, his dog, and his dignity. Such a world, Deleuze remarks, curiously enough, is already held together by clichés, the universal ascendancy of the 'reign of clichés, internally and externally, in people's heads and hearts as much as in the whole of space' (Deleuze 1986, 212). Curious since neo-realism is supposed to have found new images in response to the problem of clichés, rather than deploying these for new artistic and ethical ends.

The second aspect of the 'crisis of the action-image' appears in the opening chapter of *Cinema 2*, where Deleuze resumes the 'beyond the movement-image' story with a brief but explicit discussion of Italian neo-realism (1989, 1–24). Taking his lead from Bazin's formal aesthetic definition, Deleuze again emphasizes the 'new form of reality' in these films, which is 'dispersive, elliptical, errant or wavering, working in blocs, with deliberately weak connections and floating events' (Deleuze 1989, 1). This social reality, however, is not presented transparently; rather, it is an 'always ambiguous, to be deciphered real' that is 'aimed at', rather than recorded, and thus requires a 'new type of image' (like Bazin's 'fact-image') (Deleuze 1989, 1). Where Deleuze parts company with Bazin is over the question of 'reality', questioning Bazin's claim that neo-realism attempts to capture the new reality of post-war Europe, whether in social-historical, 'formal or material' terms (Deleuze 1989, 1). On the contrary, Deleuze asks whether it is a question of *thought* rather than 'reality' at issue in the new cinema:

> If all the movement-images, perceptions, actions and affects underwent such an upheaval, was this not first of all because a new element burst on to the scene which was to prevent perception being extended into action in order to put it in contact with thought, and, gradually, was to subordinate the image to the demands of new signs which would take it beyond movement?
>
> (Deleuze 1989, 1)

Neo-realism displays a 'philosophical' trajectory, reflecting that of modern (European) cinema: the discovery and composition of new cinematic signs (pure optical and sound situations), new images and forms of narration (time-images and crystalline narration), culminating in the emergence of a new kind of cinema 'beyond the movement-image'.

Indeed, Deleuze's philosophical reinterpretation of neo-realism clearly accords with his thesis concerning the modern (post-Kantian) philosophical reversal of the subordination of time to movement (see Deleuze 1984), coupled with his Bergsonian re-inscription of 'the essence' of cinema as re-conceptualizing the relationship between thought and time.[2] Not only does the social content of neo-realism disappear, so too does Bazin's affirmation of cinema's vocation to reveal a transfigured sense of reality. Instead, Deleuze gives neo-realism a philosophical cast as that revolutionary moment in modern cinema when film begins to 'think' cinematically in grappling with the expression of duration and of thought. Also curious in Deleuze's account of neo-realism is the minor role played by cultural-political factors or historical-ideological context. It is an account that foregrounds, rather, the aesthetic problem of images in response to the attenuated post-war sense of a meaningfully organized or coherent social reality. Indeed, the principal problem facing post-war cinema, according to Deleuze, is the breakdown of the old (sensory-motor) paradigms of narrative composition and the corrosive effects of the reign of the cultural-cinematic cliché: it is only out of this disrupted sense of world, with its discredited forms of representation, that a new kind of image might arise out of the ashes of cliché. Italian neo-realism sensed the problem ('in-itself'), but such a problem becomes self-reflexive ('for-itself') only later within the French *nouvelle vague*, with its ironic treatment of the sensory-motor action schema in response to the crisis of cliché (Deleuze 1989, 8–9 ff.).

The American response to this crisis, as remarked, is criticized for lapsing into romantic pessimism and empty parody. In either case, the problem remains that of 'finding an image' amidst the morass of clichés without lapsing into sterile repetition (Deleuze 1986, 214). The way out, Deleuze argues, is to turn to thought and time (1986, 215): the mental image (reaching its Hollywood highpoint with Hitchcock) has to become time-image (reaching its apogee in European cinema with Resnais). As we shall see, Deleuze's teleological history of post-war cinema moves from the crisis of the sensory-motor action schema, the discovery of pure optical and sound situations, and the emergence of 'crystalline' (parametric, to use Bordwell's term) narration, which heralds a new cinema capable of restoring our 'belief in this world'.

This theme is announced in *Cinema 2* by the shift from the problem of cliché (with which *Cinema 1* concluded) to the 'pure optical and sound situations' defining the new sense of reality in post-war European cinema. Deleuze cites a number of canonical scenes from classic neo-realist films: the pregnant maid Maria making coffee and quietly considering her bleak future in *Umberto D.*; the suicide of the boy Edmund [Edmund Moeschke] in *Germany Year Zero*, who 'dies from what he sees' (Deleuze 1989, 2); Karin's [Ingrid Bergman's] devastating revelation of the horrors of everyday reality in *Stromboli*; the conversion of grieving Irene [Ingrid Bergman] in *Europa '51*, who is transfigured by her visions of the poor and experience working in a factory; or the shattering experience of the female tourist Katherine [Bergman again] in *Viaggio in Italia*, whose experience of images and visual clichés is one in which 'she discovers something unbearable, beyond the limit of what she can personally bear' (Deleuze 1989, 2). Neo-realism, with its pure optical and sound situations that no longer extend into action, becomes 'a cinema of the seer and no longer that of the agent [*de voyant, non plus d'actant*]' (Deleuze 1989, 2). It inaugurates a new kind of cinema – centred on the experience of time, the trauma of memory, the disorientation of space, and the collapse of agency – by introducing a new regime of images and signs.

Such is Deleuze's second version of the 'beyond the movement-image' thesis, which emphasizes the emergence of pure optical and sound situations with Ozu, neo-realism, and the French New Wave. It is no longer the problem of the cliché that matters but that of responding – culturally and artistically – to a dispersed, disorganized world where sensory-motor action schemas have become ineffectual or inoperative. Unlike the first version, it is what defines Italian neo-realism (the proliferation of purely optical and sound situations), as distinct from the sensory-motor situations of the action-image within older forms of realism (Deleuze 1989, 2). Spectator identification with characters gives way to the presentation of them as a kind of spectator; the sensory-motor situation falters and gives way to pure optical and sound situations that outstrip the motor capacities of characters that now appear as visionary seers rather than motivated agents. The main characteristics of the crisis of the action-image – the 'voyage' or trip/ballad narrative form, the multi-plication of clichés, characters indifferent to the events that befall them, the relaxing of sensory-motor relations – are now presented as the preliminary conditions for the post-war appearance of pure optical and sound situations that herald the new time-image cinema.

There are a number of interesting issues that arise here with respect to cinematic ethics. The first is that the crisis of the action-image is linked with ethical evaluation, the need to create new images in response to the 'intoler-able' (see Barker 2014), and sustaining meaning in the face of waning belief in the coherence of the world as an arena of motivated action. One can find here a significant parallel with Cavell: the ethical moment of responding to the 'intolerable', to that which goes beyond our powers to imagine or to represent, is an experience that requires a revaluation of the ordinary. There is little doubt that such experiences reflect, at cultural-historical levels, the traumatic effects of WWII and the disruption of received (sensory-motor) modes of cultural meaning-making. In response, the new cinema – for Deleuze, mostly post-war European film – is thus dedicated to exploring time, thought, and new forms of subjectivity. It does so by confronting what is 'intolerable' in everyday social reality, while revealing the possibilities of ethical-political reorientation opened up by the cinematic exploration of time and thought.

3. Deleuze's existential imperative: belief in this world

Deleuze adopts what we might call a more 'existentialist' register in the third aspect of his account of post-movement-image cinema: the problem of *belief in the world*, which arises as a result of the breakdown of prevailing representational frameworks (the sensory-motor schema applied to narratives of historical meaning and political emancipation). In other words, it is now the problem of cinema and *nihilism* that now becomes the focus of cultural-philosophical attention: the need to renew our 'reasons to believe in this world' in the face of scepticism, lack of conviction, brutality and violence. Deleuze's modernist wager is that cinema can diagnose, respond to, and perhaps overcome, nihilism: it provides an ethical experience of meaning – via images exploring time and thought – in response to the crises of meaning afflicting the post-war world. We might call this a cinematic ethics of immanent conversion: an existential affirmation of the world through its aesthetic re-enchantment, an experience revealed through, and given expression by, the cinema.

Echoing Cavell's concern with scepticism, for Deleuze cinema is the art form most able to respond to the problem of nihilism – our collective loss of belief in the world as an arena of meaning and value – in an age that lacks conviction about the power of art to transform our experience. Deleuzian cinematic ethics thus concerns the relationship between *cinema and belief*: how does the moving image elicit conviction for us? What can cinema do when inherited paradigms of representation (what Deleuze calls sensory-motor action schemas) break down or lose their credibility? Can cinema restore a sense of belief in the world as an assemblage of images in which we no longer quite believe? Deleuze poses these questions most explicitly in the following much-quoted passage:

> The link between man and the world has been broken. Henceforth, this link must become an object of belief: it is the impossible which can only be restored within a faith. Belief is no longer addressed to a different or transformed world. Man is in the world as if in a pure optical or sound situation. The reaction of which man has been dispossessed can be replaced only by belief. Only belief in the world can reconnect man to what he sees and hears. The cinema must film, not the world, but belief in this world, our only link. [...] Restoring our belief in the world – this is the power of modern cinema (when it stops being bad). Whether we are Christians or atheists, in our universal schizophrenia, *we need reasons to believe in this world*.
>
> (Deleuze 1989, 171–172)

In this thought-provoking passage, Deleuze describes nihilism as a 'cinematographic' experience of the world: it involves a loss of belief, a disconnection between perception, affection, and action, a reduction of the world to one in which images saturate our experience, yet evacuate the world of meaning, leaving its horizons indefinite and opaque. Transcendent sources of belief or mythic beliefs in progress (religion and ideology) no longer justify the world; rather, the world itself has become 'a bad film' in which we no longer really believe (or know how to act). The 'pure optical and acoustical situations' that defined post-war cinema have mutated, in our present context, into an all-pervasive, cognitively distracting audiovisual culture defined by a fragmented state of atomized immersion and incessant proliferation of enervating cliché. What Deleuze describes here, in short, is a cinematic version of the Nietz-schean problem of nihilism: the loss of belief in inherited, prevailing sources of normative value and moral-cultural meaning in modernity.

What can film do in the face of such crises in meaning? This is the central ethical question of modern cinema: can it give us 'reasons to believe' in a world mediated by images, where cinema's power to elicit conviction has waned? Can we construct an ethics and politics of the image that could respond to the 'destruction of experience' (Benjamin) – shared, historically meaningful experience – within a fully mediatized modernity? Such questions provide a motivation for Deleuze's existential wager, which bets on cinema as a creative response to the moral-cultural nihilism undermining the conditions of social-political agency – a condition that cinema can either exacerbate or to which it can respond ethically. We require, as a response to nihilism, a reanimation of existential-vitalist belief in the link between human beings and the world, in the immanence of thought and life. As Deleuze remarks:

> Which, then, is the subtle way out? To believe, not in a different world, but in a link between man and the world, in love or life, to believe in this as in the impossible, the unthinkable, which nonetheless cannot but be thought. [...] It is this belief that makes the unthought the specific power of thought, through the absurd, by virtue of the absurd.
>
> (Deleuze 1989, 170)

Deleuze advocates an existential affirmation of the immanent link to the world, a link articulated in thought and expressed through cinema, one that might enable us to retrieve the ethical relationship between thought and life. Philosophy can join with cinema as cultural media with the power to invent forms of life and provide reasons to maintain fidelity with the world. More specifically, this means rethinking what it means to be human, beyond the body/mind dualism that, through its opposition between a corrupted material-sensuous realm and an unattainable ideal-metaphysical realm, leads to scep-ticism. Our salvation, so to speak, in response to such scepticism, lies in 'simply believing in the body' as the ground of our existence, 'before dis-course, before words' (Deleuze 1989, 172–173), creating art that enables us to reconnect with the world in an embodied manner. Both Cavell and Deleuze thus emphasize the potential of cinema to serve as a means of evoking ethical experience as an aesthetic response to cultural scepticism or moral nihilism, whether via creative self-transformation or an existential affirmation of our embodied being-in-the-world.

Questioning Deleuze's cinema of belief

The question that arises here, however, is whether Deleuze's account of existential belief in our embodied relationship with the world is adequate to those challenges to which it responds. A number of critics have questioned Deleuze's claims concerning the (ethico-philosophical) significance of belief in post-war cinema (Bernstein 2012, Rancière 2006). These criticisms can be summarized as follows: the 'Eurocentrism' objection (Martin-Jones), the 'theological/nihilism' objection (Bernstein), the 'agency' objection (Bernstein again), and the 'dualism' objection (Rancière). I shall outline each of these objections in turn, and offer some critical remarks in response before articulating my own critique of the limitations of Deleuze's cinematic ethics.

The first criticism concerns the 'Eurocentrism' of Deleuze's account of the breakdown of the sensory-motor schema, crisis of the action-image, and advent of time-image cinema, as a consequence of the historical traumas of the Second World War. As David Martin-Jones has argued, Deleuze's account extrapolates from the history of American and European cinematic traditions, inflating a local or specific cultural-historical episode into a general thesis on the post-war 'crisis of the action-image' heralding the 'modern' cinema of time (Martin-Jones 2011, 10–16). But this takes one (dominant) historical-cultural possibility or historico-philosophical narrative as paradigmatic of cinema and cultural history in general, and thus ignores or overlooks the 'multiple modernities' in cinematic history and cultural practices across the globe. Correcting for this Eurocentrism, Martin-Jones argues, would mean treating the 'crisis of the action-image' as a dispersed, pluralized, but also widely shared cultural-historical phenomenon that appears during distinctive periods of political crisis or historical rupture. It need not be confined to Europe (or Hollywood) or indeed to the post-war period, and can reappear, in altered and hybrid forms, across diverse historical and cultural contexts. Latin American, African, Indian, and South-East Asian cinemas all offer examples of such 'crises of the action-image', and these innovative cultural variations on time-image cinema suggest a more pluralist, post-Eurocentric way of thinking through Deleuze's cinematic philosophy. Martin-Jones, we should note, does not criticize Deleuze's account of the shift from movement-image to time-image cinema *per se* but rather its overly Eurocentric focus; his critique offers an argument to 'decolonise' Deleuze's film philosophy, transforming it in response to the pluralist cultural and historical realities of contemporary world cinemas.

The second criticism is the 'theological leap/nihilism' critique of Deleuze's account of the shift to time-image cinema. According to J. M. Bernstein (2012), in the course of elaborating the consequences of this shift, Deleuze adopts a religious-theological, rather than historico-political, account of the crisis of meaning in the modern world. As a consequence, Deleuze cannot 'explain why movies matter to us', Bernstein claims, nor explain the shift from movement-image to time-image cinema in ways that do justice to cinema's fundamental concern with representation, narrative, and action (Bernstein 2012, 78). Moreover, the 'ontological' case Deleuze makes for the shift from movement-images to time-images cannot account for the traumatic effects of historical experience, or for the modernist response to this trauma. For Deleuze's ontological argument consistently subordinates the primacy of action (movement-image) to the primacy of belief (time-image), while also relying on a Bazinian account of realism that Deleuze's account of the shift to time and thought was meant to displace (Bernstein 2012, 78). The emergence of the time-image, for Deleuze, occurs as a consequence of the fact of our 'no longer believing that an ideal-preserving fit between action and world is available' (Bernstein 2012, 80). Following the traumatic experience of war, post-war cinema is no longer a cinema of agents but one of 'seers taking in the scope of its horror and injustice, which seem, prima facie, impervious to transformation' (Bernstein 2012, 80). The consequence of this is a diminution of the sense of human agency, our historical capacity for collective or trans-formative action; once images are no longer 'tailored to the needs of human action', the cost of their demise is 'the cost of human action within a viable human life (each 'I' is part of an ethically substantive 'We'), where action is the soul of movement' (Bernstein 2012, 80). In a word, Deleuze's account of the crisis of the action-image leading to the birth of time-image cinema remains caught within the very nihilism it aims to overcome.

The alternative to action, for Deleuze, is belief: modern cinema responds to this crisis of action when it provides reasons to believe in the world – an existential shift that Deleuze lays out, according to Bernstein, 'as a version of Kierkegaard's leap of faith in which the belief in the world replaces belief in God' (2012, 81). Bernstein's objection centres on Deleuze's 'irrationalist' pro-fession of faith in an aesthetic of the absurd, the demand to believe in the link between humanity and the world, 'in love or life, to believe in this as the impossible, the unthinkable, which none the less cannot but be thought. … It is this belief that makes the unthought the specific power of thought, through the absurd, by virtue of the absurd' (Deleuze 1989, 170). According to Bernstein, Deleuze's invocation of 'the absurd' disqualifies any reasons we might have for caring about modern cinema, or art more generally, since 'the absurd, the impossible, is as readily available without aesthetic mediation as with it' (Bernstein 2012, 81). For Bernstein, then, Deleuze's reversion to an 'irrationalist' philosophy of belief – the leap of faith required to believe in the 'unthinkable', 'the absurd', as revealed by art – undermines the modernist credentials of his otherwise persuasive, if derivative, account of modern cinema. Indeed, Bernstein even claims that Deleuze's account of time-image cinema is quasi-theological, for it 'demands that movies take on the lineaments of religious faith, belief in its most regressive sense being all that is left to agents for whom no actions or possibilities of action remain' (Bernstein 2012, 81). An irrationalist aesthetic of faith and existential conviction replaces the modernist project of believing in the (historically and politically) transformative power of art. Once again, Deleuze's 'leap of faith' into the irrational and absurd is an expression of, rather than a response to, the experience of nihilism.

Deleuze's 'premodern' account of the cinema of belief, for Bernstein, is thus tantamount to an aestheticist expression of the 'return to religion' characterizing much contemporary European philosophy. Even Deleuze's 'belief in the body', whether the corporeal figures of 'spiritual masochism' or Bazin's aesthetic redemption of the everyday, is designed to 'match the exigencies of the time-image', that is, the existential claims made on behalf of a cinema of time and memory (Bernstein 2012, 81–82). Indeed, the notion of belief in post-war cinema, Bernstein claims, appears to serve as 'a critical alternative to notions like catharsis, aesthetic experience, and love of the world' (2012, 82). In this sense, Bernstein agrees that Deleuze's cinematic ethics centres on the problem of belief and its role in response to the breakdown of narrative frameworks of meaning (or what I am calling the more general cultural condition of nihilism in post-war modernity). Deleuze's emphasis on a 'cinema of belief' (rather than catharsis, aesthetic experience or love of the world) thus raises the question whether his account can show 'how these works succeed in connecting affect and world', and if so, how this connection can be understood in a way that 'does not track back to the possibilities of human action' (Bernstein 2012, 82).

To be sure, Bernstein does note the 'existentialist' dimension of Deleuze's account of the need to valorise 'belief in the world'; however, he underplays the significance of these existential-ethical aspects (the link to Kierkegaard and Nietzsche as well as Dreyer and Bresson), dismissing Deleuze's references to 'belief' or 'faith' as only ever reflecting a regressive shift towards a religious recuperation of cinematic art that bespeaks a naïve or uncritical modernism. Deleuze's claim concerning the need for 'belief in this world', however, is not just a dogmatic 'religious' or 'theological' reworking of the disappointed (political) hopes of aesthetic modernism. Rather, it emphasizes the existential dimensions of the condition of modern nihilism, acknowledging the importance of cultural-historical conditions of meaning, and the enabling role of mean-ingful narrative accounts of social-political agency (including ideology). While emphasizing the 'existential' dimensions of this condition, Deleuze points out how the conviction that such narratives can elicit has been undermined, leading to a diffuse crisis of social agency and cultural-political innovation. The cinema of belief, which marks a shift towards time and thought rather than movement and action, signals an aesthetic response to the debilitating nihilism that renders implausible our inherited frameworks of narrative (and ideological) meaning. Deleuze's philosophical engagement with cinema, in short, is not only an exercise in philosophical typology and the construction of concepts but an exercise in cinematic ethics and cultural politics.

In a similar vein, Paola Marrati (2006) defends Deleuze's account of the 'crisis of the action-image' as both philosophical and political, arguing that the *Cinema* books are works in political philosophy as much as philosophy of film. For in these works, Marrati claims, Deleuze articulates a philosophical (but also aesthetic) response to the crisis of meaning and agency – the 'crisis of the action-image' – that finds expression in modern cinema. Indeed, by analysing the specificity of cinema, Deleuze is led, moreover, to 'analyze in detail *forms of action and agency* that contribute to understanding the 'crisis' afflicting both liberal and Marxist-inspired political theories' (Marrati 2006, x–xi). The cinematic turn towards time, affect, thought, and belief are not only philosophical but cultural-aesthetic responses to a crisis in the 'grand narratives' of politics defining the post-war world. In this respect, the action-form Deleuze explores in the *Cinema* books extends far beyond an analysis of movies. Rather, his analyses offer an implicit reflection on the conditions of meaning that 'corresponds to liberal and historicist notions of subjectivity and agency' (Marrati 2006, xi). The rise of time-images in cinema, moreover, should not be understood as implying the 'end of agency' but, 'on the contrary, an effort to think agency anew, along different lines prescribed by liberalism and historicism' (Marrati 2006, xi). From this point of view, Deleuze's account of time-image cinema, including the cinema of belief, thus heralds, in philosophical and ethico-political terms, the cultural-historical emergence of new ways of thinking and acting in response to the 'crisis' in social-political agency afflicting the post-war world.

As will be elaborated below, however, I would suggest that Deleuze's 'cinema of belief', in the end, is more ethical than political: it is oriented more towards affective, philosophical, and creative responses towards our cultural-historical situation (as mediated through transformative cinematic experience), than to a distinctive collective project of social-political transformation aided by the motivating power of a revolutionary cinema. Indeed, Deleuze's ambiguous adherence to the modernist conviction that both individual and collective forms of politics can be transformed through the power of art signals one of the more questionable aspects of his cinematic philosophy, for the project of cinematic modernism has been significantly transformed since the 1980s in response to changes in the historical, cultural, aesthetic, and technological possibilities of contemporary global cinemas. This development points to a further tension in Deleuze's cinematic ethics. The ethical aspect of Deleuze's account, on the one hand, evokes an existential imperative to respond to nihilism by elaborating, cinematically, 'reasons to believe in this world'; on the other, Deleuze's *Cinema* books remain wedded to a 'political modernism' that has become questionable within our pluralized, technologically-mediated, historical-cultural worlds. Bringing these two aspects together coherently is one of the main challenges facing Deleuze's cinematic philosophy.

Bernstein's second criticism is more telling (2012, 82 ff.): namely, that Deleuze's account of the emergence of time-image cinema fails to account for

1) the necessary persistence of action-image oriented narrative (and the fact that the sensory-motor schema remains necessary for any meaningful action to be possible); and 2) the specific nature of the response to historical trauma, which requires a more critical and activist response than reverting to passive contemplation, religious belief, or an aesthetic vision of the 'intolerable' in everyday life. It requires, rather, a cultural 'working through' of historical memory that can afflict traumatized historical subjects either by cutting them off from the past or by evacuating the present of meaning. Both dimensions of the subjective and affective effects of historical trauma are explored in Alain Resnais' *Hiroshima mon amour* (1959), a film with a much deeper cultural-historical and ethical significance, Bernstein argues, than instantiating Deleuze's Bergsonian account of the shift to time-image evocations of co-existing 'sheets of past' (2012, 83). Moreover, as Bernstein's nuanced reading of *Hiroshima mon amour* attests, such arguments require close analysis of cinematic works in order to defend the kind of film-philosophical claims that are made in their name – something for which Deleuze's impressively broad, but frustratingly piecemeal, use of cinematic examples can be criticized.

Bernstein is right to articulate the limitations, from an historical perspective, of Deleuze's account of post-war cinema, and to point out the shortcomings in Deleuze's rather superficial treatment of the effects of historical trauma – a term which does much work in Deleuze's account of post-war cinema but receives little theoretical elaboration or justification. And Bernstein's impressive analysis of *Hiroshima mon amour* shows the importance of the ethico-political dimensions of the 'crisis of the action-image', which requires more considered film-philosophical treatment than Deleuze's brief, and rather formalistic, accounts of the transformation of the agent into a seer, and his under-theorized reliance on the effects of historical trauma on memory, affect, and agency.

In response, however, Deleuzians could argue that Deleuze does not set out to offer a 'history of cinema' or do philosophical film criticism, but to extract the specific concepts of the cinema (in a philosophical typology), thereby staging an encounter between cinema and philosophy conducive to thinking 'the new'. It is here, however, that we strike another difficulty: the tension between this 'formalist' aspect of Deleuze's *Cinema* books, with their uncritical reliance on historico-cultural factors in order to account for cinematic and philosophical shifts in style and meaning (see Rancière 2006, 107–123). Although Deleuze presents a typology of concepts and signs belonging to modern cinema, this analysis also implies a critique of the historico-cultural conditions to which modern cinema responds (the trauma of post-war historical experience, the modernist struggle against cliché, the ethico-political need to resist 'the intolerable', and the need to reinvent political cinema within specific historical-political contexts in which 'the people are lacking'). These two dimensions of Deleuze's project – the formal-typological and the historical-philosophical – stand in an uneasy, unstable relationship with each other; and this is nowhere more evident than in Deleuze's account of the causes of the crisis of the action-image and consequential turn to a cinema of time and thought, the body and belief.

Deleuze's fable: Rancière's critique

Jacques Rancière offers what is perhaps the best known recent critique of Deleuze's philosophical engagement with 'cinematographic modernity' (2006, 107), claiming that Deleuze's account of the 'two ages' of cinema – an organic 'action-image' cinema oriented by the sensory-motor schema, and a discontinuous 'time-image' cinema manifesting a liberated sense of duration – is both incoherent and implausible (Rancière 2006, 108). Deriving from well-known historical accounts of the shift from classical to modern (post-war) cinema (Bazin, Burch, and Schefer), Deleuze's model relies, Rancière argues, on an implausibly dualistic and linear model of cinematic history that underplays the hybridity and 'impurity' of moving images. Giving Bazin's theses on realism a philosophical-temporal cast, Deleuze defines the new image-regime with reference to the 'autonomous temporality' of the time-image and the 'void' separating it from other images (Rancière 2006, 107). Unlike the 'rational' organization of images linked according to sensory-motor relations, we now have a non-totalizable, 'irrational' set of autonomously temporal images expressing pure optical and sound situations. Such images no longer organize perception and affection in order to extend these into action; rather, they now command a disorienting 're-arrangement from the void', decoupled from other images via 'irrational' cuts, and thereby open themselves up to time and thought via their own 'virtual' images (Rancière 2006, 107–8).

Rancière's first criticism focuses on Deleuze's mapping of the distinction between movement- and time-images directly onto an historical rupture affecting both cinematic and cultural practices. He questions, moreover, the plausibility of dividing cinema into two discrete 'ages': an 'organic', sensory-motor, action-image oriented cinema obeying laws of 'classical' narrative; and a 'crystalline' modern time-image cinema exploring 'parametric' narrative styles (to use Bordwell's term). This rupture raises many questions, not least the relationship between cinema and history. As Rancière asks, 'how are we to think the relationship between a break internal to the art of images and the ruptures that affect history in general?' (2006, 108). In this regard, Deleuze repeats, Rancière contends, the modernist gesture of narrating the development of each art form as a quest to realize its own essence, with cinema finally realizing its historical and philosophical vocation as a moving expression of duration (Rancière 2006, 108). Since Deleuze denies, however, that he is presenting a 'history of cinema,' offering instead a philosophical typology of images within a Bergsonian metaphysics of 'matter-light in movement' (Rancière 2006, 109), how are we then to understand the historicist aspect of the 'rupture of the sensory-motor link' (Rancière 2006, 109)? Deleuze relies upon, without properly explaining, the *historical rupture* represented by the traumatic experience of war in order to account for the *conceptual shift*, underpinned by Bergsonian metaphysics, from the regime of movement-images to time-images expressing thought and duration.

Indeed, in the face of the evident difficulties that arise in demarcating movement-images from time-images, Rancière charges Deleuze with proposing a 'fictive' account of this conceptual distinction that exaggerates their differences and artificially separates and distributes them across the historical caesura represented by WWII. As Rancière argues, the affection-image already undermines the distinction between movement-image and time-image, for it expresses the qualities and potentialities of the 'any-space-whatevers' said to compose the pure optical and sound situations belonging to the time-image as such (2006, 112). For this reason, a cinematic modernist like Bresson, as Rancière points out, can appear as an exemplary case of affection-image cinema (which isolates pure or virtual qualities but as still part of a sensory-motor schema) and of time-image cinema (which interrupts this schema via the presentation of pure optical and sound situations evoking time and thought): 'The very same images examined in the first book as the components of the movement-image reappear in the second book as the constitutive principles of the time-image' (Rancière 2006, 112). The theoretical distinction between movement-images and time-images, along with their distinctive narrative 'logics', collapses to reveal a coalescing of the two that straddles both historically-grounded forms of image-regime. Again, this raises the question of the relationship between Deleuze's ontology of cinematic images and his critical history of post-war cinema: 'How can a classification among types of signs be split in two by an external historical event?' (Rancière 2006, 114).

This difficulty, for Rancière, becomes manifest in Deleuze's discussion of examples of the crisis of the action-image. Indeed, these examples are presented allegorically, expressing such a breakdown in narrative or thematic terms (the faux-cum-real amputee knife thrower in Tod Browning's *The Unknown* (1927), the child-seers in Italian neo-realist movies such as *Germany, Year Zero*, 'Jeff' [James Stewart] in Hitchcock's *Rear Window*, and so on). The Hitchcock examples are telling: situations of paralysis or motor inhibition are presented allegorically as alluding to the crisis of the action-image that introduces pure optical and sound situations (like the case of Scottie in *Vertigo*). Such 'paralysis', however, is evidently also usually 'an aspect of the plot, a feature of the narrative situation' (Rancière 2006, 115). Indeed, films like *Vertigo* and *Rear Window* remain, contra Deleuze, strongly driven by action-image dynamics within sensory-motor situations – will 'Jeff' [James Stewart] be able to intervene and save Lisa [Grace Kelly] from being killed? will Scottie [Stewart] resolve the mystery of Carlotta's haunting death and uncover her husband's murderous plot? – while at the same time being films with a highly reflexive conscious-ness of cinematic spectatorship. As Rancière points out, 'the logic of the movement-image is not at all paralysed by the fictional situation'; rather, the vertigo and immobility of the protagonist only render more complex the sensory-motor machinations necessary to resolve their sophisticated plots (Rancière 2006, 116).

The alternative is to understand Deleuze's readings of these films as 'allegories of the rupture of the sensory-motor link'; but, if so, this suggests that movement-image and time-image cannot be as sharply distinguished as Deleuze claims (Rancière 2006, 116). They co-exist, rather, within a hybrid plurality of image-making forms characteristic of the romantic-modern aesthetic regime of the arts, where the latter is defined by the co-existence of conscious and unconscious, intentionalist and automatist, popular and experimental aspects of the moving image. There is no pure breach between action-image and time-image cinema; rather, there are plural, hybrid forms that demand a more fluid mode of engagement than Deleuze's formalist typology of images mapped onto a linear, dualistic model of cinematic history. Deleuze can thus be criticized here, ironically enough, for applying a pre-given philosophical paradigm to the mobile thinking of cinema, rather than thinking about cinema in a manner that keeps philosophy mobile, open to transformation, which is surely Deleuze's intention.

Rancière offers as evidence his readings of Rossellini's post-war films (2006, 125–142): contra Deleuze, Rossellini does not depict icons of contemplative seeing, inert trauma, or ethical belief so much as a kinetic-materialist physics of bodies that undermines Marxist, theological, and moral-ethical interpretations of his work. Rancière's aestheticist/materialist reading of neo-realism thus emphasizes the action-driven, movement-oriented elements of these films – not to mention their complex engagement with melodrama – as against Deleuze's selective philosophical citing of such films as instances of time-image cinema (Rancière 2006, 125 ff.). For Deleuze, the latter express a collapse of the sensory-motor schema, a dissolution of goal-directed narrative, a foregrounding of pure optical and sound situations, the transformation of the agent into a 'seer', and an expression of existential disorientation in face of the 'intolerable' and the 'unthinkable' (Deleuze 1989, 169). Rancière thus challenges Deleuze's 'allegorical' construal of neo-realist film, suggesting that their use of 'any space-whatevers', moments of stasis, attenuation and proliferation of plot, are testimony to the irreducibly 'impure' character of *both* movement-images and time-images. The cinematic hybridity and unique complexity of such films attest to the dangers of imposing any philosophically formalized conceptual-historical schema upon actual works of cinema.

Rancière's intervention via his alternative readings of neo-realist film raises an important issue rarely addressed in the voluminous commentaries on Deleuze: the philosophical status and aesthetic validity of Deleuze's film interpretations. It is clear that Deleuze's discussion of the crisis of the action-image depends heavily on the plausibility of his film interpretations, which serve both to 'illustrate' the kind of philosophical claims Deleuze is making and to suggest ways of conceptualizing the aesthetic experience that such films afford. Yet Deleuze's typically brief, selective, and narrative-focused discussions of individual films do not readily allow for detailed critical engagement or hermeneutic interpretation. Deleuze's remarks on classic Italian neo-realist films are a case in point: these films are presented as exploring pure optical and sound situations (rather than expressing 'social content') articulating a 'world out of joint' to which agents no longer feel connected, or capable of responding to through meaningful action. A contemplative theatre of trauma and dissociative experience of duration replaces the sensory-motor schema underlying what Deleuze calls the 'hodological' (agency-oriented) space of perception, affection, and action. On the one hand, as Bernstein notes, this tends to undermine these films' potential to articulate various forms of social, moral, and political agency, despite the traumatic circumstances and historical experiences of their protagonists. On the other, as Marrati claims, they also attempt to open up the possibility of rethinking agency and ethico-political experience in a context in which 'classical' schemata of representation and meaning (including socio-political ideologies) have begun to lose their credibility.

A cinematic critique?

It is hard to see, however, what kind of 'politics' this would amount to, and how cinema figures in its articulation and propagation. Despite her suggestive remarks, Marrati does not elaborate either how cinema might achieve this aim, or what this 'post-ideological' Deleuzian politics looks like. Although Deleuze does explore the question of a new kind of political cinema (in his account of 'minor cinema'), I would suggest that it is cinematic *ethics* (rather than politics) at stake in his discussion of the significance of neo-realism. Despite the evident 'loosening' of classical narrative form that Deleuze identifies, most post-war neo-realist films, such as Rossellini's 'War Trilogy' (*Rome, Open City, Paisan*, and *Germany, Year Zero*) nonetheless remain strongly narrative-driven, with numerous plots and sub-plots that are clearly 'sensory-motor' in structure and orientation, even if the protagonists are pluralized, spread across different scenarios, and representative of a more general situation of crisis.

Each vignette in *Rome, Open City*, for example, is a mini action-image narrative with suspenseful, dramatic tension; the spectator's moral allegiances are engaged in strongly 'partisan' terms in sympathy with the beleaguered locals in their constrained and covert struggles against their Nazi occupiers. These films employ emotionally-engaging forms of genre (melodrama), coupled with 'realist' documentary framing and footage, situating these within affectively-charged narrative scenarios (within the disruptive context of the war and its disorienting aftermath) in order to elicit and direct the spectator's moral-political allegiance. It is hard to read such films, as Deleuze does, independently of their moral motivations, socio-political content, and strong narrative emotionalism, adducing them as evidence supporting a philosophically ambiguous thesis (between historical and conceptual rupture) concerning the radical shift in cinematic meaning and practice in the post-war European context. Rather, we might think of them, I suggest, as engaging in a 'cinematic critique' mediated via images: a cinematic ethics articulated through emotional engagement, imaginative involvement, and critical reflection, evoked aesthetically by pluralistic, even fragmentary forms of cinematic narrative, but directed against the background social, historical and political conditions of existence in which the films were made and viewed.

From cinema of belief to minor cinema

Unlike Cavell's more individualist focus on moral perfectionism as a response to (cultural and moral) scepticism, Deleuze does include a more collective, political dimension in his cinematic ethics, arguing that cinema has the capacity to constitute a missing community, to create a 'people to come', without recourse to historical teleology or political totality. Indeed, in *Cinema 2* (1989, 215 ff.), Deleuze explores how a political cinema might respond to the nihilistic 'crisis' of narratives underpinning collective forms of socio-political agency. Classical cinema assumed the existence of 'a people' – an historically unified, socially cohesive, or potentially organized political community – that could either be mobilized towards revolutionary action (Soviet cinema) or whose democratic ideals could be affirmed in the face of moral-political corruption (Hollywood cinema). In both American democratic and Soviet revolutionary cinema, Deleuze claims, 'the people are already there, real before being actual, ideal without being abstract'; hence the ideologico-political aspirations of classical cinema as an 'art of the masses' capable of constituting a new community that finds itself reflected and projected on screen (Deleuze 1989, 216). As Deleuze observes, however, the utopian political hopes of cinema were soon dashed, first by Hitler's harnessing of the propaganda potential of cinema, then by Stalin's crushing of the revolutionary aspirations of 'the people' within communism, and finally by the cultural loss of belief in the unifying democratic ideals of American community, whether as harmonious cultural 'melting pot' or as destined 'seed of a people to come' (Deleuze 1989, 216). As a consequence, modern cinema could be political only by recognizing that the pre-given political communities addressed by classical cinema are lacking (Deleuze 1989, 216). Following the withering of belief in the 'grand narratives' of modernity,[3] post-war political cinema – Deleuze mentions the Straubs and Resnais, as well as Kafka, Klee, and the idea of a 'minor literature' (Deleuze and Guattari 1986) – finds its vocation in showing 'how the people are what is missing' (Deleuze 1989, 215).

Deleuze identifies three aspects to the modern political cinema. As mentioned, the first is the recognition of, and creative response to, the problem of the 'missing people' (Deleuze 1989, 217). South American and African 'Third Cinema' are cases in point, transforming the aspirations of twentieth-century revolutionary cinema by inventing or anticipating a 'people to come', and doing so from the margins of a dominant (whether colonialist or imperialist) cultural tradition. Third Cinema defines itself by moving beyond the Holly-wood cinema of individualist narrative (First Cinema), the aestheticism and chauvinism of European art cinema (Second Cinema), towards a self-defining cinema that posits a collective – a pluralist vision of 'many peoples' – that does not yet exist, but which this cinema will contribute to creating as a collaborative cultural-political work (see Solanas and Getino 1976). It represents what Deleuze calls a 'minor cinema': one that 'deterritorialises' (decodes or deconstructs) dominant cultural codes and forms of representation in the name of an open-ended process of 'becoming-revolutionary' promising to transform social and political reality.

The second feature of minor cinema, to quote a phrase, is that 'the personal is political'. Recalling what Deleuze and Guattari (following Kafka) call a 'minor literature' (1986), minor cinema shows how the private – or the everyday – is itself imbued with, or revelatory of, the historical and political forces defining an individual's world (Deleuze 1989, 219–221). Whether through the co-existence of familial and social spheres, of old and new ways, filmmakers like Glauber Rocha or Pierre Perrault explore this erasure of the boundary between the private and political while also enacting the 'impossibility' that defines Third cinema: the impossibility of speaking using the dominant voice, the impossibility of doing so independently of prevailing codes, and the impossibility of not speaking or of not showing 'the intolerable' as it manifests in everyday life. In the absence of any definitive 'revolution', there are only creative, resistant ways of giving collective voice or testimony to everyday struggles within con-flicted historical and political circumstances. Minor cinema thus participates in an 'anarchic' process of becoming-revolutionary rather than anticipating a definitive revolutionary event to come. The 'loss of belief' in a revolutionary cinema gives way to a renewed sense of political engagement that articulates the multiple ways in which the everyday can become a new sphere of politics – an ethics of resistance and a politics of experimentation. This represents the third aspect of a minor cinema, the filmmaker's task of contributing to the pro-duction of '*collective utterances*' (Deleuze 1989, 222): expressing the polyglot perspectives of the marginal and the excluded, those whose personal plight reveals the politics in which they are embedded, whose stories demand to be seen and heard despite the 'impossibility' of communicating that defines their cultural situation (Deleuze 1989, 222–223).

Deleuze's fascinating account of 'post-revolutionary' cinema opens up new ways of thinking about how film can be at once ethical and political. In arguing for the possibility of a minor cinema that functions in the absence of 'the people', that explores how the private sphere reveals a deeper political reality, and that shows how the 'impossibility' of the subjected minority's position – being unable to speak, being unable to speak outside the dominant discourses, yet still needing to speak 'in one's own voice' – creates a space for collective (political) utterance, Deleuze offers a vision of 'minor cinema' that brings together the ethical and the political without relying on ideological dogmas or utopian idealization. The 'loss of belief' in revolutionary cinema finds a response in the emergence of a minor cinema, a political cinema without 'the people', coupled with an ethical cinema of 'belief in this world'. This is Deleuze's response to the crisis of political modernism that, as D. N. Rodowick argues (1994), has afflicted the paradigm of 'progressive' political cinema since the 1970s.

The difficulty, however, is that Deleuze's account of minor cinema and the cinema of belief assumes that these two strands of post-war cinema can work together in ways that are synergistic. What is less clear is precisely how this might be so. Existential belief in the world evoked by the contemplative cinema of the 'seer' who eschews action in favour of thought seems sharply at odds with the political affirmation of a creative becoming-revolutionary that would allow a 'missing people' of dispersed minorities to articulate their shared social-political experience of the intolerable. Indeed, Deleuze's cinematic ethics and politics vacillates between these two poles without bringing them together coherently or explaining how they might be able to interact: we have, on the one hand, an existentialist-vitalist belief in the world, the aesthetic imperative to affirm the ethical link between thought and life, to think the 'impossible' as an ethical affirmation of existence; and on the other, a 'prefigura-tion of a people who are missing' (Deleuze 1989, 224), a political commitment to a 'coming community' (Agamben), however dispersed, pluralist, and fragmen-tary, coupled with a utopian belief in cinema's power to criticize the present in order to 'summon forth' a new people and a new earth (Deleuze and Guattari 1994, 99). On the one hand an existential leap, on the other a revolutionary faith. In both cases, we have an existential-vitalist wager: a betting on belief that acknowledges the crisis of cinema and culture today – against the shadowy background of global capitalism – but which also retains a modernist faith in cinema's power to renew the world and summon forth a 'new human being', even if only virtually through art.

The challenge for Deleuzians, then, is to account for this belief in a becoming-revolutionary, in affirming the 'deterritorialising' power of cinema, while acknowledging that our world – the technologically-mediated, audiovisual world of global capitalism – is itself a deterritorialising plane of fluxes and flows, of mutating identities and proliferating desires. The modernist creed of a revolutionary transformation of culture through art – as though art were somehow separate from the world – is itself a key element in the crisis of belief that Deleuze so deftly identifies. This is the challenge for all cinematic philo-sophies that turn to the aesthetic power of cinema to renew our belief in the world, where this pervasive and immersive image-world is itself experienced as a defective source of belief. Only a belief, in cinematic art, can save us (to being Heidegger and Deleuze perversely together); but it is precisely such a belief – the modernist belief in the transformative power of art – that has come to be viewed with scepticism or indifference within our thoroughly mediatized, socially fragmented, globally commodified life-worlds.

A further question looms. What if we cannot or do not wish to give up this belief in cinema? How can the legacy of modernist cinema, with its promise to transfigure our experience, and perhaps transform our subjectivity, be inherited and elaborated today? If the modernist tradition of revolutionary political cinema has been challenged, what are the prospects for a cinema of ethical resistance and political reinvention? A number of filmmakers, both past and present, have responded to such questions with ingenious creativity and imaginative daring, showing how diverse kinds of film can engage in cinematic ethics – as the final three chapters of this book will show in depth.

***

For all of Deleuze's welcome contributions to cinematic ethics (and politics), some persistent questions remain unanswered. Deleuze assumes, rather than shows, that cinema retains its power, despite the climate of scepticism or condition of nihilism within which we exist, to transfigure our experience and transform our subjectivity. The question that arises, of course, is how cinema can do this: what are the processes by which cinema elicits affective responsiveness, emotional engagement, and critical reflection? It is remarkable that, despite Deleuze's theorization of the sensory-motor action schema and its role in 'classical' action-image narrative cinema, there is no account of the role of *emotion* either in relation to perception or action in Deleuze's *Cinema* books (Deleuze's idiosyncratic concept of affect, precisely, is not the same as emotion, especially in his Spinozist-Bergsonian-Nietzschean (anti-subjectivist and transpersonalist) understanding of the term; yet it is called upon to do the conceptual and explanatory work that emotion would ordinarily do in accounting for the cinematic structuration, subjective responses, and cognitive effects of 'classical' movement-image cinema). It is one thing to assert, as Deleuze does, that the 'essence' of cinema concerns the expression of thought through images of duration, but quite another to explain, without recourse to just-so metaphysical accounts, how this might be possible or what processes come into play in our experience of them. It is one thing to claim that cinema can provide us with 'reasons to believe in this world' or even articulate the 'impossible' experience of the marginalized and excluded. It is quite another to give an account of how cinema achieves this ethical and political vocation; how it engages, motivates, mobilizes, and transforms viewers into something other than they were, eliciting new ways of thinking and feeling, which is another way of saying how film can be philosophical – the idea of cinema as ethics.

To answer these questions, I suggest, requires a shift of perspective: both from the therapeutic-aesthetic response to scepticism enacted through moral perfectionism in cinema (Cavell); and from the speculative exploration of time and thought coupled with an existential affirmation of belief and the possibility of a collective 'minoritarian' becoming through cinema (Deleuze). We need to consider, rather, not just 'what cinema can do' (as Deleuzians might put it) but *how* cinema does what it does, and thus, more concretely and empirically, how it might serve as a medium of ethical experience. To do this, we need to consider more closely those narrative-related dimensions of cinematic spectatorship that are given short shrift in Deleuze's vitalist-existentialist form of cinematic ethics: namely, the intimate and inseparable connections between affective responsiveness, emotional engagement, critical reflection, and moral evaluation. We need philosophical perspectives, in short, that can open new ways of thinking about how affect, emotion, and cognition work together in our ethical experience of film. The next chapter takes up this challenge and addresses the 'affective' turn in film theory, exploring how both phenomenological and cognitivist approaches can contribute to developing a more comprehensive account of cinematic ethics.

Notes

1 Cf. 'Here Cavell, alone with Gilles Deleuze in recent scholarship, proposes not just an ontology but an ethics of cinema' (Rodowick 2007, 63).
2 Cf. 'But the essence of cinema – which is not the majority of films – has thought as its higher purpose, nothing but thought and its functioning' (Deleuze 1989, 168).
3 To cite a few examples, the Enlightenment ideal of the 'perfectibility of man', the inevitability of a utopian revolutionary communism, the peaceful spread of democratic freedom through the globalization of capitalism, rational moral and historical progress ensured through the technological mastery of nature, and so on.

Bibliography

Barker, Joseph. 'Visions of the Intolerable: Deleuze on Ethical Images', *Cinema: Journal of Philosophy and the Moving Image*, 6, Susana Viegas (ed.), 'Deleuze and Moving Images' (2014): 122–136.
Bernstein, J. M. '"Movement! Action! Belief?" Notes for a Critique of Deleuze's Cinema Philosophy', *Angelaki: Journal of the Theoretical Humanities*, 17.4 (2012): 77–93.
Bogue, Ronald. 'To Choose to Choose – to Believe in this World'. In *Afterimages of Gilles Deleuze's Film Philosophy*, edited by D. N. Rodowick, 115–134. Minneapolis: University of Minnesota Press, 2010.
Boljkovac, Nadine. *Untimely Affects: Gilles Deleuze and an Ethics of Cinema*. Edinburgh: Edinburgh University Press, 2013.
Bordwell, David. *On the History of Film Style*. Cambridge, MA: Harvard University Press, 1997.
Cavell, Stanley. *The World Viewed: Reflections on the Ontology of Film*. Enlarged Edition. Cambridge, MA and London: Harvard University Press, 1979.
Choi, Jinhee and Frey, Mattias (eds). *Cine-Ethics: Ethical Dimensions of Film Theory, Practice, and Spectatorship*. London and New York: Routledge, 2014.
Deleuze, Gilles. *Cinema 1: The Movement-Image*. Trans. Hugh Tomlinson and Barbara Habberjam. Minneapolis: University of Minnesota Press, 1986 [1983].
Deleuze, Gilles. *Cinema 2: The Time-Image*. Trans. Hugh Tomlinson and Robert Galatea. Minneapolis: University of Minnesota Press, 1989 [1985].
Deleuze, Gilles. 'The Brain is the Screen: An Interview with Gilles Deleuze'. Trans. Marie Therese Guirgis. In Gregory Flaxman (ed.), *The Brain is the Screen: Deleuze and the Philosophy of Cinema*, 365–373. Minneapolis: University of Minnesota Press, 2000.

Deleuze, Gilles. *Kant's Critical Philosophy: The Doctrine of the Faculties*. Trans. Hugh Tomlinson and Barbara Habberjam. London: The Athlone Press, 1984.

Deleuze, Gilles and Guattari, Felix. *Kafka: Towards a Minor Literature*. Trans. Dana Polan. Minneapolis: University of Minnesota Press, 1986.

Deleuze, Gilles and Guattari, Felix. *What is Philosophy?* Trans. Hugh Tomlinson and Graham Burchell. New York: Columbia University Press, 1994.

del Rio, Elena. *Deleuze and the Cinemas of Performance: Powers of Affection*. Edinburgh: Edinburgh University Press, 2012.

Flaxman, Gregory (ed.). *The Brain is the Screen: Deleuze and the Philosophy of Cinema*. Minncapolis: University of Minnesota Press, 2000.

Foster, Hal (ed.). *Postmodern Culture*. London: Pluto Books, 1985.

Jameson, Fredric. *Postmodernism, or the Cultural Logic of Late Capitalism*. London: Verso Books, 1991.

Kennedy, Barbara M. *Deleuze and Cinema: The Aesthetics of Sensation*. Edinburgh: Edinburgh University Press, 2002.

King, Alisdair. 'Fault Lines: Deleuze, Cinema, and the Ethical Landscape'. In Jinhee Choi and Mattias Frey (eds), *Cine-Ethics: Ethical Dimensions of Film Theory, Practice, and Spectatorship*, 57–75. London and New York: Routledge, 2014.

Marrati, Paola. *Gilles Deleuze: Cinema and Philosophy*. Trans. Alisa Hartz. Baltimore: The Johns Hopkins University Press, 2006.

Martin-Jones, David. *Deleuze, Cinema, and National Identity*. Edinburgh: Edinburgh University Press, 2006.

Martin-Jones, David. *Deleuze and World Cinemas*. London/New York: Continuum, 2011.

Nietzsche, Friedrich. *The Will to Power*. Trans. Walter Kaufman and R. J. Hollingdale. New York: Vintage Books, 1968.

Pisters, Patricia. *The Neuro-Image: A Deleuzian Film-Philosophy of Digital Screen Culture*. Stanford: Stanford University Press, 2012.

Powell, Anna. *Deleuze and Horror Film*. Edinburgh: Edinburgh University Press, 2005.

Rancière, Jacques. *Film Fables*. Trans. Emiliano Battista. Oxford and New York: Berg Books, 2006.

Rodowick, D. N. *The Crisis of Political Modernism: Criticism and Ideology in Contemporary Film Theory*. 2nd Edition. Urbana: University of Illinois Press, 1994.

Rodowick, D. N. *Gilles Deleuze's Time Machine*. Durham and London: Duke University Press, 1997.

Rodowick, D. N. *The Virtual Life of Film*. Cambridge, MA and London: Harvard University Press, 2007.

Rodowick, D. N. 'The World, Time'. In D. N. Rodowick (ed.), *Afterimages of Gilles Deleuze's Film Philosophy*, 97–114. Minneapolis: University of Minnesota Press, 2010.

Rodowick, D. N. *Philosophy's Artful Conversation*. Cambridge, MA and London: Harvard University Press, 2015.

Sinnerbrink, Robert. 'Film-Philosophy'. In Warren Buckland and Edward Branigan (eds), *The Routledge Encyclopedia of Film Theory*, 207–213. Abingdon and New York: Routledge, 2014.

Solanas, Fernando and Getino, Octavio. 'Towards a Third Cinema'. In Bill Nichols (ed.), *Movies and Methods. An Anthology*, 44–64. Berkeley: University of California Press, 1976.

Filmography

Bicycle Thieves [*Ladri di biciclette*]. Dir. Vittorio De Sica (Italy, 1948)
Europe '51 [*Europa '51*]. Dir. Roberto Rossellini (Italy, 1952)

Germany Year Zero [*Germania, anno zero*]. Dir. Roberto Rossellini (Italy, 1948)
Hiroshima mon amour. Dir. Alain Resnais (France/Japan, 1959)
Journey to Italy [*Viaggio in Italia*]. Dir. Roberto Rossellini (Italy/France, 1954)
Paisan [*Paisà*]. Dir. Roberto Rossellini (Italy, 1946)
Rome, Open City [*Roma, città aperta*]. Dir. Roberto Rossellini (Italy, 1945)
Stromboli. Dir. Roberto Rossellini (Italy/USA, 1950)
Umberto D. Dir. Vittorio De Sica (Italy, 1952)
The Unknown. Dir. Tod Browning (USA, 1927)

4 Cinempathy: phenomenology, cognitivism, and moving images

[Film] succeeds in short-circuiting the rigid surface cultural blocks that shackle our consciousness to narrowly limited areas of experience and is able to cut directly through to areas of emotional comprehension.

Stanley Kubrick on *2001* (quoted in Frampton 2006, 164)

Some of the most innovative philosophical engagement with cinema and ethics in recent years has come from phenomenological and cognitivist perspectives in film theory. This trend reflects a welcome re-engagement with cinema's potential for ethical transformation, that is, with the idea of cinema as a medium of ethical experience. Such an approach challenges the sceptical view, familiar from 1970s film theory, according to which cinema contributes to the construction of dominant 'subject positions' and thereby reproduces ideology through the manipulation of spectator subjectivity. In this chapter, I explore the implications of the recent 'affective turn' in film theory (with its focus on affective, empathic, and embodied responses to cinema), examining the ethical implications of phenomenological approaches to affect and empathy, emotion and evaluation, care and responsibility. The oft-criticized 'subjectivism' of phenomenological theories, I argue, can be supplemented by recent cognitivist approaches that highlight the complex forms of affective response, emotional engagement, and moral allegiance at work in our experience of moving images. At the same time, the cognitivist temptation towards reductionism or inadequate accounts of aesthetic experience can be avoided by way of 'thick' phenomenological description and hermeneutic interpretation. I will explore this exciting crossover between phenomenological and cognitivist approaches to both empathy and sympathy as intimately related dynamic processes (a 'cinempathy') involved in emotional engagement and ethical responsiveness. My claim is that this kind of empathic ethics is at work in many films: film provides a powerful means of enacting the affective temporal dynamic between empathy and sympathy, emotional engagement, and multiple perspective-taking. Taken together, these elements of cinematic ethics offer experientially rich, context-sensitive, and ethically singular forms of imaginative engagement in social situations that reveal the complexities of a cultural-historical world. I elaborate this thesis by analysing a key sequence from

Asghar Farhadi's *A Separation* (2011), a film that offers a striking case study in cinematic ethics.

The affective turn in film theory

As Eisenstein, Noël Carroll, and David Bordwell have all remarked, the power of movies resides in their capacity to elicit emotional engagement (Eisenstein 1991, Carroll 1985, Bordwell 1989). Yet until the recent 'affective turn' (roughly since the late 1990s/early 2000s), topics such as emotion, emotional engagement, affect, not to mention empathy and sympathy, were largely ignored by the dominant schools of film theory (structuralist, semiotic, Marxist, and feminist forms of psychoanalytic film theory). As is well known, film theory of the 1970s and 80s focused on theorizing 'desire' and questioning 'pleasure', critically analysing the manner in which movies manipulate spectator subjectivity, channelling spectator desire through ideologically structured forms of 'identification' in order to reproduce dominant ideological (and gendered) 'subject positions'. Psychoanalytic film theory had little interest in 'emotion' or 'affect' because its focus lay elsewhere, namely in the unconscious and ideological processes that contributed to the formation of (gender and class) identity. Marxist critical film theory, on the other hand, argued that the dominant forms of narrative (Hollywood) cinema, with their emphasis on emotional engagement, moral individualism, and narrative closure, provided ideologically manipulative, compensatory forms of narrative pleasure that contributed to the depoliticization of the masses and ideological valorization of the American (capitalist) way of life. Emotion and affect were relegated to the domain of the regressive, 'irrational' responses of manipulated spectators. Only a critical cinema – along with an activist film theory – could unmask or subvert these ideological processes through the progressive modernist gestures of rupturing conventional codes, refusing closure, exposing the film production process, and forcing critical self-reflection on the part of the spectator. Both psychoanalytic and critical film theory thereby shared in the philosophical suspicion of emotion as the pernicious 'other' of a critical reason that would emancipate oppressed subjects through theoretical illumination and ideological demystification.

Today things appear very different, with film theory in recent years undergoing related affective and ethical turns. One striking aspect of this development is the manner in which aesthetic and ethical dimensions of film are increasingly understood as complementary, even coincident, features of our experience of movies. As Jinhee Choi and Mattias Frey remark, the 'ethical turn' 'stresses the particular affective nature of film spectatorship' such that 'perceptual and sensorial engagement with film is considered ethical in and of itself, not merely as a moral ground to connect reality and others outside the self' (2014, 1). As Choi and Frey point out, research in analytic aesthetics and philosophy of film, by contrast, tends to focus on the problem of the relationship between aesthetic and moral value and the ethical implications of this relationship for practices of criticism and aesthetic evaluation: does the moral value or attitude expressed in a work of art affect how we judge or evaluate the aesthetic qualities of the work or its artistic achievement? 'Autonomists' argue that aesthetic value is and should be kept distinct from moral value, which implies that a work enjoys aesthetic autonomy from whatever moral judgments one may make concerning the attitudes or values expressed in and by the work; 'moralists', on the other hand, argue that aesthetic and moral value cannot be so readily separated, hence that the moral values or attitudes expressed in and by the work do affect our evaluation of its aesthetic qualities or artistic achievement.[1] An autonomist can acknowledge the artistic achievement of Leni Riefenstahl's *Triumph of the Will*, for example, despite its purpose and content as a work of Nazi propaganda; a moralist, by contrast, rejects this separation and would claim that the film's promotion or expression of Nazi ideology neutralizes or vitiates any putative artistic achievement by interfering with the achievement of its artistic aims. As we shall see in the chapters that follow, it is precisely where there is a conflict or dissonance between aesthetic expression and moral-ethical meaning that we find the most challenging, thought-provoking cases of cinematic ethics.[2]

The 'affective turn' across the humanities has put affect, emotion, 'the body', and subjectivity back on the agenda, opening up new forms of ethico-political reflection. Emotion and affect are now central issues in film theory, which has been rejuvenated by contributions from philosophy, empirical psychology, cognitive theory, neuroscience, and evolutionary biology (see Carroll 2008, Coplan and Goldie 2006, Gaut 2010, Grodal 2009, Pisters 2012, Plantinga 2009, Stadler 2008, Laine 2011, M. Smith 1995, Allen and Smith 1997, G. Smith 2003). Philosophy of film – in both 'Continental' and analytic-cognitivist guises – has criticized the psychoanalytic paradigm and developed new ways of thinking about affect, emotion, and the ethico-aesthetic experience of cinema (an aesthetic encounter that opens up varieties of ethically significant experience). Psychoanalytic film theory, moreover, has been challenged by cognitivist psychology, which offers explanatory theories dealing with phenomena relevant to cinematic experience such as affective response, emotional engagement, cognitive understanding and moral-critical evaluation. In this sense, the 'affective turn' coupled with the explosion of philosophical interest in cinema – what many today call the 'philosophical turn' – has renewed some of the key questions of 'classical' film theory (as explored in Hugo Münsterberg's *The Photoplay*, for example), in particular, how to understand cinema's power of emotional engagement and hence its ethical significance.

The phenomenological-affective turn

The broad sweep of recent phenomenological approaches in film studies, from Vivian Sobchack's work to various forms of affect theory, offer concrete and focused explorations of embodied subjective experience. Indeed, the turn to phenomenological theories focusing on affective experience – both from the spectator perspective and in relation to cinematic expression – has become so influential that we can talk of an 'affective turn' in film-philosophy (see Stadler 2014, 29). Phenomenological approaches, foregrounding the experiential aspects of cinema, put the human subject back into the picture, albeit a subject defined by its 'affects', its corporeality, and its embodied difference. Once again, we find an emphasis on 'the body' – often left theoretically under-defined – rather than on consciousness or the mind/brain in its embodied 'being-in-the-world'. Such theories are generally eclectic, deriving in part from classical and post-war phenomenology (Husserl, Merleau-Ponty, and Heidegger), as well as drawing on feminist, culturalist, 'Continental' as well as cognitivist sources (see Barker 2009, Casebier 1991, Laine 2011, Marks 2002, 2000, Sobchack 2004, 1992, Stadler 2008). All of them tend to affirm the centrality of 'first person' experiential perspectives that can be applied not only to the theorization of spectator response – sometimes even attributing 'subjective' traits or qualities like 'embodiment' or 'intentionality' to the film itself (Barker 2009, Frampton 2006, Laine 2011, Sobchack 1992). Crossover theorization drawing, for example, on phenomenological and cognitivist, or Deleuzian and neuroscientific approaches, is becoming more common (Laine 2011, Pisters 2012, Stadler 2008). These hybrid approaches provide a rich interdisciplinary theoretical matrix for exploring the complexities of affect and emotion, including empathy and sympathy, in regard to the aesthetic and ethical experience of cinema.

Nonetheless, the 'standard' challenge facing phenomenology, broadly construed, is how to avoid the charge of *subjectivism*: to articulate and account for the relationship between first-person phenomenological description and more general theoretical explanation. How to connect the first-person, experientially rich, *description* of a phenomenon (say affect) to the empirically grounded, *explanatory* theory of the causal mechanisms (physiological and neurological) underlying subjective phenomena? This question, I note, is just as pertinent, from the opposite direction (from explanation to description), for the recent proliferation of work using cognitivist and neuroscientific approaches to ethics, aesthetics, and, of course, philosophy of film. Phenomenological approaches offer rich, 'thick' descriptive theories of various aspects of cinematic experience. At the same time, they are not in a position – given their character as descriptive – to offer causal explanatory accounts of the phenomena in question. This is the point, however, at which phenomenology and cognitivism can meet, the former providing a rich descriptive theory of phenomena relevant to cinematic experience that the latter can analyse in empirically-grounded, causally explanatory terms.

A brief history of cognitivism

Despite a still uneasy relationship with historicist and 'theoretical' camps within film theory, cognitivism now presents itself as one of the most developed alternative approaches to the once dominant semiotic-psychoanalytic paradigm. In broad terms we can describe cognitivism as an empirically-grounded, naturalistic approach to film that rejects 'speculative' theory in favour of 'piecemeal' theorization (Bordwell and Carroll 1996). This broad approach enquires into various aspects of film experience using the tools of cognitive psychology and theories of mind, which for their part often draw on neuroscientific theories and philosophy of cognition emphasizing (depending on orientation and commitments) computational, functional, modular, or embodied processes of cognition. Although early forms of cognitive theory indeed modelled the brain as operating computationally (using the algorithmic processes of the computer as an analogy for how our brains process information), more recent forms of cognitive theory have moved away from this computational model in favour of modular, network, and, more recently, embodied, embedded, extended, and enactive conceptions of mind (the '4E model of cognition' or 4EA model, which includes the 'affective' aspect; see Clark 2008, Menary 2007, 2010).

Commencing in the 1980s and into the 1990s, a number of film theorists (such as Joseph Anderson 1996, Edward Branigan 1984, Noël Carroll 1985, 1988, David Bordwell 1985, 1989, Gregory Currie 1995, Torben Grodal 2009, Carl Plantinga 2009, and Murray Smith 1995), challenged the psychoanalytic-semiotic paradigm of film theory and adopted instead a variety of cognitivist approaches to the theorization of film, analysing a range of relevant problems including audiovisual perception, emotional engagement, narrative understanding, emotion and genre, and film interpretation (see Bordwell and Carroll 1996, Allen and Smith 1997, Plantinga and Smith 1999, and more recently, Nannicelli and Taberham 2014). Cognitivist theorists reject the long-standing Platonic prejudice that reason and emotion are opposed, agreeing with Aristotle that they are complementary modes of human cognition that enable us to understand and respond to the world through practical action. They assume that spectators respond to cinema using the same cognitive modes of perception, emotion, and understanding as occur in everyday experience; hence they argue that film theory can draw on cognitive theory and psychology in order to better theorize the complex forms of cognitive engagement at play in experiencing and understanding movies.

From an initially marginalized position in the 1990s, cognitivism has developed into a flourishing research programme tackling many of the traditional problems of 'classical' film theory. In conjunction with philosophical aesthetics, cognitivist theories have been developed to explain film spectatorship and the understanding of narrative film, while stressing the importance of emotional engagement for cognitive experience more generally. In more recent work, cognitivist approaches are being extended to areas often considered the preserve of more 'Continental' approaches in aesthetics and film theory (avant-garde, experimental, and modernist forms of film, for example) as well as theorizing some of the broader aesthetic, cultural, and technological aspects of film, including questions of aesthetic evaluation, genre, and the impact of digital media (see Nannicelli and Taberham 2014).

According to critics of cognitivism, however, contentious issues still remain that mark the limits of this paradigm's explanatory power, particularly with reference to the relationship between epistemology and ethics (Rodowick 2007). One problem is how to deal with *ideology* and the cultural-historical dimensions of film reception. As a 'naturalistic' theory – one that posits causal scientific explanations of phenomena explicable in terms of the laws of nature – critics argue that cognitivism has difficulty accounting for the role of ideology, along with cinema's historical and political dimensions, without risking some version of the 'naturalistic fallacy' (assuming that because a phenomenon can be *explained* in terms of natural laws it can also be *justified* by appeal to such laws). Even if we could produce an evolutionary explana-tion of, say, racism or sexism, that would still leave open the normative question of its moral wrongness or its cultural-political dangers, which is not a question readily addressed using scientific theories. It is one thing to explain the appeal of action movies with high levels of violence, or the fascination exerted by pornography, quite another to draw normative conclusions about the desirability or otherwise of such popular forms of audiovisual culture.[3]

Other critics acknowledge that cognitivism offers powerful explanatory theories of the underlying causal processes involved in our experience of cinema but that this does not mean it provides a suitable hermeneutic framework for film interpretation or aesthetic evaluation (see Frampton 2006, 106–107; Sinnerbrink 2011, 51 ff.). Even if we have a general explanatory theory of the evolutionary usefulness or neurological basis of narrative or genre, this may not be particularly enlightening when applied to particular film examples or offer sufficient resources to evaluate film from an aesthetic perspective. The danger of 'reductionism', in a word, looms large for such critics, who accuse cognitivism of distorting or downplaying important aesthetic, hermeneutic, and ethico-political dimensions of cinema by reducing these to underlying elements of a naturalistic theory of mind that pays scant attention to the role of social or cultural-historical contexts in our engagement with the world.

These objections, however, are not necessarily conclusive: cognitivists can respond that naturalistic theories explaining perception, emotion, cognition, and so on, can provide a firmer, more empirically-grounded basis for theorizing the role of affective response, emotional engagement, and cognitive understanding in the operations of ideology through film (see Plantinga 2009, 190–197). The presumed opposition between 'cognitivism' and 'culturalism' may be a false or misleading one. Or they may argue that the charge of 'reductionism' is misguided because the 'conflation' of levels of explanation is as much a pro-blem for hermeneutic theories as naturalistic ones (for example, the tendency to treat film interpretation as providing hermeneutic 'evidence' for the validity of a theoretical approach, whether psychoanalytic, Deleuzian, phenomenological, and so on). Moreover, recent forms of social cognition and 4EA theories of cognition are at pains to incorporate the role of social interaction, social-cultural context, language and culture, distributed cognition, and external/technical cognitive prostheses in our conscious engagement with the world. The point, rather, is to tailor one's theories to the phenomena in question, and to be scrupulous about the level of description, analysis, or explanation to which one is committed: to avoid, in short, indulging in theoretical 'overreach' (using a specific theory to go beyond what it can legitimately cover).

Finally, cognitivism is a relatively new research paradigm within film theory, one that has many schools and strands that are still being developed and applied to an increasing number of topics, problems, and cases. There is no one model of cognitivist theory; and the multiple uses to which these various strands can be put are now being explored in exciting ways (see Nannicelli and Taberham 2014). Despite the scepticism of some theorists, it would be unwise to pre-judge how successful applying cognitivist, neurological, evolutionary theories to aesthetics will be, especially with regard to the critical analysis of particular films. Rather than dismissing the possibility that such a paradigm could offer a framework compatible with, or conducive to, detailed film interpretation, aesthetic evaluation, or moral-ethical judgment, we should look to see what kind of theoretically enlightening work can be done using such approaches and what critical insights different kinds of cognitivist analyses might yield. We could mention here, for example, the growth in cognitivist, neuroscientific, and evolutionary-biological readings of art cinema, which attempt to posit explanatory accounts of the manner in which it generates the kind of dissociative, imaginative, poetic, or 'meaning-saturated' responses that it does (Grodal's analyses (2004) of von Trier's films, for example). So rather than reject the cognitivist approach in regard to aesthetics (and ethics) *tout court*, it would behove sceptical film-philosophers to adopt a more open, pluralistic attitude, experimenting with a dialectical approach to competing theories, acknowledging their strengths and supplementing their weaknesses, while aiming at a more comprehensive theoretical perspective that can do justice to the complexity of our cinematic experience.

A more productive path, I suggest, is thus an interdisciplinary one: drawing on the 'subjective' perspective of phenomenological as a descriptive approach to cinematic experience, and the 'objective' orientation of cognitivism that aims to develop explanatory theories concerning central features of our experience of movies. In this way a pluralist and pragmatist perspective can help counteract the unfortunate tendency towards theoretical sectarianism and solipsism in some areas of film theory and philosophy. Recent 'hybrid' forms of film theory, for example, attempt this kind of 'synthesising' approach – crossing disciplinary boundaries as well as the 'analytic/Continental' divide – supplementing the 'subjectivism' of phenomenology with the 'objectivism' of cognitivism, but also striving to remain true to the complexity of the phenomena under consideration. For affect and emotion, including empathy and sympathy, are protean and ambiguous; they demand a range of theoretical descriptions and a plurality of explanatory models. In this pluralist and pragmatist spirit, I turn to consider affective and emotional engagement in film in order to explore further how narrative cinema can evoke varieties of ethical experience.

Affect and emotion

I commence with a thesis: adopting phenomenological and cognitivist approaches to affect and emotion can help us better explain the processes involved in our aesthetic and moral engagement with film. The first challenge, however, is to describe the phenomena in a manner that is accurate without being unwieldy. On the one hand, emotions are readily understood in everyday experience and in ordinary language; they are constitutive of our personal identity and ability to engage in social interactions. On the other, the theorization of emotions involves a complex and confusing array of approaches focusing on different levels of explanation and diverse aspects of emotional experience. Most theorists agree (de Sousa 1987, Goldie 2002, Plantinga 2009), however, that emotions include a *physiological* aspect (changes in autonomous physiological processes); a *psychological* aspect; an *affective* or *'feeling'* aspect; a *sensory-motor* or *action-oriented* aspect; and an *evaluative* or *cognitive* aspect. When I am angry I experience physiological changes in my body (accelerated heartbeat, muscle tension, adrenaline flow), changes in my psychological state (increased aggression or a desire to 'act out'), in my affective state (feeling tense, a sense of agitated arousal), linked with a rapid cognitive appraisal, judgment, or evaluation of my situation (a belief that I have been wronged, a construal of the other's behaviour as posing a threat). My anger has an object, which serves as the reason for my getting angry (e.g. a reckless driver swerving in front of me), and it enables me to evaluate my situation promptly and act accordingly (e.g. to take evasive action). Emotions condense these affective, bodily, and cognitive responses in a manner that enables the rapid evaluation of my situation and the taking of appropriate action depending on how I respond to having the particular emotional responses that I do in a given situation.

Analyzing emotions from a phenomenological and cognitivist perspective reveals a number of constitutive elements. To list the most salient:

1 emotions are temporal and episodic: they unfold in time, have a definite duration, and are generally transient phenomena;
2 they arise and develop according to feedback from our bodies and from our environment: our emotional life, as Plantinga observes, 'occurs in streams that continuously evolve in response to everchanging construals, actions and action tendencies, bodily states, and feelings', any of which can serve as feedback to modify our subsequent emotional responses (Plantinga 2009, 60);
3 emotions are intimately related to narratives; they can be triggered by acquired 'paradigm scenarios' (de Sousa 1987), namely, characteristic

patterns of feelings, actions, and reactions, organized in narrative terms, that occur in specific situations leading to a 'learned' emotional response; my emotional state is thus shaped by the kind of narrative meaning through which I make sense of my identity and describe my emotions to others, usually through shared narrative schemata;

4   emotions vary in duration and intensity, waxing and waning over time, varying in affective amplitude;

5   emotions are often mixed or ambiguous: primary emotions (anger, fear, disgust, happiness, sadness, and surprise) are often discrete and identifiable, yet emotions usually occur in complex affective clusters or overlapping combinations that can be difficult to define. Plantinga mentions, for example, the simultaneous horror and fascination felt in response to 'a monster in a horror film', a complex of emotional responses that combines contrary affective valences (negative and positive) and conflicting action tendencies (repulsion and attraction);[4]

6   emotions are distinct from moods, which are more global, encompassing, diffuse, and 'world-disclosing' (Heidegger 2010 [1927]). To be more precise, emotions have intentional objects (fear of a speeding car, of losing one's job, of getting cancer), whereas moods tend to lack a definite intentional object, so can be 'free-floating' or, as Heidegger has it, oriented towards our 'being-in-the-world' in general (2010 [1927]). From a hermeneutic point of view, emotions can be understood in terms of reasons (I was angry with you because of what you said to me), whereas moods have more dispersed causes (physical fatigue, environmental factors, physiological changes, the aesthetic qualities of my surroundings; although some 'existential' moods seem to lack a definite object or singular cause). Nonetheless, moods and emotions remain intimately related, moods priming us for particular emotions, and particular emotions being enhanced or diminished by background moods;

7   emotions can be further 'primed' or 'cued' according to discrete environmental factors, background mood, mental outlook, and ongoing emotional dynamics; and, finally,

8   we can have propensities towards certain emotional responses ('character traits') that make up an emotional disposition (someone prone to anger, someone habitually cheerful, consistently calm and measured, someone who enjoys risk and thrills, someone who tends towards fear or anxiety) as opposed to emotions as occurrent states (a flash of anger, a sense of joy). These general features of emotions come into play during our aesthetic experience of cinema, which, in Ed Tan's (1995) nice phrase, can be aptly described as an 'emotion machine'.

Definitions of emotion are legion. As Peter Goldie (2002) points out, however, there are two aspects that any definition of emotion should capture: namely the *affective* or feeling aspect, and the *cognitive* or appraisal aspect.

Although emotions involve and express feelings they are also linked to, or expressive of, appraisals that have a cognitive dimension (sometimes involving definite beliefs or propositional attitudes, for example, but also including non-propositional forms of affective appraisals or what Goldie calls 'feeling towards' an object). At the same time, emotions are complex phenomena that comprise a number of overlapping elements, both affective and cognitive. Following Robert C. Roberts, Carl Plantinga defines emotional responses as *concern-based construals* (2009, 55–56 ff.) that are at once cognitive, relational, intentional, and embodied. Robert Solomon (2003) defines them as *cognitive judgments* that work through feeling more than reasoning. Peter Goldie (2002) describes the intentionality of emotions as a phenomenological *'feeling towards'* that expresses both a concern and a potential for action, without necessarily being 'intellectual' or 'cognitive' in the narrower sense of these terms. Contra common criticisms of cognitivist theory, this view of emotions as affective-cognitive forms of judgment or construal does not imply the banishment of unconscious pro-cesses from our cognitive experience. On the contrary, Plantinga points to the crucial role of the 'cognitive unconscious' in our engagement with others and the world; consciousness requires unconscious cognitive operations and 'automatic' responses to various stimuli in order to facilitate our successful emotional and practical engagement with our environment (2009, 50). Affective responses (bodily feelings, sensations, corporeal states) often occur in ways that are involuntary, or below the threshold of conscious intention; yet they orient and qualify emotional responses and prime our bodies to take appropriate action depending on our emotional-cognitive appraisal of a situation. Emotions thus provide a cognitive-evaluative, sensory-motor way of responding rapidly and adroitly to complex social situations within our culturally diverse life-worlds.

A Brief History of Empathy ('Einfühlung')

One of the central ethical topics in the recent focus on emotion has been the role of, and relationship between, empathy and sympathy. Yet these are hardly new ideas. The roots of the notion of 'sympathy' lie in eighteenth century English moral philosophy and psychology of the sentiments. Adam Smith's 1759 treatise *The Theory of Moral Sentiments*, for example, defines sympathy as 'fellow-feeling for the misery of others' accompanied by 'passion of the mind', offering a 'naturalistic' moral psychological account of our shared human propensity towards sympathetic concern for others. Rousseau too regarded compassion as rooted in the human sentiment of *pitié*, which takes the place of morality in the hypothetical 'state of nature' before the estab-lishment of a social contract: 'It is therefore quite certain that pity is a natural sentiment which, by moderating in each individual the activity of the love of oneself contributes to the mutual preservation of the entire species' (Rousseau 1992 [1755], 38). For both Smith and Rousseau, this compassionate concern for the suffering of others provides an affective basis for mutually beneficial altruism that offsets our natural desire for self-preservation and thus provides a 'natural' foundation – based upon our innate sense of fellow-feeling or moral sympathy – for the development of social and political community.

Hume also offers a 'non-cognitive' account of the foundation of morality in a theory of moral sentiments, which derive from our feelings of pleasure and displeasure in the exercise of sympathy in regard to the suffering of others (Hume, 1896 [1739], Bk III). Moral sentiments of approval or disapproval – experienced as pleasurable or displeasurable – are emotional responses to the impartial contemplation of another person or their actions independently of one's self-interest. Hume's account of sympathy, moreover, merges with what we would today call *empathy*, which involves adopting a first-person perspective from which we imagine the subjective experience of another: 'By our imagination we place ourselves in his situation, we conceive ourselves enduring all the same torments, we enter as it were into his own body, and become in some measure the same person as him, and thence form some idea of his sensations' (Hume 2002 [1759], 1ff.) Our capacity to discern the underlying 'passions' shaping another person's actions leads to the moral emotions of approval or disapproval that ground how we judge desirable or undesirable character traits (virtues or vices). Morality, for Hume, thus depends upon the feeling of sympathy coupled with empathy in our imaginatively construed social relations with others.

It is 'empathy', however, that has become an intensive focus of research in recent years for many moral philosophers, psychologists, and film theorists (see Coplan and Goldie 2011, IX-XLVII, and Coplan 2011). The term is of recent provenance (in English), but it has a fascinating history stretching from German romantic aesthetics to hermeneutics (see Currie 2011 and Nowak 2011). It appeared as a translation (by Titchener in 1909) of the German term *Einfühlung* developed by German aesthetician Theodor Lipps (although the term itself goes back to J. G. Herder, Friedrich and Robert Vischer, before being taken up by Dilthey and Schleiermacher). As Nowak notes, the eighteenth century concept of *Einfühlung* originally referred to 'the possibility of exploring the human psyche by empathizing with other people', and was later used to 'describe the relation between humankind and nature' (Nowak 2011, 302). Herder emphasized the manner in which we can perceive similarities with the human within nature, endowing it with a consciousness and (symbolic) meaning that can be experienced empathically (as a 'mystical union'). For German romantics like Schelling, Novalis and the Schlegel brothers, *Einfühlen* described the experience of overcoming the separation of subject and object in the aesthetic experience of nature and of art (Nowak 2011, 309). Herder then applied the notion of *Einfühlung* to the interpretation of texts, arguing that one could experience the ideas of an artist or author through an 'empathic' projection that opens up a text's inner symbolic meaning.

Hegelian philosopher Friedrich Theodor Vischer (1807–1887) elaborated the concept, focusing on how objects, whether living beings or works of art, can become endowed with a spiritual or symbolic meaning. Vischer's son

Robert then used *Einfühlung* to refer to 'the viewer's active participation in a work of art', defining it as 'a mutual experience of exchange between the body and the perceived object' (Nowak 2011, 304). Robert Vischer's contribution was to shift the focus to the viewer or spectator, who now became the source of the aesthetic experience of meaning and recipient of an intensified sense of sensuous vitality. Although criticized for its 'subjectivism', Vischer's *empathic aesthetics* – the enlivening 'transference' of subjective feeling to the sensuous form of objects – claimed that one could 'feel one's way into' (the core meaning of *Einfühlung*) the emotional and symbolic meaning of objects through an immersive aesthetic encounter.

Theodor Lipps went a step further, arguing that *Einfühlung* describes the process by which the viewer comes to experience the 'emotional states of the object' expressed through its sensuous, symbolic, and visual aspects (Nowak 2011, 306). Empathy, for Lipps, is thus a form of aesthetic 'identification'; a 'merging of subject and object' in which one 'participates' in the object's inner meaning through symbolic communication. Empathy can be experienced, moreover, in relation to four different kinds of objects – the psychological-emotional life of human beings, the psyche of animals, nature, and works of art – where we respond to facial expression, corporeal similarities, gesture and comportment, mimetic affinities, and symbolic form (Nowak 2011, 306). It can even be applied to historical objects, opening the possibility of an empathic hermeneutics in which the historian is able to enrich our cultural-historical understanding through aesthetic practices of narrative and symbolic interpretation – an idea taken up in romantic hermeneutics via the notion of *Verstehen*. Suffice to say, the fascinating history of *Einfühlung* within German romantic aesthetics and hermeneutics offers many exciting insights that could contribute to contemporary film-philosophical discussions of empathy and sympathy. Two recent contributions to this line of inquiry, for example, are Currie's (2011) discussion of 'empathy for objects' as a mode of bodily simulation, and Smith's account of empathy and the 'extended mind' thesis, which explores the devices of cinema as '*cognitive prostheses*' enabling an expansion and enhancement of empathic and imaginative engagement (2011, 109).

Empathy and sympathy ('cinempathy')

Against the background of this fascinating history, a brief glance at research literature on empathy and sympathy reveals a bewilderingly complicated situation: there are disputes over the meaning of these terms, whether they designate two discrete emotional capacities, whether the distinction between them is confused, whether they are better used as synonyms, whether they name imaginative operations, whether they work through the 'simulation' of another's emotional response, whether empathy means that I share *the same* emotional state as another, a *congruent emotional state* (Plantinga), or imagine myself experiencing an emotional state. And so on.

When it comes to film theorization the complexities proliferate: empathy is often identified with 'identification' (with characters and their emotional states), which is itself a contested term. Some theorists identify empathy with 'pre-conscious' involuntary responses such as *affective mimicry* or *emotional contagion* (the tendency to 'unconsciously' mimic the affective states and expressions of others or to 'catch' their emotional state through the mirroring of facial expression and bodily gesture). Others, such as Amy Coplan (2011, 2006), argue that empathy should not be identified with affective mimicry or emotional contagion since these are non-voluntary affective responses whereas empathy – as the capacity to imagine and respond emotionally to the experiences of another, while maintaining a discernible self-other distinction – requires a complex imaginative construal of the other's situation along with a cognitive-emotional evaluation of their expressions, intentions, and actions. Some theorists, moreover, go on to identify empathy (and sympathy) as key to our capacity for moral perception (the ability to discern, recognize, or be attentive to the moral predicament or sufferings of others). Martha Nussbaum (1992) and Stanley Cavell (2004, 1996, 1981), for example, suggest that literature and film can be regarded as an artistic means of exercising and thus cultivating and refining our moral imaginations, which in turn opens up the possibility of enhancing our capacity for moral understanding and promoting the exercise of ethical conduct (see Prinz 2011 for a contrary view). A number of theorists pursue the idea of mental simulation as a way of capturing how we relate, emotionally and imaginatively, to fictional characters (Currie 1995, Feagin 1996, Knight 2006). Schiller's romantic ideal of art serving as a means of educating the senses towards moral maturity through the free play of the imagination thus finds in cinematic empathy a new lease of life.

Instead of working through this tangled web, I shall focus on the distinction between empathy and sympathy, arguing that it remains important for film-philosophy, even though the phenomena in question tend to coalesce (I should note that I am referring to empathy and sympathy here as imaginative capacities to respond emotionally to the situation of others rather than using the more ordinary sense of these terms as an expression of emotional solidarity or moral support). One of the most useful ways of distinguishing these, as Alex Neill observes (2006), is to describe sympathy *as feeling for* someone while empathy is *feeling with* him or her. I feel sympathy for my friend who has just lost her father, without experiencing a state of grief as such; yet at his funeral I might feel empathy for her and find myself grieving and crying along with her family. Here one could say that sympathy spills over into empathy, and empathy over into sympathy, intensified by affective mimicry and emotional priming due to the particular features of the social situation (a funeral) with its relevant 'paradigm scenarios' (de Sousa 1987). From a phenomenological perspective, empathy and sympathy can be described as poles between which we are 'moved' perceptually *and* affectively: poles marking two distinct yet related kinds of subjective perspective-taking having different but related emotional dynamics and evaluative valences (more immediate, immersive, and affective in the case of empathy, more mediated, reflective, and normative in the case of sympathy). As I shall elaborate below, this is crucial for understanding how cinema engages us at once empathically and sympathetically in a mobile, kinetic, and dynamic manner; that is, understanding how cinema can both express and evoke ethical experience.

The case of empathy and sympathy with regard to fictional characters is also intriguing: they do not exist as persons do, yet I can have a sympathetic response to them while being aware of their fictional nature. To resolve any potential paradox (Radford's so-called 'paradox of fiction'), theorists have pointed to the 'pretend' (Walton 1990) or 'simulated' (Currie 1995, 2011; Currie and Ravenscroft 2002) character of these emotions, or alternatively to the *imaginative* character of empathy (and sympathy) (Plantinga 2009, Stadler 2013): the capacity to imaginatively adopt the other's perspective, either from a first-person point of view (empathy) or from an observer or witness perspective (sympathy). I imagine the other's grief and can either experience it myself – or experience 'congruent emotional states' (Plantinga) like sorrow or sadness – or else imagine the emotional response the other might be experiencing (without actually having that same emotion myself). Murray Smith (1997, 412–430), for example, describes this, drawing on Richard Wollheim, as *central* versus *acentral* imagining: in central imagining (empathy) I imagine the other's emotional state from his or her point of view, while in acentral or *peripheral* imagining, I imagine it from an 'observer' or third-person perspective (without having the emotion as such). In watching a mother struck by grief over the death of her son (Mrs O'Brien [Jessica Chastain] in Terrence Malick's *The Tree of Life* or Manuela [Cecilia Roth] in Almodóvar's *All About My Mother*) I can imaginatively participate in her emotional experience despite knowing she is fictional, and despite being neither a mother nor having experienced this kind of devastating loss. I am also moved, both emotionally and audio-visually, such that I adopt, depending on the mode of cinematic presentation, now a central, now a peripheral perspective on her experience of grief at learning of her son's death. Empathic and sympathetic responses are elicited here as part of an unfolding affective and emotional dynamic involving the interplay of point of view, expressive gesture, emotional contagion, and imaginative-cognitive evaluation of what we are seeing on screen. All of these processes come into play in the empathic and sympathetic emotional engagement with characters in a given fictional situation with its relevant paradigm scenarios (de Sousa, 1987).

Part of cinema's power, in short, is to elicit the kind of affective mimicry or emotional contagion responses that prime us for empathy and sympathy; but in order to experience these responses we need to be already engaged within a cinematic 'world': immersed in a meaningful context of action, with its own distinctive 'mood', qualities, and norms (see Plantinga 2012, Sinnerbrink 2012, Yacavone 2015). We also need to have encountered certain situations, formed certain views of the characters, evaluated their particular situation, imagined – or simulated – their subjective experience or emotional responses to what befalls them, moving effortlessly from first person to third person or from central to peripheral perspectives thanks to the aesthetic devices of cinematic composition (involving mood setting, emotional cueing, point of view, shot selection, audio effects and musical accompaniment, colour, lighting, *mise en scène*, performance and gesture, alterations in visual perspective, and so on). Orchestrating all of these elements is part of the art of cinematic direction: the orchestrated, dynamic elicitation of aesthetic responses using all the devices of cinematic composition, temporal dynamics, and dramatic presentation to create a plausible, convincing cinematic world capable of engaging us affectively, emotionally, and cognitively.

Within what Plantinga (1999, 239–255) calls 'scenes of empathy' – scenes usually focusing on the expressive features of the human face, and designed to elicit empathic responses – we typically find a number of features that correspond to the elements of emotional engagement. These include the use of close-ups and long takes focused on facial expressions and bodily gestures, magnifying the expression of affect and emotion but also ensuring sufficient duration for an emotional dynamic to be established. There is the selective use of visual and aural cues (lighting, shadow, colour, music, vocalization, sound effects) but also stasis and movement of the camera (stasis to allow duration and expression to be perceived, and movement to express kinetic resonance and generate affective excitation). As Murray Smith (1995, 1997), Carl Plantinga (1999), Julian Hanich (2010), Jane Stadler (2008), and others have noted, it is not simply point of view (POV) shots (showing the visual perspective of a character) that suggest empathic involvement. Rather, it is more often reaction shots (showing either the object of the character's attention or the character's own emotional responses) that generate the effective forms of empathy and sympathy.[5] Long takes on their own will not suffice; rather, they must be combined with alternating distinct points of view in order to create an intensive, dynamic, space within which emotional expression and the elicitation of empathy and sympathy become explicitly manifest and non-verbally communicated.

Instead of discrete forms of emotional engagement that remain independent of each other, cinema can render the dynamic movement between poles of empathy and sympathy in an experientially rich manner. It can encourage shifting between central and peripheral imagining, thus enabling spectators to both inhabit and observe, emotionally engage with and ethically evaluate, the fictional characters with whom we align ourselves within a cinematic world. This movement between poles of empathy and sympathy – or what Jane Stadler calls the 'compassionate gaze' (2014, 27 ff.) – reflects, I suggest, the phenomenological experience of emotional-cognitive engagement that other theorists have described using concepts of sympathy or compassion, *Einfühlung* or empathy. Both active and passive dimensions of affective involvement are at play here: in moving (and being moved) between perspectives with differing affective, emotional, psychological, and evaluative dynamics, we are placed as spectators so as to have a more complex experiential (both affective and reflective) engagement with, and ethically significant responsiveness to, the drama unfolding on screen and the cinematic world to which it belongs. We could therefore describe this dynamic movement between poles of empathy and sympathy as a *cinempathy*: a cinematic/kinetic expression of the synergy between affective attunement, emotional engagement, and moral evaluation that captures more fully the ethical potential of the cinematic experience. This temporally extended sense of empathic-sympathetic involvement, I suggest, offers a more dynamic, kinetic way of articulating cinematic empathy compared with the rather static, 'punctual' model of theorizing empathy and sympathy that often prevails in contemporary film theory.

Cinempathy in *A Separation*

To consider this dynamic movement between empathic and sympathetic perspectives, let us turn to Asghar Farhadi's Iranian familial drama *A Separation* [*Jodaieye Nader az Simin*] (2011), a remarkable case study in empathic cinematic ethics. To give some narrative background, the three protagonists, Nader [Peyman Moaadi], Simin [Leila Hatami], and their daughter Termeh [Sarina Farhadi] are shown at a crucial juncture in the ongoing domestic drama – a marital separation and custody dispute – that is tearing apart this ordinary Iranian family. The father, Nader, who is committed to staying in Iran to look after his ailing father, is fighting with the mother Simin, who wants to remove their daughter Termeh from being raised and educated in a country undergoing, the film suggests, a conservative-religious turn.

In the midst of their attempts to either reconcile or to separate, the parents have hired a domestic/carer, Razieh [Sareh Bayat], to look after Nader's dementia-afflicted father while Nader and Simin are at work (she is a teacher). Razieh has her own domestic dramas to contend with, including a frustrated, alienated husband, Hojjat [Shahab Hosseini], who cannot find work, and a pregnancy (concealed from her employers) that is giving her difficulties. Struggling to look after the confused and unpredictable old man, and to keep an unexpected, urgent doctor's appointment, Razieh chains the sleeping grandfather to his bed while she slips out of the house to keep her appointment. In the meantime, Nader returns home with Termeh to find his chained father collapsed on the floor, looking for all intents like he might have died. Upon Razieh's return, a major fight erupts, with Nader dismissing Razieh from her job and ordering her to leave the house immediately. The fight is further exacerbated by Nader's discovery that an amount of money is missing – the precise amount Razieh would have been owed for her final wages, which casts suspicion on her as having taken it without permission.[6] She returns, however, to protest her innocence and a more physical dispute begins, with Nader sharply pushing her out the door, causing her to fall down the stairs and injure herself (stairs that were mopped up earlier after Razieh's younger daughter dropped a rubbish bag on them). Upon receiving news of Razieh's fall, Nader and Simin head directly to the hospital, where they learn that she has been diagnosed with a miscarriage.

The subsequent dispute between Nader and the injured woman's husband threatens to get violent. Simin and Nader become increasingly estranged as the dispute with the injured couple spills over to their own marital dispute over whether to stay together so that Nader can care for his father or to separate so that Termeh can grow up elsewhere. Distressed by Termeh's increasing unhappiness, Simin attempts to broker a deal between the two families; she sympathizes with the injured woman caught in the middle but also desperately wants to resolve the escalating dispute. As we shall see, the central dispute between the couple concerns Simin's pragmatic attempts to resolve the situation, and Nader's principled refusal to pay any compensation (or 'blood money') because it would mean assuming guilt for what has happened (while carrying the risk that he may go to prison, thus leaving Termeh and Nader's father worse off than before).

In the scene that I wish to discuss, Simin has returned from negotiating with Razieh and her husband Hojjat, managing to secure their tentative agreement to accept a reduced amount of 'blood money' (Hojjat initially refuses but is persuaded by his family since they desperately need the money). She now has to persuade Nader to agree to this compromise deal, principally for the sake of his daughter's well-being, but also to save what is left of their disintegrating marriage. The sequence begins with an important mood-setting image – a domestic 'still life' shot from the apartment balcony of laundry on a drying rack swaying lightly in the breeze – which cuts to a long shot of Simin seated on the bed, looking pensive and concerned. As the sound of the door is heard off-screen, we see Simin seated on the bed, framed by the doorway, anxiously preparing herself to reveal to Nader that she has negotiated a financial settlement. The long-take shot frames the pensive Simin waiting as Termeh arrives home from school, enters the bedroom where her mother is seated, quickly intuiting her mother's distress. They embrace in silence, the camera holding on their embrace, their faces concealed from us in a poignant moment of empathic intimacy. Again, the shot holds on the backs of the two embracing figures, witnessing their emotional embrace in a long-take, waiting patiently, with a discreet, unobtrusive intimacy, for what they do next. Termeh wants her mother to stay, but Simin knows she has to deal with Nader first.

Simin enters the kitchen where Nader is packing away the shopping. The camera remains close, but not intrusively so, a slight wobble adding to the sense of intimate realism and durational dynamics. As is evident through his refusal to meet her gaze, Nader is unwilling to hear of her negotiated deal with the injured couple. She asks him to sit down at the table, the camera alternating between shots of Nader, viewed in profile, refusing to meet her gaze, and Simin, viewed almost front-on, her face open and pleading, light illuminating her face. Simin addresses Nader directly, whereas Nader is obliquely positioned, his face more dimly lit, clearly resisting her offer, visually and emotionally, of a way to resolve the dispute. As she explains to him what she has brokered, the camera alternates between their contrasting perspectives, the shots of Simin focusing on her direct, open face, whereas the shots of Nader show his more guarded profile and resistant gestures. He then fixes her with his gaze, pointing his finger at her, saying sharply that she had no right (as a wife and as a woman) to 'go behind his back' and negotiate directly with the injured couple, adding firmly that he will not agree to a financial settlement that would imply his guilt or responsibility for what has happened.

Simin is concerned for his safety, but also tries to persuade him by appealing to his sympathy for the adolescent Termeh, who is deeply distressed by the familial dispute (and will soon be shown sitting in the room adjacent to the kitchen, having heard their argument unfold). Nader claims that Termeh must be handling things since she has agreed, thus far, to stay with him; Simin, choking up, asks why does he think Termeh has stayed, and 'chosen' him, answering that it is clearly in order to prevent their separation: she knows that Simin will not leave (either her family or the country) without her daughter. During this sequence, the shot rhythm slowly accelerates, accentuating the sense of escalating tension and rising conflict as the exchange grows more heated. Another shot of Nader in profile, again turning away, suggests that he has not grasped this about his daughter, nor about his wife, or considered the gravity of the situation much beyond his staunch refusal to admit liability – a moment of insight that only seems to steel his resolve to refuse Simin's offer of a resolution to the conflict engulfing the family. He gets up and moves to the sink, once again turning his back to her, as the argument continues to unfold, now shifting ground, as we are about to be shown through a different camera placement.

The camera perspectives are now altered, with Simin shown in profile, and Nader's face shown more directly as he attempts to give his reasons for refusing Simin's offer of help. Simin remains seated at the table and begins to cry, accusing her husband of putting the money and his own pride ahead of his daughter's safety and well-being. Nader responds by saying it is nothing to do with money but about acknowledging guilt, which he refuses to do. The shots alternate, gathering momentum and building a rhythm that evokes the escalating tension and antagonism between them. Once again Nader asserts his authority, wagging his finger, claiming defensively that she 'has no right to do anything', turning his back to her again and walking away. If I didn't interfere, Simin responds, you would still be in jail, a retort that stops him dead; he turns around slowly to tell her that she should revoke the bail money because he does not want to be free on her account. Here there is a pause in the intensity of the camerawork, the more static shots framing both characters tightly within the confines of the domestic space – the walls, the table, the doorway – visually accentuating the escalating tension and oppressive sense of there being no way open for resolving the dispute.

As the argument escalates, the characters are reframed in a different part of the house, the camera revealing their agitated movement across various internal spatial thresholds. Nader leaves the kitchen and crosses to the lounge room, where Termeh is seated, clearly upset, having heard her parents arguing about her next door. A shot through an open doorway reveals Nader tending to his ailing father, as Simin strides past in a blur. Here as throughout the film, the camera creates a densely textured, emotionally charged sense of domestic space, characters framed by doorways, moving through hallways, past windows and glass panes reflecting their faces and gestures. These heavily 'framed' shots mark the many domestic obstacles to communication and conflicting lines of 'separation' expressing the escalating tension of this domestic drama. This is no more evident than in the crucial boundary space surrounding the front door, the decisive threshold between domestic and social worlds marked by the door frame, landing, and stairs.

The concluding part of this sequence is marked by the conflicting movement of the characters towards other parts of the house and towards the outside, and the interrupted, obscured visual presentation of the characters both separated and struggling with each other. As Nader tends to his father, Simin crosses the doorway in front of the old man's room, heading towards Termeh, who is now shown seated, from above and behind, obscured behind a wooden internal glass door and window frame. An important dramatic caesura now occurs: Simin decides to abandon her attempt to persuade Nader (and return to the family home), instructing Termeh to leave the house with her. Termeh pleads with her mother to stay and an argument ensues, which is only partially

Figure 4.1 Still from *A Separation*, Dir. Asghar Farhadi (2011)

shown but mostly heard offscreen: Simin screams at Termeh that they must leave, making sure that Nader, who is shown seated and listening with his father in an adjacent room, hears her accusation that he values the blood-money (15 million) more than his daughter's life. As the fight escalates, Simin's screaming and Termeh's crying can be heard offscreen as the camera holds on Nader and his father, and then cuts away to Simin and Termeh now locked in a very different embrace than the one at the beginning of this sequence – a tearful grappling between mother and daughter expressing their conflict and distress rather than their sympathy and understanding. Simin abandons her task of reconciling with Nader and storms out of the house, telling Termeh to meet her at the car, with Termeh, in tears, begging her to stay. The shot rhythm has now slowed again, allowing us to take stock of the intense emotional dynamic of the conflict and the aftermath of the familial fight.

As her mother leaves the house, a devastated Termeh returns to her room to collect her bag and belongings, turning to her father, pleading with him to accept her mother's offer of the money and a resolution to the crisis. The rhythm of shots has died down, the camera holding steadily on the exhausted Termeh, allowing the audience to reflect upon the conflict and how it might conclude. Nader refuses, again, stating that it is not about the money or reconciling with her mother but about the principle at stake. Termeh reminds him, pleadingly, that he had said that the dispute wasn't really serious: 'It got serious,' replies her father, as we see Termeh, standing in mid-shot, suddenly break down, burying her face in her hands and collapsing on the couch. This physical gesture or expression of emotional overload acts as an affective release for the sequence, providing a visual, corporeal expression of the pent-up, inchoate mixture of emotions that have marked this tense, seemingly irresolvable, three-way conflict. Nader tries to comfort her, advising her to join her mother until her exams are over. Termeh then turns to him, faces him, revealing that her mother had planned to move back home today and even had packed her belongings in the car in preparation. In response, he again turns to one side, cannot meet her gaze, and turns to walk away, the camera lingering on his back.

As a dejected Termeh prepares to leave the house, she passes the kitchen where Nader is standing still, looking lost in thought. He calls her back to the kitchen before she leaves and poses an 'impossible' question: if you think I am guilty, go and get your mother, and we will go and pay them the money. Caught between the desire to prevent her parents' separation, and a decision that would implicate her father in the death of the unborn child, Termeh picks up her belongings, clearly exhausted, despondent, and leaves the house. We have reached a point where actions and gestures, rather than words, communicate the truth of their situation. Nader moves to the window and watches her cross the road, the camera revealing what he sees: Simin waiting in the car, packed with luggage, joined by Termeh as the car drives away. He watches, ruminating, as the camera lingers, in a long take, on his blank expression, resolving the mood following the argument in a melancholy key, as we are invited to reflect upon the complex emotional, psychological, and moral conflict we have just witnessed.

This powerful sequence is noteworthy for its skilful evocation of a variety of sympathetic and empathic responses. It is also striking for the manner in which it 'defocalizes' the narrative away from privileging one particular protagonist and repeatedly shifts the viewer's attention – including his or her emotional engagement and moral allegiance – between Simin and Nader, offering equal weighting to their particular perspectives, thus situating their actions within an evolving, shifting emotional dynamic that reveals the complexities of their social situation. Although the argument that unfolds between them is sharply focused, intense, and realistic, the film avoids privileging one character's position over any other. Rather, the camera alternates between shots and reverse shots focusing on both characters, establishing affective alignment and emotional allegiance, but alternating these so as to capture and convey the conflicted quality of their increasingly heated exchange. The camera initially presents Simin from a frontal perspective and Nader in profile, turning away, but then changes perspective to show Nader more frontally and Simin now in profile or turning away. Simin and Termeh are initially shown embracing, their faces concealed from our view, then later as struggling and fighting, their faces again removed from sight as we hear their conflict unfold aurally off-screen. The movements of the characters alternate from seated (and heated) conversations at the kitchen table, faces open, revealed or turning away, then standing up, moving away, turning around, leaving the kitchen, crossing doorways, struggling across spatial thresholds, communicating across windows and other barriers. The camera then takes up a new perspective for the fight between Simin and Termeh by the doorway, and another perspective again on Termeh and her father, whose final ultimatum to her leaves her at a loss, concluding with lingering shot of Nader's pensive face, their future as unresolved as ever.

Throughout this sequence, long-take close-ups of facial expressions, typical of what Carl Plantinga calls 'scenes of empathy' (1999), alternate with passages of rapidly edited shots; these establish a kinetic rhythm that effectively conveys the increasingly antagonistic nature of their argument. The effect is to 'move' the viewer – visually and affectively – between these conflicting perspectives without, however, privileging one over the other, or offering one protagonist as the focalizing character from whose perspective the fight might ordinarily have been shown (for example, following and foregrounding Simin's perspective as she tries to persuade the intractably stubborn Nader to relent and agree to the compensation). Instead, the perspective shifts from Simin, to Nader, and then to Termeh and Simin, then Termeh and Nader, before concluding with Nader watching Termeh and Simin driving away. The concluding long shot of Nader also invites us to ponder what will become of the conflicted family and how their 'separation' – at multiple levels – might be overcome.

One could imagine the film, even if only temporarily, adopting Simin's perspective as she attempts to reason with Nader and make him agree to her request to resolve the situation. And to be sure, the sequence begins in this fashion (focusing on her mental and emotional preparation); but it then begins to alternate perspective-taking in a manner that 'shares' or distributes sympathetic and empathetic responses across all characters in the family, including Termeh in her conflicted relations with both her mother and her father. This practice of combining affective-empathic shots foregrounding the emotional perspective of one character with passages of dynamic, rapid-cut shots of both characters in conflict moves the viewer between both character perspectives, thus enabling a complex engagement with their conflicting points of view without privileging one or the other as the primary focus of emotional engagement or moral allegiance. The effect of this is to stymie the affective tendency to immediately 'take sides' in the dispute and rush to an emotionally-driven rapid evaluation of the situation; the aim, rather, is to encourage a sustained, emotionally dynamic, engagement with the different character perspectives involved in the conflict, and thus to invite the viewer to experience the subtle, ambiguous, and volatile mixture of emotions and attitudes informing and sustaining this familial conflict as it unfolds over time – a process that at the same time reveals important background aspects of the social, economic, and political conditions of the characters' lifeworld.

This dynamic movement across different perspectives, alternating perspective-taking in a manner that gives equal weighting to both characters, preventing hasty moralizing judgment while inviting a deeper ethical responsiveness towards the context and dynamics of conflict, is a fine example of what I am calling cinempathy: the kinetic-cinematic practice of alternating perspective-taking in a manner both sympathetic and empathic, an alternating of perspectives that opens up a deeper *intersubjective* understanding of the characters' situations from conflicting, yet intimately related, points of view. It puts the spectator simultaneously in the position of sympathetic witness and empathic protagonist, shifting between these perspectives in relation to individual characters, different character perspectives, and across their particular relationships as these unfold and ramify during the course of the conflict. It is not so much a 'merging' of self and other than a practice of imaginative perspective-taking that distributes the affective dynamic across different characters, and thereby invites subtle forms of intersubjective recognition and deeper ethical understanding in response to the dynamic complexities of social interactions. Such a cinematic-empathic approach thus provides an experientially 'thick' phenomenological description revealing the complexities of emotional responsiveness, the opaque or confused 'reasons' for acting, and the decisive significance of background and context in explaining why individuals do what they do in a given conflict. It thus provides a corrective to the otherwise 'easy' option of encouraging and facilitating hasty moral – or indeed 'moralizing' – judgments that remains abstracted from the ethical (and political) complexities of the characters' shared social situation.

This is a fine example of a cinematic ethics that shows how emotional engagement, social conflict, moral argument, and cultural-political background all contribute to understanding the reasons for an individual's behaviour. It reveals the complexity of the social situation or world in which the characters find themselves and begins to disclose some of the otherwise opaque motivations and meanings behind their actions. These actions are presented, moreover, in a manner that elicits both empathy and sympathy, from alternating perspectives, without privileging one character's perspective over another, prompting the viewer towards further critical reflection and deeper ethical understanding. This scene, and indeed the film as a whole, offers a powerful demonstration of how cinema can be used to cultivate moral perception and exercise our ethical imaginations, inviting viewers to consider all the relevant perspectives and complexities informing a particular ethical situation, the temporal and emotional dynamics that subtend social relationships, as well as the all-important role of the normative context or broader social-cultural world in which the characters are embedded.

***

In the powerful concluding scene of *A Separation*, as in the beginning, we are left, once again, in the difficult position of having to 'judge', or more precisely, of having to *respond*; but we are now invited to do so having undergone the full experience of moral uncertainty, psychological ambiguity, and social complexity that the film both evokes and explores. This cinematic experience, at once ethical and aesthetic, reveals the difficult ethical conflicts – and ambivalent moral sympathies and antipathies – underlying this singular, yet ordinary, domestic drama. The 'suspended', open ending of the film – which concludes with a long take of Nader and Simin, seated apart from each other, staring ahead and away from each other, framed by a doorway and glass panes – is itself a figure of moral *epoché*: a suspension of judgment, yet one that remains beholden to the other, expectant and attentive but at the same time precluded from hearing Termeh's fateful decision (whether she will stay with her mother or with her father). As viewers who have experienced, empathically and sympathetically, the complexities of their separation, we are thus invited to reflect, emotionally and intellectually, on what doing justice to all family members in this remarkable domestic drama would mean – an ambiguous experience of cinematic ethics in the flesh.

Notes

1   I return to this debate in my discussion of Almodóvar's *Talk to Her* in Chapter 6.

2   I shall return to this topic in my discussion of Almodóvar's *Talk to Her* in Chapter 6 and Oppenheimer's *The Act of Killing* in Chapter 7.

3   For an example of this kind of difficulty see Grodal (2009, 56–78) on the evolutionary-biological reasons why men allegedly enjoy pornography and action movies while women are supposed to prefer romances and melodramas.

4 Think of the German term *Schadenfreude* (malicious pleasure in the misfortune of another), or the Japanese *arigata meiwaku* (when one is the recipient of an unwanted favour or kindness, which makes one feel both obliged to, as well as secretly resentful of, the giver).

5 Consider recent popular cinematic examples such as Clarice Starling in *Silence of the Lambs* (1991), *The Blair Witch Project* (1999), *Dawn of the Planet of the Apes* (2014) but also the expressive characters in animated films like 'Sulley' in *Monsters, Inc.* (2001) or Gollum in *The Lord of The Rings* series.

6 The money was actually taken by Simin in order to pay for the removers shown shifting a piano out of the apartment earlier in the film.

Bibliography

Allen, Richard and Smith, Murray (eds). *Film Theory and Philosophy*. Oxford: Oxford University Press, 1997.

Anderson, Joseph D. *The Reality of Illusion: An Ecological Approach to Cognitive Film Theory*. Carbondale, IL: Southern Illinois University Press, 1996.

Barker, Jennifer M. *The Tactile Eye: Touch and the Cinematic Experience*. Berkeley: University of California Press, 2009.

Bordwell, David. *Narration in the Fiction Film*. Madison, WI: University of Wisconsin Press, 1985.

Bordwell, David. 'A Case for Cognitivism', *Iris*, 9 (Spring 1989): 11–40. Available online at: www.davidbordwell.net/articles/Bordwell_Iris_no9_spring1989_11.pdf

Bordwell, David and Carroll, Noël (eds). *Post-Theory: Reconstructing Film Studies*. Madison, WI: University of Wisconsin Press, 1996.

Branigan, Edward. *Point of View in the Cinema: A Theory of Narration and Subjectivity in Classical Film*. Berlin and New York: Mouton, 1984.

Carroll, Noël. 'The Power of Movies', *Daedalus*, 114.4 (1985): 79–103.

Carroll, Noël. *Philosophical Problems of Classical Film Theory*. Princeton: Princeton University Press, 1988.

Carroll, Noël. *The Philosophy of Motion Pictures*. Malden, MA: Blackwell Publishing, 2008.

Casebier, Allan. *Film and Phenomenology: Towards a Realist Theory of Cinematic Representation*. Cambridge: Cambridge University Press, 1991.

Cavell, Stanley. *Pursuits of Happiness: The Hollywood Comedy of Remarriage*. Cambridge, MA and London: Harvard University Press, 1981.

Cavell, Stanley. *Contesting Tears: The Hollywood Melodrama of the Unknown Woman*. Chicago and London: University of Chicago Press, 1996.

Cavell, Stanley. *Cities of Words: Pedagogical Letters on a Register of Moral Life*. Cambridge, MA and London: Belknap Press of Harvard University Press, 2004.

Choi, Jinhee and Frey, Mattias. 'Introduction'. In Jinhee Choi and Mattias Frey (eds), *Cine-Ethics: Ethical Dimension of Film Theory, Practice, and Spectatorship*, 1–14. New York and London: Routledge, 2014.

Clark, Andy. *Supersizing the Mind: Embodiment, Action, and Cognitive Extension*. Oxford: Oxford University Press, 2008.

Coplan, Amy. 'Catching Characters' Emotions: Emotional Contagion Responses to Narrative Fiction Film'. *Film Studies: An International Review*, 8 (2006): 26–38.

Coplan, Amy. 'Understanding Empathy: Its Features and Effects'. In Amy Coplan and Peter Coplan (eds), *Empathy: Philosophical and Psychological Perspectives*, 3–18. Oxford: Oxford University Press, 2011.

Coplan, Amy and Goldie, Peter. 'Introduction'. In Amy Coplan and Peter Goldie (eds), *Empathy: Philosophical and Psychological Perspectives*, IX-XLVII. Oxford: Oxford University Press, 2011.

Currie, Gregory. *Image and Mind. Film, Philosophy, and Cognitive Science*. New York: Cambridge University Press, 1995.

Currie, Gregory. 'Empathy for Objects'. In Amy Coplan and Peter Goldie (eds), *Empathy: Philosophical and Psychological Perspectives*, 82–95. Oxford and New York: Oxford University Press, 2011.

Currie, Gregory and Ravenscroft, Ian. *Recreative Minds: Imagination in Philosophy and Psychology*. Oxford: Oxford University Press, 2002.

de Sousa, Ronald. *The Rationality of Emotion*. Cambridge, MA: The MIT Press, 1987.

Eisenstein, Sergei. *Selected Works. Volume II. Towards a Theory of Montage*. Michael Glenny and Richard Taylor (eds). Trans. Michael Glenny. London: BFI Books, 1991.

Feagin, Susan. *Reading with Feeling: The Aesthetics of Appreciation*. Ithaca, NY: Cornell University Press, 1996.

Frampton, Daniel. *Filmosophy*. London: Wallflower Press, 2006.

Gaut, Berys. *A Philosophy of Cinematic Art*. Cambridge: Cambridge University Press, 2010.

Goldie, Peter. *The Emotions: A Philosophical Investigation*. Oxford and New York: Oxford University Press, 2002.

Grodal, Torben. 'Frozen Flows in von Trier's Oeuvre'. In Torben K. Grodal, Bente Larsen, and Iben Thorving Laursen (eds), *Visual Authorship: Creativity and Intentionality in Media*, 129–168. Copenhagen: Museum Tusculanum Press, 2004.

Grodal, Torben. *Embodied Visions: Evolution, Emotion, Culture, and Film*. Oxford: Oxford University Press, 2009.

Hanich, Julian. *Cinematic Emotion in Horror Films and Thrillers: The Aesthetic Paradox of Pleasurable Fear*. New York: Routledge, 2010.

Heidegger, Martin. *Being and Time*. Trans. Joan Stambaugh. Albany: State University of New York Press, 2010 [1927].

Hume, David. *A Treatise of Human Nature*. L. A. Selby-Bigge (ed.). Oxford: Clarendon Press, 1896 [1739].

Hume, David. *The Theory of Moral Sentiments*. Knud Haakonssen (ed.). Cambridge: Cambridge University Press, 2002 [1759].

Knight, Deborah. 'In Fictional Shoes: Mental Simulation and Fiction'. In Noël Carroll and Jinhee Choi (eds), *Philosophy of Film and Motion Pictures: An Anthology*, 271–280. Malden, MA: Basil Blackwell, 2006.

Laine, Tarja. *Feeling Cinema: Emotional Dynamics in Film Studies*. New York and London: Continuum, 2011.

Marks, Laura U. *The Skin of the Film: Intercultural Cinema, Embodiment, and the Senses*. Durham: Duke University Press, 2000.

Marks, Laura U. *Touch: Sensuous Theory and Multisensory Media*. Minneapolis: University of Minnesota Press, 2002.

Menary, Richard. *Cognitive Integration: Mind and Cognition Unbounded*, Basingstoke: Palgrave Macmillan, 2007.

Menary, Richard (ed.). *The Extended Mind*. Cambridge, MA: The MIT Press, 2010.

Nannicelli, Ted and Taberham, Paul (eds). *Cognitive Media Theory*. Abingdon and New York: Routledge, 2014.

Neill, Alex. 'Empathy and (Film) Fiction'. In Noël Carroll and Jinhee Choi (eds), *Philosophy of Film and Motion Pictures: An Anthology*, 247–259. Malden, MA: Basil Blackwell, 2006.

Nowak, Magdalena. 'The Complicated History of Empathy', *Argument*, 1.2 (2011): 301–326.

Nussbaum, Martha. C. *Love's Knowledge: Essays on Philosophy and Literature*. Oxford: Oxford University Press, 1992.

Pisters, Patricia. *The Neuro-Image: A Deleuzian Film-Philosophy of Digital Screen Culture.* Stanford: Stanford University Press, 2012.

Plantinga, Carl. 'The Scene of Empathy and the Human Face on Film'. In Carl Plantinga and Greg M. Smith (eds), *Passionate Views: Film, Cognition, and Emotion*, 239–255. Baltimore and London: The Johns Hopkins University Press, 1999.

Plantinga, Carl. *Moving Viewers: American Film and the Spectator's Experience.* Berkeley, CA: University of California Press, 2009.

Plantinga, Carl. 'Art Moods and Human Moods in Narrative Cinema', *New Literary History*, 43.3 (Summer 2012): 455–475.

Plantinga, Carl and Smith, Greg M. *Passionate Views: Film, Cognition, and Emotion.* Baltimore and London: The Johns Hopkins University Press, 1999.

Prinz, Jesse. 'Is Empathy Necessary for Morality?' In Amy Coplan and Peter Goldie (eds), *Empathy: Philosophical and Psychological Perspectives*, 211–229. Oxford: Oxford University Press, 2011.

Rodowick, D. N. 'An Elegy for Theory', *MIT Press Journals*, 122 (October 2007): 91–109.

Rousseau, Jean-Jacques. *Discourse on the Origin of Inequality.* Trans. Donald A. Cress. Indianapolis: Hackett Publishing, 1992 [1755].

Sinnerbrink, Robert. *New Philosophies of Film: Thinking Images.* London and New York: Continuum, 2011.

Sinnerbrink, Robert. '*Stimmung*: Exploring the Aesthetics of Mood', *Screen*, 53.2 (Summer 2012): 148–163.

Smith, Greg M. *Film Structure and the Emotion System.* Cambridge: Cambridge University Press, 2003.

Smith, Murray. *Engaging Characters: Fiction, Emotion, and the Cinema.* Oxford: Oxford University Press, 1995.

Smith, Murray. 'Imagining from the Inside'. In Richard Allen and Murray Smith (eds), *Film Theory and Philosophy*, 412–430. Oxford: Oxford University Press, 1997.

Smith, Murray. 'Empathy, Expansionism, and the Extended Mind'. In Amy Coplan and Peter Goldie (eds), *Empathy: Philosophical and Psychological Perspectives*, 99–117. Oxford: Oxford University Press, 2011.

Sobchack, Vivian. *The Address of the Eye: A Phenomenology of Film Experience.* Princeton: Princeton University Press, 1992.

Sobchack, Vivian. *Carnal Thoughts: Embodiment and Moving Image Culture.* Berkeley: University of California Press, 2004.

Solomon, Robert. C. 'I. Emotions, Thoughts and Feelings: What is a "Cognitive Theory" of the Emotions and Does it Neglect Affectivity?' *Royal Institute of Philosophy Supplement*, 52 (2003): 1–18.

Stadler, Jane. *Pulling Focus: Intersubjective Experience, Narrative Film, and Ethics.* New York and London: Continuum, 2008.

Stadler, Jane. 'Affectless Empathy, Embodied Imagination and *The Killer Inside Me*', *Screening the Past*, 37 (2013). Available online at: www.screeningthepast.com/2013/10/affectless-empathy-embodied-imagination-and-the-killer-inside-me/#_edn3

Stadler, Jane. 'Cinema's Compassionate Gaze: Empathy, Affect, and Aesthetics in *The Diving Bell and the Butterfly*'. In Choi and Frey (eds), *Cine-Ethics: Ethical Dimension of Film Theory, Practice, and Spectatorship*, 27–42. New York and London: Routledge, 2014.

Tan, Ed S. *Emotion and the Structure of Narrative Film: Cinema as an Emotion Machine.* Marwah, NJ: Lawrence Erlbaum Associates, Inc., 1995.

Walton, Peter. *Mimesis as Make-Believe: On the Foundations of the Representationalist Arts*. Cambridge MA.: Harvard University Press, 1990.
Yacavone, Daniel. *Film Worlds: A Philosophical Aesthetics of Cinema*. New York: Columbia University Press, 2015.

Filmography

A Separation [*Jodaeiye Nader az Simin*]. Dir. Asghar Farhadi (Iran, 2011)
All About My Mother [*Todo sobre mi madre*]. Dir. Pedro Almodóvar (Spain/France, 1999)
The Blair Witch Project. Dir. Daniel Myrick, Eduardo Sánchez (USA, 1999)
Dawn of the Planet of the Apes. Dir. Matt Reeves (USA, 2014)
Monsters, Inc. Dir. Peter Docter, David Silverman, Lee Unkrich (USA, 2001)
The Silence of the Lambs. Dir. Jonathan Demme (USA, 1991)
The Tree of Life. Dir. Terrence Malick (USA, 2011)
Triumph of the Will [*Triumph des Willens*]. Dir. Leni Riefenstahl (Germany, 1935)
2001: A Space Odyssey. Dir. Stanley Kubrick (USA/UK, 1968)

Part III

PERFORMING CINEMATIC ETHICS

5 The moral melodrama (*Stella Dallas,* *Talk to Her*)

Music, moods, worlds, abandonment, subjection, dispossession – of course; we are speaking of melodrama.

Stanley Cavell (1996, 222)

[Melodrama] refers not only to a type of aesthetic practice but also to a way of viewing the world.

Christine Gledhill (1987, 1)

Film theorists have long linked genres with emotional responsiveness, investigating how genres can modulate or manipulate our emotional engagement with film. Less attention, however, has been given to the question of how genre, emotional response, moral perception, and ethical experience are related. One genre (if it is indeed a genre) that brings together these aspects in dramatic fashion is the melodrama, which, as Laura Mulvey once quipped, remains 'a magnificent obsession' for film theory (1996, 19). Mulvey's observation has proved prescient. Following Thomas Elsaesser's groundbreaking work (1972 [1987]), and Peter Brooks' seminal study (1976), studies of melodrama have flourished over recent decades. Initially taken up in the context of literary-historical studies of cinema, scholars in the 1980s turned to feminist and psychoanalytic film theory, as well as Althusserian-Marxist analyses of ideology in Hollywood cinema, to which we can now add, among other approaches, phenomenological, cognitivist, queer, and Deleuzian perspectives on melodrama (see Mercer and Shingler 2004, del Rio 2008, and Zarzosa 2013). Linda Williams (1998, 42) has even claimed that the melodramatic mode is definitive of Hollywood narrative cinema, a claim that has profound implications for how we understand the history, aesthetics, and prospects of narrative film. So what is melodrama, or, more broadly, the melodramatic imagination? How does this relate to cinema, and, in particular, the idea of cinematic ethics?

Cinema, from its silent beginnings, has maintained a close relationship with literary and dramatic forms of melodrama, which in its dictionary sense refers to 'a dramatic narrative in which musical accompaniment marks the emotional effects' (Elsaesser 1987, 50). As remarked, film theory also embraced the idea of melodrama, not only as an aesthetic style and cinematic genre but as an expressive mode found in literature, drama, and cinema (Elsaesser 1987, Gledhill 1987, Williams 1998). Debate still continues, however, over whether it is best understood as a genre, a style, a mode, an aesthetic sensibility, or a 'world-view' that has moral-ethical, even political significance (see Mercer and Shingler 2004). Linda Williams has made the provocative claim that melodrama should no longer be regarded as a 'mode of excess' (to use Peter Brooks' phase), to be contrasted with the 'realism' of classical Hollywood, but rather as 'the fundamental mode of popular American moving pictures' (1998, 42). For Williams, melodrama is not a specific genre (like the Western or musical), nor a 'deviation' from classical realist narrative, typically found in the traditions of 'women's films', 'weepies' or the family melodrama. Rather, melodrama should be understood as the 'foundation' of the classical Hollywood movie, a 'peculiarly democratic and American form that seeks dramatic revelation of moral and emotional truths through a dialectic of pathos and action' (Williams 1998, 42). Such a conception of melodrama allows us to understand the pervasive nature of the 'melodramatic imagination' within popular American (Hollywood) cinema, and its capacity to organize, shape, and influence a variety of genres (leading to variations such as the male melodrama, war-melodrama, crime melodrama, and so on). Although controversial, Williams' expansion of the concept of melodrama to a shared 'mode' encompassing a variety of cinematic genres, aesthetic forms and moral themes opens up the field of inquiry in new and exciting ways.

To this expanded field, we can add the philosophical, especially the moral-ethical, dimensions of melodrama. Cavell (1996), as we have seen, has claimed melodrama as a *philosophical* genre, indeed a case of 'film as philosophy'. As noted in Chapter 2, what Cavell calls the 'melodrama of the unknown woman' defines a genre of film or series of narratives, interacting versions of a story or myth, 'that seems to present itself as a woman's search for a story, or of the right to tell her story' (Cavell 1996, 3). Thanks to their dramatization of the relationship between knowledge and scepticism, moral transgression and moral perfectionism, melodramas of the unknown woman, along with remarriage comedies, can stake a claim to philosophical significance. Indeed, they are Hollywood films, Cavell claims, noted for their 'working out of the problematic of self-reliance and conformity, or of hope and despair, as established in the founding American thinking of Emerson and Thoreau' (1996, 9). Cavell's emphasis on the philosophical significance of melodrama is laudable, though I shall question whether Emersonian perfectionism is the best way to understand the ethical dimensions of melodrama, using Cavell's reading of *Stella Dallas* as my case study.

In this chapter, I explore the idea of the 'moral melodrama': films that use melodrama, understood as expressive mode, style, or genre, to elicit forms of affective responsiveness and emotional engagement that open up a space for sympathetic ethical understanding achieved through aesthetic means. Moral melodrama elicits emotional engagement with a view to exercising our moral perception and thus deepening our ethical understanding; it invites forms of moral reflection that confirm cinema's potential as a medium of ethical experience. To elaborate this idea, I explore the idea of melodrama as an expressive mode, and offer a critical discussion of Cavell's approach to melodrama ('melodramas of the unknown woman') as a form of moral perfectionism, arguing that such an approach, while sensitive to the ethical possibilities of individualist self-transformation with a democratic community, struggles to deal with the 'excessive' dimensions of melodrama that reveal or express the tensions, limits, or contradictions of the world within which the characters are embedded. The affective intensity, emotional pathos and hyperbolic aesthetics of melodrama point, rather, to the otherwise inarticulable clash between individual desires or social aspirations and the possibility (or impossibility) of their practical fulfilment within the normative context of a given social-cultural world. My case studies here will be two films, a classic maternal melodrama, King Vidor's *Stella Dallas* (1937), and Almodóvar's contemporary 'male melodrama', *Talk to Her* (2002). Both films offer striking cases of moral melodrama showing how emotional engagement, aesthetic excess, and the experience of normative ambivalence can be understood as experiential ways of exploring and engaging in cinematic ethics.

The melodramatic imagination

Film genres have long been associated with the expression and generation of emotion. We talk of thrillers, suspense movies, horror films, screwball comedies, and the melodrama (from the Greek *melos* and French *drame*, the musical drama coined by Rousseau and first theorized by Diderot). Deriving from post-revolutionary French musical drama, and nineteenth century Victorian 'Gaslight' musical drama (with its stock characters, moral Manicheanism, and exaggerated plots featuring women in peril), melodrama developed early in the history of narrative cinema and seemed particularly suited to silent film (the 'Victorian' melodramas of the early teens, for example, or the 'Fallen Woman' melodramas of the 1920s). It became transformed – thanks in part to the imposition of production codes in the 1930s banning explicit sexual displays and depictions of adultery – into a sophisticated, popular, 'feminine' Hollywood genre in the 1940s and 50s (the heyday of romantic, domestic, and family melodramas), including some fascinating generic hybrids (Nicholas Ray's *Johnny Guitar* and Robert Aldrich's *Kiss Me Deadly*, for example) before disappearing during the 60s and 1970s (with the exception of Fassbinder's Sirkian-Brechtian reworking of the genre in films such as *The Bitter Tears of Petra von Kant* (1972) and *Ali: Fear Eats the Soul* (1974), the latter inspired by Sirk's *All That Heaven Allows* (1955)). Pedro Almodóvar is perhaps the most celebrated of contemporary filmmakers working with melodrama, while elements of melodrama can be found in many generically hybrid, contemporary films (von Trier's *Breaking the Waves* (1996), Aronofsky's *Black*

Swan (2010), Fincher's *Fight Club* (1999), Gondry's *Eternal Sunshine of the Spotless Mind* (2004), and Malick's *The Tree of Life* (2011), to name a few). Despite its waxing and waning fortunes in the Anglophone world, it has remained a consistently popular genre in various 'World' cinemas (in Latin America (*telenovelas*) and South East Asia cinema, for example), and has found a new lease of life in extended television serial dramas (such as *Mad Men* (2007–2015) and *The Sopranos* (1999–2007), as well as pioneering 'cinematic' television series such as Lynch's *Twin Peaks* (1990–1991) and von Trier's *The Kingdom* (1994)).[1]

The use of music in melodramatic narrative is well-known and contributes an essential element to its organisation. As Elsaesser remarks, the elements of melodrama can be seen and heard as comprising a 'system of punctuation, giving expressive colour and chromatic contrast to the storyline, by orchestrating the ups and downs of the intrigue' (1987, 50). He defines it as a specific body of work (exemplified by Hollywood family narratives of the 1940s and 50s), deriving from a long history of theatrical and literary antecedents, and expressing, in cinematic form, 'a particular, historically and socially conditioned *mode of experience*' (1987, 43). Gledhill too emphasizes its breadth as a mode of cultural-historical experience expressed in a variety of intellectual and artistic forms, identifying it as 'an epistemological and imaginative paradigm across nineteenth-century culture and thought,' which goes beyond literature and drama to include the works of Darwin, Marx, and Freud (1987, 20). Classical melodrama emphasized emotion, musical punctuation, romantic longing, psychosexual intrigue, moral and social transgression, improbable events, chance and coincidence, a Manichean dualism between virtuous heroes or heroines (innocent or misunderstood) and evil villains (often charming or seductive). This emphasis on innocence persecuted and emotional involvement within a morally ambiguous situation remains a mainstay of melodrama, whether it uses conventional melodramatic elements or recasts the melodramatic content using 'realist' effects or style (as in von Trier's *Breaking the Waves*, for example). As Linda Williams remarks:

> If emotional and moral registers are sounded, if a work invites us to feel sympathy for the virtues of beset victims, if the narrative trajectory is ultimately more concerned with a retrieval and staging of innocence than with the psychological causes of motives and actions, then the operative mode is melodrama.
>
> (1998, 42)

To emotional and moral registers, we can add particular varieties of aesthetic expression. Brooks (1976) famously described melodrama as the 'mode of excess', one in which the intense desires, hyperbolic emotions, or Manichean struggles of characters exceed the conventional frameworks of moral norms or social expectations, and hence cannot find explicit articulation within narrated speech or via dramatic resolution. These find indirect expression, rather, through aesthetic means: in the case of cinema, through music, colour, movement, gesture, *mise en scène*, or performance. It is thus a genre both celebrated and denigrated for its disruptive, discontinuous emotional dynamics (what Elsaesser called melodrama's characteristic 'letting-the-emotions-rise and then bringing them suddenly down with a thump' (1987, 60)); its sometimes 'excessive' aesthetic stylization and overt symbolization (using colour, *mise en scène*, performance, and musical punctuation to generate emotion and modulate mood); and its ambivalent sense of tragedy, without cathartic resolution (melodrama as 'tragedy that doesn't quite come off'), within a constricted or contradictory moral-social order that is revealed as limited or flawed. Lending itself to psychoanalytic and ideological readings, melodrama is often associated with the Freudian idea of a 'return of the repressed', according to which whatever remains unacceptable in the psychological or social life of characters – or impermissible within the ideological framework of the narrative – 'returns' in the form of aesthetic or dramatic excess. Echoing literary romanticism, the encounter with madness, illness, sexual transgression, death and sacrifice remain staples of melodrama, as is the conviction that emotional response, however discontinuous, reveals a deeper social and psychological truth than reasoned action or adherence to social convention.

How could such a genre be apt for the communication of philosophical insights? What grounds the claim that melodrama can be an ethically significant genre? Many critics have noted the link between melodrama and morality, most famously in Peter Brooks' discussion of the melodramatic imagination as an aesthetic approach to the post-secular world that attempts to articulate its implicit or hidden moral significance in the absence of divine or religious sources of moral authority. For Brooks, melodrama arises in response to the loss of overarching religious or spiritual grounding of morality, and attempts to find, in the dramas and conflicts of everyday life, elements of a hidden moral meaning or order that he called the 'moral occult': 'the domain of operative spiritual values which is both indicated within and masked by the surface of reality' (Brooks 1976, 5). Echoing Nietzsche's diagnosis of the modern condition of nihilism – the displaced quest for alternative sources of transcendent moral meaning after the cultural-historical event of the 'death of God' – Brooks describes the 'moral occult' as no longer functioning within a metaphysical system but as 'the repository of the fragmentary and desacralized remnants of sacred myth' (1976, 5). It recalls a kind of 'cultural unconscious' or quasi-mythic realm of cryptic moral meaning that remains suppressed or obscured within post-Enlightenment rationalist culture, but which finds continued expression in (romantic) art and literature, including, more recently, varieties of cinema and cinematic genres. From this point of view, the melodramatic imagination represents a cultural paradigm of moral meaning, a cultural-historical mode of experience that 'in large measure exists to locate and articulate the moral occult' (Brooks 1976, 5).

The melodramatic mode, from this perspective, is an aesthetic attempt to reveal the 'moral legibility' of a secular social order that is both riven by social contradictions and no longer unified by shared (religious or theological) moral foundations. It can thus be understood as the inheritor of tragedy within the post-heroic or prosaic age of modernity, taking up the cultural-moral role of aesthetic justification of existence that Nietzsche (1967 [1872]) had earlier envisaged as the task of a re-born tragic art in modernity. The idea that melodrama can reveal an obscured moral legibility in the modern world, making manifest tensions afflicting the sphere of the family, social expectations concerning gender, and disavowed hierarchies of social privilege, continues to make it a focus of intensive theoretical reflection and historical-cultural inquiry.

Cavell's moral perfectionist reading of *Stella Dallas*

All of these possibilities are evident in King Vidor's *Stella Dallas* (1937), the subject of one of Cavell's defining presentations of a moral perfectionist approach to the melodrama of the unknown woman. His chapter in *Contesting Tears* ('Stella's Taste: Reading *Stella Dallas*') is largely reproduced in his later book, *Cities of Words* (2004), accompanied by a reflective chapter on Ibsen's *The Doll House*. The latter chapter substantiates Cavell's claim that Stella and her sisters are cinematic descendants of Ibsen's Nora, who famously leaves her family and husband, escaping suffocating domestic conformity in favour of an uncertain future. The stakes of this moral perfectionist reading, however, are philosophical, shaped by what Cavell calls his 'preoccupations':

> with intersections between cinema and philosophical scepticism, between scepticism and tragedy and melodrama, hence (it turned out) between scepticism and gender, and between the main traditions and two institutional formations of Western philosophy, and between each of these traditions and psychoanalysis.
>
> (Cavell 1996, 199)

A number of correspondences and conflicts are articulated here: an encounter between cinematic genre, the question of gender, and analytic versus Continental philosophical traditions, and the role of psychoanalytic film theory, and so on. The central question, however, is whether *Stella Dallas* is to be read as a story of self-sacrifice or one of autonomous choice; whether we understand the film to be an eradication of Stella as woman and mother, typical of the ideological operations of Hollywood melodrama, or as a vindication of her struggle to find a non-conformist feminine identity – one mediated by cinema's transformative powers – beyond the constraints of a domestic, conservative world in which marriage may be neither possible nor desirable.

How does Cavell read Stella Dallas (the character)? For Cavell, Stella is unknown, both in the sense of lacking self-knowledge, thus needing an education as to the reality of the world to which she aspires, and 'unknown' in the sense of being 'isolated', that is, misrecognized by her husband and others within her social world (even, in the end, by her own daughter). The ironies of misrecognition are staples of melodrama, which trades on our allegiance with a troubled or frustrated 'woman on the verge' who is subject to a variety of misunderstandings of her actions, her motivations, and of her moral character.

This point is clearly at issue in the clash between Cavell and feminist critic Linda Williams, for whom *Stella Dallas* exemplifies the melodramatic motif of feminine 'self-sacrifice', and culminates with the erasure of Stella as 'both a woman and a mother' (Williams 1984). Williams' influential reading of the film commences with the experience of a female spectator (as reported by a character in Marilyn French's novel, *The Women's Room* (1977)), who describes the 'shock of recognition' in viewing the film's moving final scene: Stella [Barbara Stanwyck] anonymously witnessing from the street, through an exposed window, the wedding of her daughter Laurel [Anne Shirley] to upper-class beau Richard (Dick) Grosvenor [Tim Holt], while the rain beats down on her tear-stained face. As the crowds gather and a policeman tries to move the crowd along, she is allowed to watch, in anonymous privacy, the climactic kiss between bride and groom, before drifting away into the night, her face illuminated in the darkness and disappearing off-screen with a teary but triumphant smile. Williams takes up the sense of recognition expressed in French's character's response to the scene ('How they got us to consent to our own eradication!'), asking how the film attempts (and yet fails) to reconcile the sacrificial model of motherhood with Stella's social roles as wife and woman.

The key question, in Williams' spectator-focused response, is how such a film, as a maternal melodrama focusing on the 'mother-daughter knot' (Williams 1984, 5), elicits conflicted responses from a female spectator. Stella's final scene, for example, not only valorizes maternal sacrifice but expresses tearful pride and joyful satisfaction in the accomplishment of Stella's task in relation to her daughter. Indeed, for Williams, the maternal melodrama's strategy of devaluing the actual mother while celebrating the institution of motherhood is clearly evident in *Stella Dallas*. So too is the melodramatic mode's wish-fulfilling tendency towards a personalization and domestication of the social, economic, and ideological forces shaping the characters' situation; in Williams' words, the 'acting out of the narrative resolution of conflicts derived from the economic, social, and political spheres in the private, emotionally primal sphere of the family' (1984, 4). Williams' psychoanalytic reading (1984) thus emphasizes the 'enigma' of the female or, more precisely, the maternal gaze, as well as the reflexive exploration of the desires and pleasures informing female cinema spectatorship. She also challenges feminist critiques that posit a 'passive' female spectator who simply accepts the valorization of maternal self-sacrifice in the film, arguing that the viewer takes a more active, reflective stance towards the film's ambivalent 'resolution' of the conflict between the roles of mother and woman by 'erasing' Stella from both in a melodramatic release of emotion.

Against other psychoanalytic-feminist readings that make both Stella and the female spectator unwitting victims of patriarchal ideology, Williams underlines the conflicted role of the female spectator in response to the film, both 'recognizing' the maternal conflict between self-sacrifice and independence, while actively reflecting on these alternatives within the constraining social situation that Stella confronts.

Cavell takes up the conversation on melodrama, adding his own (male) voice to the debate, by challenging Williams' critical reading of the film (1996, 197 ff.). He rejects the feminist critique that posits Stella as an unwitting victim of social and cultural forces beyond her control, rather than the subject of her own active (but imperfect) form of perfectionist self-education. According to Cavell, like other female characters in the melodrama of the unknown woman, Stella rejects marriage as the path towards self-transformation, attempting instead to find an alternative form of feminine identity, which puts her at odds with her social milieu and male romantic partners. At the same time, this melodramatic exploration of the 'irony of human identity' – and in particular the 'unknownness' of the woman in need of acknowledgement and self-education as to her own identity – is accompanied by the self-reflexive exploration of the medium of film, which finds in the 'unknown woman' of melodrama one of its great subjects. Such films are remarkable for their success in realizing the potentially transfiguring aesthetic and expressive power of moving images in relation to the (particularly female) face and persona – in this case, the discovery, through the film's unfolding, of Barbara Stanwyck as a 'star'.

Cavell understands the 'standard reading' of the film to take Stella as being 'oblivious' to the social transgressions she (innocently) commits, and for the most part unaware (as we are not) of the vulgarity of her fashion sense and boisterous social manners. According to this reading, one seemingly endorsed by Williams, Stella only realizes the degree to which she is hampering her daughter's chances at social and personal happiness (by joining the household of her wealthy father and new stepmother and marrying into a higher social class), after her disastrously vulgar display at the posh Hotel Mirador resort where Stella and Laurel have been staying together. They have come to this resort with different, but complementary motives in mind: Laurel to socialize her friends and new beau Richard Grosvenor, and Stella to show Laurel a good time in the kind of environment of which Stephen would have approved. As a consequence of overhearing Laurel's friends gossiping that the scandalously dressed woman was actually Laurel Dallas's mother, Stella realizes her mistake and resolves to find a way to ensure that Laurel will be forced to undergo the 'pain of individuation' (to cite Nietzsche) and to leave Stella's home once and for all. Stella thus orchestrates a plan: playing the vulgar, uncaring, 'bad' mother whose provocative social and sexual displays will make her unacceptable to Laurel, thus forcing her loyal, loving daughter out of the maternal nest, and thereby cleansing her of future social stigma by erasing any connection with her earthy, working-class mother. This will clear the way – emotionally and socially – for Laurel to take up the role prepared for her as a fully-fledged member of the Dallas/Morrison family with all the social advantages this will afford, not least that of acquiring a 'mother she can be proud of' (to quote Stella): Mrs Helen Dallas/Morrison, Stephen's new wife.

Stella's 'Christmas tree' display

In one of the film's most famous sequences, and the one upon which the debate between Cavell and Williams turns, Stella makes a dramatic appearance at a posh country club (the Mirador Hotel), where her daughter Laurel is mingling with rich 'society' types, her new beau Dick Grosvenor, and their college friends. Stella's gaudy costume – an elaborately prepared ensemble of floral prints, frills and feathers, leopard-skin pumps, clanking jewellery, jaunty hat, and white fox stole – provokes ridicule and scorn, as she saunters through the courtyard crowd, loudly tipping a busboy responding to her inquiry as to where Mrs Grosvenor (Dick's mother) might be. The film goes to considerable lengths to dwell on Stella's preparation for her display – her choice of outfit and accessories all designed for maximum 'shock' effect – while also being careful not to ridicule her. At the same time, however, the film does not shy away from showing the excessive, confronting manner in which Stella attempts to attract attention to herself and robustly assert her 'stylish' but earthy persona in this intimidating social milieu. As she continues her ostentatious parade, heading slowly towards the milk bar/kiosk, we see some of the college kids sharing gossip about the dreadful 'Christmas tree' display they've just witnessed. Too wrapped up in her romantic excitement with Richard, Laurel fails to notice, reflected in a wall mirror, her mother entering and loitering in the kiosk. When she becomes aware that her mother is the subject of the scandalized gossip, Laurel flees in tears to avoid the humiliation of being 'outed' as the vulgar woman's daughter and having her déclassé social origins exposed.

For Williams, this is one of the key moments of the film, one that reveals Stella's ignorance of her social disgrace. It is the most extreme instance of Stella's social transgressions that inadvertently risks the 'isolation of mother and daughter from the upper-class world to which they aspire to belong but into which only Laurel fits' (Williams 1984, 13). Indeed, one of the basic conflicts at the heart of the film, Williams claims, 'comes to revolve around the *excessive presence* of Stella's body and dress', her flaunting of an 'exaggeratedly feminine presence that the offended community prefers not to see' (1984, 13). This showy display of femininity, however, only 'emphasises her pathetic inadequacy' no matter how many 'ruffles, feathers, furs, and clanking jewellery that Stella dons' (1984, 13). Stella's strategy of flamboyant display backfires in the eyes of her upper-class audience, who regard her, in contrast with the discreet charm of Mrs Morrison, as a tasteless travesty of 'what it means to be a woman' (1984, 13).

As Williams observes, this exaggerated display is nowhere more evident than in the Hotel Mirador sequence, where Stella and Laurel have ventured 'for their one fling at an upper-class life together' (1984, 13). On the one hand, Stella asserts her own flamboyant taste ('I've always been known to have stacks of style') against the restraint and decorum of the upper-class world. Her sense of style, Williams adds, is 'the war paint she applies more thickly with each new assault on her legitimacy as a woman and a mother' (1984, 14). On the other, Stella 'is as oblivious as ever to the shocking effect of her appearance', Williams claims, which she goes on to describe as 'a grotesque parody of Stella's fondest dream of being like all the glamorous people in the movies' (1984, 15). It recalls the key scene earlier in the film when Stella and Stephen do go to the movies, their first and fateful date, where we see a spellbound Stella, entranced by the movie, ask Stephen to teach her how to act and speak like the glamorous figures she has been admiring on screen.

In any event, Stella is unaware, Williams claims, of the disastrous effects of her extravagant display, and of the social humiliation it will cause her daughter. It is only after a moment of revelation in the train carriage when she overhears Laurel's friends mocking her garish appearance that finally she understands, from her daughter's perspective, 'the reality of her social situation' as 'a struggling, uneducated woman doing the best she can with the resources at her disposal' (Williams 1984, 15). It is *this* vision of herself from Laurel's perspective, sympathetic and loving yet aware of Stella's lack of social graces, that convinces Stella to embark on the exaggerated 'masquerade' that will force Laurel away from Stella and towards the Morrison/Dallas household and thus into a more 'desirable' social world.

This is precisely the centre of Cavell's disagreement with Williams' reading of the film as a melodramatic study in maternal self-sacrifice. Williams claims that Stella is oblivious to the effect of her garish garb, and only realizes her social transgression after overhearing the gossip on the train home. Cavell claims that Stella 'knows exactly what her effect is there, that her spectacle is *part of* a strategy for separating Laurel from her, not the catastrophe of mis-understanding that causes her afterward to form her strategy' (Cavell 1996, 201). According to Cavell, Stella decides to put this strategy into effect (adopting an off-putting persona to make Laurel leave) after the disastrous Christmas Eve impromptu dinner plan, which is cancelled once Stephen decides, thanks to the sudden appearance of a drunken Ed Munn, to decline Stella's invitation and leave with Laurel on the next train. The concluding shot of Stella, watching Stephen close the door behind him, the camera lingering on her back, is the moment of reflective 'self-absorption, of self-assessment', Cavell claims, when she decides on her plan for Laurel to leave her home (1996, 203).

Cavell thus questions the assumption that Stella's 'Christmas tree display' is unknowing, oblivious, or naïve. Indeed, he goes so far as to claim that feminist critics like Williams subject Stella to the same 'ironic misinterpretations' (1996, 201) that other characters perpetrate against her, misreading her deliberate strategy of provocation as an unwitting display of ignorance. According to Cavell, Williams' claim that Stella is 'oblivious' is refuted by Stella's 'massively authenticated knowledge of clothes, that she is an expert at their construction and, if you like, deconstruction' (1996, 201). A number of key scenes, for example, show that Stella is not only a talented dressmaker but knows how to 'dress to impress' (for example, when she first captures Stephen's attention at his office in the factory, and in Mrs Morrison's praise of Laurel's beautiful dresses, all designed and made by Stella). Cavell's reading of her character centres on the question of Stella's *taste*: her taste in clothes, her knowledge of costume and its effects, and her taste, or rather distaste, for the life she thought she desired (social mobility and domestic fulfilment through marriage). Stella's decision to make a display of herself was an expression of her 'taste': a deliberate act, part of a strategy, to shock or confront those 'who have no taste for her' (1996, 202), and thus to ensure that Laurel embraces her new social life with her 'tasteful' father and stepmother.

This strategy of sartorial and behavioural provocation – alienating her daughter from herself in order to set Laurel free – is a resolution of Stella's sceptical bind: her realization that, while she remains committed to being a mother, she no longer aspires to the fantasy of social mobility that once moved her. It is a form of self-discovery, an affirmation of her non-conformist identity as a woman who has rejected marriage but also begun separating herself from her role as mother. Indeed, this deliberate strategy can be viewed as part of Stella's self-education: her realization that the world of social privilege she once so admired in Stephen ('just like people in the movies') is not for her, is not to her taste. Cavell thus offers an affirmative reading of Stella's emotional journey towards moral self-education and transformative ethical agency – an unconventional case of Emersonian ethical self-reliance.

At a more cinematic level, Stella's showy display is also a reflexive commentary on the 'communication' between women that occurs via the movies. One example is when Mrs Morrison realizes the degree to which Stella was prepared to release Laurel into her new social world with the Dallas/Morrisons ('can't you read between those pitiful lines' she asks Stephen, as they consider Stella's fictional letter to Laurel announcing that she will marry Ed Munn, her remark also implicitly addressed to the audience). This 'cinematic' communication between women reaches its apogee in the film's famous concluding sequence, Laurel's society wedding at Mrs Morrison's splendid house. In preparation for the ceremony, Mrs Morrison insists that the curtains be left open, a gesture presumably enabling Stella to witness her daughter's marriage from the perspective of an anonymous spectator, gazing at the spectacle through the window frame/film screen. Finally, in the film's most famous shot, an emotionally transported Stella walks slowly away from the wedding scene, gazing into the night with an enigmatic smile (recalling her expression after being captivated by the movies on her first date with Stephen); a moment of emotional intensity and painful self-restraint that we might call an instance of the domestic sublime. Here too, Cavell claims, we encounter the film's communication of Stella's self-transformation: namely, the film's declaration of Barbara Stanwyck as a star.

Stella's class

There are many admirable features in Cavell's provocative reading of *Stella Dallas*. The first is his treatment of it as a case of 'cinematic ethics', one in which the melodrama of the unknown woman is also an expression of (imperfect) Emersonian moral perfectionism; one in which Stella learns to 'become who she is' by rejecting marriage, and her youthful fantasies of social glamour ('just like in the movies'), while enabling her daughter to pursue her own version of this kind of social and marital happiness, one that Stella no longer shares. My questioning of this moral perfectionist reading, however, turns on the question of 'class', understood here as aesthetic style, as social status, and as economic situation. Can Cavell's moral perfectionist approach to melodrama acknowledge those 'suppressed' dimensions of (class, gender, and social) identity – elements that find expression through aesthetic, emotional, dramatic, and cinematic means – that cannot be acknowledged, realized, or fulfilled within the melodramatic world the woman inhabits? Despite Stella's evident 'knowledge of clothes' on display throughout the film, one can argue that it is Stella's desire for 'class', in the sense of social status as much as style and glamour, that comes undone when she proves unable, or unwilling, to be satisfied with Stephen's 'doll house' world of social propriety or Laurel's world of genteel elegance (as personified by Mrs Morrison). Stella's social transgressions – her raucous laughter and 'loud' display in the railway carriage; Stephen's discovery of Stella and Munn entertaining themselves while minding infant Laurel; Munn destroying a moment of possible reconciliation between Stella and Stephen just as they are about to share an impromptu Christmas dinner – all link Stella with Munn, if not romantically (she regards him as an avuncular friend), then socially and domestically (he is more 'her crowd' than Stephen's bourgeois world, but also becomes an object of moral sympathy for Stella when she realizes he has hit hard times).

These transgressions or improprieties link Stella with Munn in ways that thwart her aspirations to 'class': to take her proper place as Stephen's wife within a superior social world. As foreshadowed by the early scene at the River Club, which centres on Stella's socially inappropriate desire to 'hang out' with Munn's racing crowd rather than her husband's respectable but boring business colleagues, Stella makes it clear to Stephen that she finds her new domestic world – and his social respectability – lacking in vitality and enjoyment. It is not just that Stella realizes she does not wish to persist in marriage or that she deliberately tries to push Laurel towards the social privileges afforded by Stephen and Mrs Morrison. Rather, the barrier to her desire for moral perfectionist self-realization is not only her gender but her social class, both of which, in their dialectical interactions, cannot be readily reconciled within her divided social and cultural world. It is this complex relationship between class and gender that teaches her that the world she formerly aspired to, and that her daughter now desires, is not for her, not where she can find herself, not where she can become who she is. Stella's ethical drama has to do with her conflicted desire for class, the attraction/repulsion towards it that Stephen and his social world elicits from her, yet also prevents her from realizing or enjoying. How well does Cavell's moral perfectionist reading of the film encompass Stella's ambivalent desire for social class, her desire to be an unconventional 'single' mother as well as an independent, non-bourgeois, woman?

As remarked above, Cavell's central claim is that Stella knows very well the effect of her vulgar display at the Hotel Mirador, and that she begins her plan to push Laurel towards social respectability just after the disastrous Christmas Eve dinner:

> I take the mark of its beginning to be precisely the close of the sequence of her final lesson from Stephen as he reneges on his expansively thoughtful suggestion that he and Laurel take a later train.
>
> (Cavell 1996, 203)

The concluding shot of Stella standing in her black dress, back to the camera, in front of the closed door, is held for some time, 'calling attention to itself', which suggests, for Cavell, a moment of 'thought under collection in privacy' (1996, 203). The Hotel Mirador sequence that follows he takes to be an 'initial attempt to send Laurel away' that 'backfires': Laurel is drawn all the closer to her mother after realizing that she did hear her friends in the train gossiping, and so has been nobly 'sacrificing' herself in offering to let Stella live with Stephen and Helen.

The very next scene, however, before the 'Christmas tree' display, is of Stella confronting Stephen's lawyer, who inquires whether she would object to a divorce. Stella is dressed, moreover, in a flamboyant manner and projects a sceptical, streetwise persona, clearly suspicious of the lawyer's (which is to say Stephen's) underlying motives. She asks whether Stephen's request to divorce is really so that he can now marry Mrs Morrison; but also makes clear that she fears this will mean she loses Laurel to her husband's new family. This is a crucial scene in the film, especially for the Hotel Mirador sequence that follows, yet it is a scene that Cavell and Williams both ignore. There are two ways we can approach it: either as Stella's sincere expression of her fear that she will lose Laurel, or that she is acting a role, pretending to be outraged as part of her 'plan' to push Laurel towards her new family (as Cavell maintains). If Stella is being sincere, then she is expressing her desire to prevent Stephen and Helen taking full custody of Laurel, and vows to make sure that she does not lose her daughter to the new couple. Indeed, she defiantly announces that, if that is the sort of lifestyle to which Laurel aspires, she will also show Laurel a good time, taking her to expensive hotels and the like, but will make sure that Stephen foots the bill. To confirm this, the very next shot is a close-up of Stella signing the Hotel Mirador bill as 'Mrs Stephen Dallas'. This important scene thus frames the Hotel Mirador sequence as Stella's attempt to show Stephen and Laurel (not to mention their society crowd) that Stella will not be pushed aside, that she is willing to assert herself as Laurel's mother, thus resisting the prospect of Laurel being 'stolen' away from her (all while insisting on her continued identity as 'Mrs Stephen Dallas').

If she is not being sincere, however, if she is already executing her plan to 'push' Laurel away (as Cavell suggests), then it becomes hard to understand why Stella would put on this curious performance solely for the benefit of Stephen's lawyer. Why would she proclaim that she will not allow Stephen and the new Mrs Dallas to 'take Laurel away' from her if this is supposed to be what Stella desires for her anyway? Cavell's reading of the film overlooks this crucial framing scene, which casts doubt on how Stella can be both hatching a plan to push Laurel towards Stephen and Helen, while also professing that she will fight their attempts to take Laurel away from her.

Another problem with Cavell's account of Stella's vulgar display is that her 'plan' risks being damaging to Laurel, the very person whose future happiness is what Stella desires most. Laurel's horror at discovering it was her mother parading through the hotel grounds 'like a Christmas tree' is painfully evident to the spectator. Laurel is presented sympathetically, with an emotionally-charged build-up showing her enjoying herself with Dick's friends, cycling together as a carefree group, the two shy lovers sharing a chaste kiss, with Dick offering her his pin, the young couple oblivious to the scandal erupting around them. The suspense over the imminent destruction of Laurel's romantic happiness is almost unbearable, as is the idea that she will be socially humiliated once it becomes public that she is Stella Dallas's daughter. All of this risks being destroyed – and with it Laurel's chances at happiness – by her mother's vulgar antics. Stella may well succeed in 'pushing' Laurel away but on pain of destroying her chances of being accepted into the world to which she aspires – a high price to pay for Stella's realization that domestic respectability was not what she thought it was.

To be sure, the question of Stella's attitude to motherhood is a complex one. It is clear that she is ambivalent about its constraints but also deeply loves her daughter; yet she is misrecognized as the unconventional kind of mother she aspires to be ('something more than a mother', a remark Stella makes while attempting to 'push' Laurel away by feigning a relationship with Ed Munn). Stella's smile at the end of the film thus remains enigmatic, even ironic. Not just an expression of her 'completed education', her emancipation from the strictures of marriage and motherhood (which will now be 'perfected' by her daughter). The smile expresses a sense of triumph that Laurel has crossed that subtle class divide that Stella, in the end, did not desire to transcend, remaining, as a consequence, ambiguous in her solitude or, to use Cavell's term, in her 'unknownness'.

As remarked, Cavell's version of events faces the difficulty of explaining the lawyer scene just prior to the Hotel Mirador sequence; it also commits us to taking the melodramatic scene of communication between the two mothers – Stella visiting Helen to discuss the delicate topic of Laurel coming to live with the Dallas/Morrisons – as an artful piece of deception rather than an expression of emotional intimacy. This scene, a master class in melodramatic emotional display, shows a visibly moved and contrite Stella, touched by Helen's gracious response to Stella's delicate request that Helen 'take' Laurel into her new family once she marries Stephen. Stella shows vulnerability in her awkward conversation with Helen, a gesture which Helen, despite their differences in social class, style, and demeanour, gracefully acknowledges. It thereby anticipates the 'reciprocal' moment of acknowledgement at the end of the film when Helen insists on the curtains being drawn so that Stella can witness the wedding between Laurel and Richard and thus see the culmination of their private agreement. The emotional tenor of this scene, the changed demeanour evident in Stella's speech and manners, the sincerity of Helen's sympathetic response, all suggest to the viewer that this is not a carefully staged performance but rather a genuine change of heart: a realisation that Stella's former strategy was wrongheaded, even self-centred, forgetting or overriding Laurel's feelings and desires, however much these differ from Stella's own.

This account of the film chimes with elements of Cavell's moral perfectionist approach, but it also emphasizes a key element that is passed over in his interpretation of Stella's moral ambivalence towards marriage and motherhood: the issue of class. The barrier facing Stella is not just that of reconciling being a mother with being a woman (as Williams argues), or rejecting marriage in favour of a self-education as to her own identity (as Cavell maintains). Rather, it is the question of class (and its intersection with gender, with being a woman, a mother, but also a social being, a mother of a certain social standing, status, and social class, whose daughter aspires to a higher class); the manner in which the constraints of her situation of economic and social dependency (and its associated stigma) profoundly shape and define Stella's conduct and her possibilities. Indeed, Stella's decision, and her future, whatever we make of it, cannot be divorced from her social status as a déclassé 'single mother': her conflicted struggle to advance herself socially, and, more ambitiously, her daughter, across a subtle barrier of class, wealth, education, and social distinction. The drama of Stella's decision to separate herself from Laurel's life – for Williams, a sign of the film's 'erasure' of Stella as mother and as woman; for Cavell, an autonomous decision that enables her to discover her new identity – cannot be separated from the melodrama of desiring class, both as style and as social and economic status, even if this is what Stella ultimately rejects, acknowledging her own ambiguous identity 'between' incompatible social worlds.

This is an ideological aspect of *Stella Dallas* – and of melodrama more generally – that Cavell's moral perfectionist approach struggles to articulate: how the conditions of a character's world shape her quest for ethical self-transformation, and, more profoundly, how the 'impossible' desires that this social world stimulates yet cannot satisfy, find visual expression in an aesthetic of excess, of hyperbolic performance, and an ambivalent mood of melancholy self-affirmation. If melodramas of the unknown woman are domestic tragedies without cathartic resolution, playing out the cultural aporias of gender and class, their aesthetic presentation of the possibilities of moral perfectionism will remain conflicted, excessive, and incomplete – a 'tragic' moral perfectionism that, to use Elsaesser's phrase, 'doesn't quite come off' (1987, 65).

The emotional excessiveness of the film's famous concluding scene is a case in point: far from being sentimental tears at finally seeing her daughter happily married, Stella's silent display of emotion condenses many elements of her character and situation, not to mention conflicting features of the narrative arc, into a 'private' space of viewing, emotional expression, and bodily communication: Stella's self-sacrifice, her uneasy but independent manner of relating roles of mother and of (no longer married) woman, her sense of having traversed the fantasy of marrying up – of upward social mobility achieved through romantic union – only to find that this was not for her, not to her taste, not her style, however much it remains part of Laurel's world, her romantic fantasy and social desire. The circular repetition of this sequence, rhyming with the earlier sequence when Stella and Stephen go on their first date, Stella mesmerized by the movies and wanting Stephen to educate her into his social world, finally resolves itself through Laurel's successful achievement of social mobility through advantageous marriage. Stella's smile, while chewing on her scarf as she did earlier with Stephen after the movies, is also a Stoic rejection of this social world, of the institutions and norms that uphold it, in favour of her own unconventional mode of feminine social identity ('something more than a mother'), however alone it leaves her on the obscured edges and margins of this world. The 'domestic sublimity' of this moment is a melodramatic expression of all the conflicting dynamics at work in Stella's divided subjectivity and social worlds that could not find direct expression in the narrative as such.

Moral melodramas such as *Stella Dallas* run up against the individualist limits of this perfectionist ethic of self-transformation within the difficult familial, social, economic, and cultural circumstances in which characters find themselves – whether as women, as mothers, or as social outsiders. Indeed, this feature of melodrama has been recognized as one of its defining features and sources of aesthetic novelty as well as ideological limitation. As noted previously, the melodramatic mode often takes on the quality of cultural 'wish-fulfilment', 'acting out the narrative resolution of conflicts derived from the economic, social and political spheres in the private, emotionally primal sphere of the family' (Williams 1984, 4). This is a source of its emotional intensity but also marks a limit to what it can articulate of the broader currents shaping the domestic world of the protagonists and their interpersonal struggles. Melodrama can delineate these background forces, but only obliquely, indirectly, suggesting them in aesthetic or dramatic ways rather than articulating them directly in narrative terms. They point, through emotional excess, to the fractures and

limits of a social world that cultivates desires for selfhood, happiness, independence, and acknowledgment, particularly in women, that often cannot be
fulfilled without that world being changed.

The challenge for Cavellian moral perfectionism is to articulate how individual self-transformation also requires recognition of how the conditions shaping
one's social-cultural situation can either foster or restrict one's exercise of
individual autonomy. The challenge is to make the transition from ethics to
politics from within moral perfectionism's individualist framework, one that
struggles to contain and explain the powerful emotional and social dynamics
buffeting the female characters, especially, who remain caught between their
conflicted and divided subjective and social worlds (notably, in relation to
marriage, family, and social recognition through career, and so on). To be
sure, Cavell makes forays in the direction of social community and politics (in
Cities of Words (2004)), arguing that moral perfectionism is linked to an
'Emersonian' democratic ethics of communal sociability. But Cavell's readings
of melodramas like *Stella Dallas* tend to avoid the political question of the
social conditions of the woman's desire for creative self-transformation within
the conflicted social and subjective worlds of the melodrama. Stella's struggle
with the entwined challenges of gender and class – to reconcile marriage,
motherhood, and the 'pursuit of happiness' within a social class to which she
aspires but does not belong – dissolves in Cavell's affirmative reading of her
self-education as a form of moral perfectionist self-transformation mediated
by the cinematic exploration of feminine identity.

These critical reflections suggest the need to question Cavell's moral-
perfectionist individualism in favour of a more complex dialectic between
individual and social-cultural world, to find a more 'Hegelian' (rather than
Emersonian) model of melodrama as tragedy without catharsis – a model
that situates the exercise of individual autonomy within an intersubjective
relational network of social-cultural norms, practices, and institutions – one
that articulates the contradictory demands or desires that are engendered by,
yet remain unsatisfied within, our modern world (I explore this idea further in
the following section). In many ways this is one of the most suggestive features
of cinematic ethics: the idea that narrative film can not only evoke varieties of
ethical significant experience inviting further philosophical reflection, but this
narrative focus on ethical experience can also reveal tensions, conflicts, or
contradictions shaping and defining a particular social-cultural world – an
aesthetic disclosure of some of the complex background historical and social
forces shaping individual and social identity.

Talk to Her

Some of these concerns are addressed in more recent forms of moral melodrama, which inherit and renew the genre while putting it to new cinematic
and ethical uses. In such films we not only find the interweaving of ethical and

social concerns, but also the cinematic exploration of troubling, confronting, or difficult ethical situations. Moral melodramas are particularly apt at evoking complex forms of ethically ambivalent experience, eliciting simultaneously sympathetic and antipathetic responses, thereby generating a dynamic dialectic of emotional engagement and critical reflection that make these films powerful instances of cinematic ethics. One such film is Pedro Almodóvar's *Talk to Her*, an accomplished but confronting moral melodrama that shifts from the maternal to the 'male' melodrama, and from the familial to the more interpersonal and cultural-social planes. Almodóvar is a filmmaker whose body of work offers exemplary cases of the use of melodrama – as style, genre, and mode of experience – to explore a range of psychological, moral, and sexual dynamics. His films give indirect aesthetic and dramatic expression to the contradictory pressures – social, cultural, sexual, and emotional – confronting characters in difficult social and cultural circumstances, playing with the ambiguity of subjective identities as much as with cinematic genres. At the same time, his films foreground and luxuriate in the ambivalent dynamics of passionate love, the ambiguities and crossovers in sexual desire and gender identity, and the implacable forces marginalized characters face in transgressing implicit societal, cultural, sexual, and moral norms. In doing so, however, they nonetheless cultivate an enlivening sense of emotional expansiveness and ethical receptivity coupled with humour, camp, and a sense of irony. They explore the contradictory demands reflecting the cultural-historical moment of post-Franco Spain, a country emerging from political authoritarianism, and forging an alternative artistic culture in response to a repressive historical past and social uncertainties of the present (see D'Lugo 2006, 1–16; Acevedo-Muñoz 2007, 1–7; Epps and Kakoudaki 2009, 1–34). Moreover, they are beautifully crafted films that balance stylistic excess, emotional intensity, and cinematic reflexivity in ways that are at once aesthetic, philosophical, and ethical. They reveal, through a combination of aesthetic stylization and emotional excess, how individuals caught in the conflicting norms of sexual and social identity manage to reinvent themselves, acknowledge each other, and create unconventional forms of community within the difficult constraints of their particular social and cultural worlds.

Almodóvar's artistic achievements and philosophical significance as a filmmaker have been acknowledged in a recent volume of the Routledge *Philosophers on Film* series, which features a number of essays dedicated to his film, *Talk to Her* [*Hable con ella*] (2002). This honouring of *Talk to Her* as an artistically and philosophically significant moral melodrama provides an ideal entry point for my engagement with the film, for it exemplifies the manner in which cinematic form, emotional engagement, and ethical experience can work together in narrative cinema. To give some background, the film tells the story of Benigno [Javier Cámara], a male nurse caring for a comatose female patient, Alicia [Leonor Watling], a beautiful dance student with whom he is obsessively in love. It also features Benigno's friend Marco [Dario Grandinetti], a journalist mourning his previous lover while in a relationship with female toreador, Lydia [Rosario Flores]. Like Alicia, Lydia ends up in hospital, also in a coma, after being gored during a bullfight. Benigno and Marco meet at the hospital where Benigno is caring for Alicia and Marco is visiting Lydia; the two men, however, have encountered each other earlier (or at least Benigno has) at a Pina Bausch dance performance. At the beginning of the film, they are shown seated next to each other, watching a performance of Bausch's piece 'Café Müller'. Benigno notices the handsome, melancholy Marco next to him, who is moved to tears by the poignant dance sequence (accompanied by Purcell's 'O let me weep, forever weep' from his opera, 'The Fairy Queen'). The mesmerizing dance features two women, in plain white shifts, their eyes closed, moving fitfully across the café floor, while an anxious male character rushes before them, clearing away the chairs so that the women avoid colliding with them. The dance prefigures the story of the two women, bedridden and comatose, and the two men caring for them, talking with each other, and, in Benigno's case, talking to comatose Alicia as though she were aware of him. In the film's dramatic climax, Benigno, whose 'benign', comical character masks a darker delusion, sexually violates the unconscious Alicia, leaving her pregnant. We do not directly witness this shocking event but infer it thanks to the allegorical presentation of a strange black-and-white silent movie (*The Shrinking Lover*), which Benigno saw the night before, found disturbing, and narrates to the unconscious Alicia before the traumatic act.

The Shrinking Lover, a remarkable film-within-the-film, is a surreal melodrama depicting a woman scientist whose immature lover impulsively drinks a 'potion' she has discovered that shrinks him to the size of a man's hand. After failing to find an antidote, the lovers escape from the man's overbearing mother and elope to a hotel (the Hotel Youkali[2]), where the woman falls asleep, and the man explores the landscape of her naked body, finally stripping off and entering her vagina, enacting a symbolic act of returning to the womb. The film-within-a-film then cuts to warm colour images of liquid globules merging and parting in silence, an aesthetic 'screen' for the violation that has just taken place – an image that Almodóvar described as 'a lid' [*una tapadera*] 'to cover up what is really happening' (D'Lugo 2006, 112). When asked why he adopted such a 'dangerous' strategy – using cinematic 'masking' in order to depict the rape from the rapist's (Benigno's) perspective as storyteller – he replied: 'I did it to hide something that is going on in the film and something which the audience should not see (qtd. in Mackenzie 157)' (D'Lugo 2006, 113). The traumatic reality of sexual violation has to be filtered and mediated via Benigno's cinematic fantasy; the task of 'hiding' or 'masking' the true nature of Benigno himself, moreover, becoming more apparent as the film unfolds.

Once Benigno's monstrous act has been uncovered, he is sent to jail where he continues to mourn his 'lover' Alicia, desperately wanting to know the outcome of her pregnancy. As for Marco, he discovers that Lydia had been planning to leave him (just before her accident) in order to marry her former lover and fellow matador, El Niño de Valencia. She even tried to raise this with him, unsuccessfully, after attending the wedding of Marco's former lover, Angela [Elena Anaya] (a sequence that is shown in two parts, using interrupted flashback, across different sections of the film). Their conversation, however, was fruitless; Marco is too preoccupied with his own feelings to listen to what Lydia wanted to tell him, or to notice what her tears at the wedding revealed (that she was imagining her own future wedding to El Niño). Upon learning this tragic news, Marco leaves Madrid behind, dealing with his pain through work (going overseas and writing a travel book). When Marco reads about Lydia's death in the newspaper, he returns to Madrid, where he learns the tragic fates of Benigno and Alicia. Marco visits his condemned friend in prison, the two men sharing an interrupted intimacy that is both painful and moving.

The film's final act opens with Benigno's farewell message to Marco, hinting that he plans suicide, and Marco's desperate rush to reach his friend in prison before it is too late. He visits Benigno's gravesite, lays flowers, and begins now to talk to him. After Benigno's death, Marco moves into his late friend's flat, starts watching, just as Benigno did, the dance classes taking place across the street, and is shocked to see Alicia, seated with her walking stick, observing the students perform. The film concludes with Marco and Alicia meeting in person, at another Pina Bausch dance performance (the more sensual, optimistic piece, 'Masurca Fogo'). Alicia seems intrigued by the strangely familiar Marco, who is again moved to tears by the dance. They begin to talk, much to the dismay of Alicia's protective dance teacher Katerina [Geraldine Chaplin]. Resuming their seats in the theatre for the second act, separated by an empty seat, they smile at each other across the empty space, as an intertitle appears: 'Marco y Alicia'. Marco remarks to Katerina during the break that they need to talk later about what happened with Benigno and Alicia, and that it will be easier than she thinks. 'I am a dance mistress,' she replies, 'and nothing is easy.' The film's final images show couples slowly dancing, to sensuous and seductive music, against a verdant background, suggesting the possibility of a future relationship between Alicia and Marco.

Talk to Her is notable for being a melodrama concerned at once with ethical themes and philosophical problems. Indeed, in his Introduction to the *Philosophers on Film* volume, Noël Carroll notes that the essays on *Talk to Her* encompass issues in the philosophy of motion pictures (philosophical questions concerning the nature of the medium, representation, aesthetics, and genre); philosophy 'in' film (exploration of thematic issues via film narrative); and philosophy *through* motion pictures, offering 'significant contributions or insights to the conversation of philosophy' (Carroll 2009, 3). This is also the case, I would add, with regard to cinematic ethics: the manner in which it presents and explores complex moral situations by engaging viewers emotionally, and uses the aesthetic strategies of melodrama to explore the ambiguity of communication, the difficulty of interpreting others, the significance of non-verbal forms of expression, and the destructive effects of unthinking, 'moralizing' judgments. It is a moral melodrama that foregrounds performance, the interplay of communication and miscommunication, the limits of verbal discourse (despite Benigno's advice to his friend Marco to 'talk to her', referring to the comatose Lydia), and the value of sensuous and aesthetic forms of communication (dance, movement, touch, but also narrative film). More pointedly, it is a film that deliberately attempts to put the viewer in an 'uncomfortable' ethical position, emphasizing the moral ambivalence of our responses to Benigno as at once a thoughtful, devoted carer and a deceptive, manipulative rapist.

A number of the philosophers discussing *Talk to Her* (Carroll 2009, Pippin 2009, and Wilson 2009) emphasize, on the one hand, the value of verbal communication, taking the film's title – a quotation of Benigno's advice to Marco – as a motto, endorsed by the film, for the ethic of communication Benigno seems to embody. On the other, they also stress the inadequacy of one-sided verbal communication, or the manner in which the viewer is misled into taking Benigno as a morally admirable carer, a naïve innocent, or benign eccentric. Noël Carroll, (2009, 3), for example, describes how Benigno is presented 'as an extremely humane person, even perhaps somewhat saintly – a holy fool of sorts – at times', even though he may also strike us as 'not exactly mentally sound'. On the one hand, Benigno appears to offer a lesson in the virtue of an ethics of care, a commitment to communicating with others, regardless of their capacity to respond; on the other, he is guilty of a dreadful crime, raping a comatose woman who could in no way consent to such an act. The paradoxical figure of Benigno – at once a devoted carer and a deluded rapist – prompts moral consternation along with philosophical reflection on the inadequacy of moral judgment as the sole criterion in evaluating ethically complex situations.

Alluding to debates in analytic aesthetics concerning the relationship between morality and artistic value, A. W. Eaton (2009, 11–26) notes the ambiguity in how Benigno is portrayed, arguing that the film engages in aesthetic *amoralism*: depicting a morally flawed character in an aesthetically engaging manner, which does not detract, however, from the artistic value of the work. For some philosophers (aesthetic autonomists), works of art should be judged independently of moral criteria (a position famously espoused by Kant); for others (aesthetic moralists, like Hume), the artistic value of some works of art may be vitiated by their endorsement of morally dubious ideas or value perspectives, especially when these are presented in an aesthetically pleasing light. Leni Riefenstahl's Nazi propaganda epic *Triumph of the Will*, for example, can be judged aesthetically, according to the autonomist, despite its morally objectionable content; on the other hand, it is disqualified as art, according to the moralist, precisely because its content constitutes a moral flaw preventing it from achieving its artistic aims. What is curious about *Talk to Her*, according to Eaton, is that it succeeds in engaging the viewer emotionally, masking Benigno's morally appalling act via aesthetic means, thus confusing the viewer in their moral evaluation of his character. So successful was this aesthetic masking that many critics, for example, described the film as a 'love story' between Alicia and Benigno (Eaton 2009, 11–12). At the same time, *Talk to Her* invites the sympathetic viewer to reflect on their response to Benigno, who turns out to be something other than a 'moral saint' or 'holy fool'. This feature, for Eaton, makes *Talk to Her* an unusual case of 'amoralism' in film: one in which a moral 'flaw' (presenting an 'immoral' character in an aesthetically engaging manner) contributes to the artistic achievement, rather than failure, of the work.

Robert Pippin (2009, 27–44) also defends the evaluation of Benigno, despite his monstrous act, as a complex, divided character embodying the virtue of empathic communicative engagement with others (even in the absence of a response) as well as darker impulses reflecting his arrested sexuality. Noting the 'mythic' character of the narrative, recalling fairy tales such as Snow White, Sleeping Beauty (as well as Wagner's *Siegfried*), Pippin's focus is on exploring the moral ambivalence in our response to 'barely sane, largely delusional' Benigno (2009, 27). Despite the gravity of his crime, he observes that it does not seem entirely satisfactory to simply condemn Benigno for the rape, without also recognizing his other moral qualities (care, compassion, and communication), as well as the personal authenticity of his misguided commitment to Alicia. The inadequacy of moral judgment as the sole consideration in evaluating Benigno, Pippin argues, represents one of the most provocative and thoughtful aspects of *Talk to Her*. Indeed, it is the source of much of the moral ambivalence or 'unease' that spectators are left with, the unresolved tension between sympathy for Benigno's qualities coupled with moral repulsion for his act. Echoing Eaton, Pippin points out the Kleistian 'angel/devil' dyad defining Benigno's character, strikingly revealed thanks to Camara's brilliant performance: the angelic, naïve Benigno, caring and empathetic, replaced by a darker, harder Benigno after his sexual violation of Alicia.[3] Not only the question of personhood, as a function of recognition rather than some identifiable biological 'fact'; the inadequacy of relying solely on moral judgment (or moralism) in understanding situations as complex as those depicted in the film; the need to acknowledge the conflicted or dyadic nature of human action; the emotional and ethical commitments defining friendship; and the mythic and moral truth that cinema can present indirectly via aesthetic means – all of these elements are at play in *Talk to Her*, qualities which endow it with striking philosophical and ethical significance.

While recognizing the film's artistic achievement and exploration of moral ambiguity, Cynthia Freeland (2009, 69–83) gives voice to the feminist critique that the 'communication' here is decidedly one-way: a *talking to* rather than a *talking with*, a 'communication' without listening to or interpreting the other, and hence no real communication at all. To be sure, she acknowledges the moral value of the film as a kind of aesthetic and moral pedagogy in the virtues of communication and empathic engagement. As she points out, Benigno, unlike most other characters, does not treat Alicia as an inert object – a comatose body – but as a (potential or virtual) subject; a person who, despite her lack of consciousness, is to be recognized, treated with care, and with whom communication remains a defining possibility. Where this goes wrong, however, is in Benigno's failure to 'listen' to the other: to maintain the care, respect, and acknowledgement not only at the level of Alicia's bodily integrity but by treating her as an *actual,* rather than *imagined,* person or subject (one with whom Benigno imagines he is in love, and who he imagines loves him in return). This means that the film's motto is not so much 'talk to her' as 'interpret her': the moral understanding of others requires not only communication but interpretation and re-interpretation: the task of understanding persons being akin to that of understanding a work of art, even a cinematic work like *Talk to Her* (2009, 71). Genuine communication means the ongoing attempt to understand the other from her point of view, not only through what she says but how she communicates non-verbally. *Talk to Her* emphasizes this aspect by showing the failure of Benigno's attempt to care for Alicia, talking to her but not 'listening', not recognizing her actual condition, imagining what she is rather than attending to how she exists.

All of these readings are more or less cognizant of the moral-aesthetic trap that the film sets for the viewer: using the sympathetic portrayal of a morally flawed or damaged character who espouses the virtues of communication in order to confront the viewer with the limitations – or ambiguity – of verbal communication, an ambiguity crystallized in Benigno's advice to Marco that he should 'talk to her'. Indeed, the title itself – a quotation in the Spanish intertitle, 'Hable con ella' ['talk *with* her', quoting Benigno, which has a more casual, colloquial, and communicative sense than the English translation of

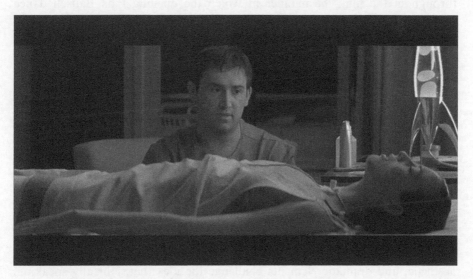

Figure 5.1 Still from *Talk to Her*, Dir. Pedro Almodóvar (2002)

'talk *to* her'] – is ironic: Benigno and Marco both 'talk to' the women they love but do not listen to them; the women being talked to cannot hear, or express themselves verbally, yet they excelled at physical communication (dancing, bull-fighting); the real communication in the film happens through touch, physical gesture, and non-verbal expression (including the allegorical silent film, *The Shrinking Lover*); Benigno, whom we may initially take as a benign, though misguided, 'angel', turns out to be a deceptive character (and unreliable narrator, especially concerning his own past and immediate present) whose guileless charm and innocent candour lull the viewer into overlooking the darker, obsessive aspects of his personality, until we are forced to re-evaluate him after the revelation of his delusory violation of Alicia.[4]

These aspects are rendered visually, expressed aesthetically, through performance and bodily expression; hence they are at odds with much of the dialogue and narrative exposition that remains the focus of most viewers' (and some critics') attention (the contrast, for example, between Benigno's 'benign', attentive massaging of Alicia and the lingering close shots of his hands kneading her flesh, intercut with brief shots of his troubled facial expression, shots that add a darker, sensual undertone at odds with the cheerful, innocent tone of his patter with the other nurses).[5] Indeed, like many melodramas, Almodóvar's films recall the Sirkian tradition of making aesthetic expression – colour, gesture, *mise en scène*, performance, music, allegory – compensate for contradictory, 'impossible', or inarticulable elements within a character's situation or world (in this case, Benigno's emotional and sexual immaturity, the stunting effects of his relationship with his domineering mother, and the deluded nature of his 'relationship' with Alicia).

Evidence for the misleading presentation of Benigno can be found throughout the film: the manner in which the opening Pina Bausch dance sequence frames the story to come, alerting us to its allegorical character, substituting dance, movement, and gesture for speech and conversation (also the role of tears as forms of emotional and physical self-expression);[6] the depiction of Benigno's stalker-like obsession with Alicia, spying on her during her dance classes, following her home after she drops her purse, making an excuse to visit her psychiatrist father in order to 'get close to her', offering an (unreliable) story as to his 'odd' relationship with his mother during adolescence, suggesting to the psychiatrist (and father of Alicia) that he might be homosexual; stealing a hairclip of hers and spying on her in the shower; the disturbing, fantasized character of the silent black-and-white melodrama, which may well be largely an expression of Benigno's imagination, rewriting Alicia's rape as a tragically doomed act of love; his peculiar behaviour after the rape, wanting to 'do the right thing' and marry Alicia, knowing that she is pregnant, much to Marco's horror, and even while in prison, imagining a future together, which, ironically, Marco will pursue: all of these non-verbal, aesthetic, and dramatic elements challenge the idea that, ethically speaking, all the male characters need to do is make the effort to 'talk to her'. Indeed, these episodes question, rather, this overly simplistic notion of communication, and suggest that the deeper ethical meanings of the stories of Benigno and Alicia, Marco and Lydia, and Marco and Benigno are expressed physically, non-verbally, and aesthetically.

A more literal, narrative-focused reading of the film might yield the view that Benigno is a morally misguided, yet admirable, character espousing an ethic of care and the virtues of empathic communication. Yet it is important to recognize that empathy is shown, throughout the film, to be in some cases a snare or ruse, a phenomenon necessary for sympathetic moral understanding but insufficient to ensure ethical clarity or soundness of judgment. Indeed, our empathy and sympathy for Benigno, while understandable and for the most part laudable, can also lead us badly astray, distorting our judgment or dissipating critical reflection, especially if we are dealing with a character skilled in emotional deception (or else subject to significant forms of self-deception). This is especially the case if we are not attentive to the indirect, but distinctively cinematic, means by which his distorted 'moral' reactions and responses are communicated (the tension between verbal presentation and visual style, between dialogue and demonstrative action, between dramatic, narrative development and background mood or tone). This only underlines, however, the ambiguous dialectic between verbal and non-verbal communication, between saying and showing, through which *Talk to Her* articulates its melodramatic ethics. If we only listen to Benigno, as he talks to Alicia, without observing and interpreting his expressions and actions, we risk missing the darker, unsettling point of this confronting moral melodrama: that it presents a sympathetic portrait of a 'psycho' (there is one scene, showing Benigno spying on Alicia from his apartment window, as his mother is heard off-screen scolding him, which seems to allude to Hitchcock's film[7]), who is also caring and loving, charmingly naïve but also cleverly deceptive, morally admirable and despicable at once. Benigno is charming, humorous, and sincere enough (or self-deceiving enough) to fool those around him into thinking that he is genuinely benign (clearly this is the case with Alicia's psychiatrist father, who permits Benigno, whom he takes to be homosexual, to be his daughter's primary carer, despite also having seen him once as a 'patient'), a liberty that allows him to fulfil his (Buñuel-like) 'Sleeping Beauty' fantasy.[8]

The film deliberately thus positions the viewer – much like the majority of the characters – in a morally ambiguous, compromising space: eliciting moral sympathy for a character who commits an appalling act upon another for whom consent is impossible; showing him to be ethically caring and sensitive to the needs of others, while being oblivious to (or delusionally unable to acknowledge) the personhood and dignity of the one he 'loves'; advocating an ethic of communicative openness while at the same time cleverly concealing his secret fantasy from those around him (apart, perhaps, from Marco), not to mention his criminal act against Alicia; and testing the limits of our capacity to judge a moral situation where conflicting impulses towards sympathy and antipathy, moral understanding and ethical condemnation, are put into play within a conflictual, unstable dynamic. It is in these senses that *Talk to Her* evokes a profoundly unsettling, ambivalent form of ethical experience – an ethical estrangement rather than engagement – that demands a considered, thoughtful response; an experience of ethical cognitive dissonance or moral self-questioning that lasts well after the movie has ended.

As in all good melodrama, the film ends with the 'too late', and 'if only', of tragedy unable to be averted. Benigno's text message to Marco is missed; Marco gets to the prison too late to prevent his suicide: if only Benigno had been told the truth about what happened to Alicia and her unborn child (the child died at birth while Alicia was miraculously awoken from her coma), then perhaps his tragic death could have been avoided (at another level, however, Benigno appears to have decided that this is the only way to be with his 'beloved', now that there is no possibility of their being reunited as a couple). Hence the final aspect of the disturbing moral ambiguity of Benigno's relationship with Alicia: the concluding romantic-tragic denouement (suicide) fits well with the film's depiction of his passionate love for her as a case of *amour fou*, which is another notable recurring feature of moral ambiguity in Almodóvar's *oeuvre* (for example, in films such as *Law of Desire* (1987), *Live Flesh* (1997), and *Broken Embraces* (2009)).

Despite this tragic denouement, the fragile possibility of a new relationship is revealed: Marco takes over Benigno's apartment after Benigno's suicide, takes up his old window view of the dance school, and is shocked to see Alicia slowly returning to her old life. In the concluding sequence, which bookends the opening one, Marco meets Alicia at another Pina Bausch performance (*Masurca fogo*), one that is less tragic, more languid, suggesting – again through movement and gesture but also through music and mood – the possibility of a reconciliation between the sexes, of the woman being both seen and heard, of being physically buoyed by her male partners, her only 'verbal' expression a short breathy sigh. The concluding scene of the film suggests the possibility of a new relationship as Alicia and Marco watch the sensuous dance together – Benigno's pointed absence adding an ironic undertone to this thought-provoking moral melodrama, one that not only plays with our capacity for moral empathy/sympathy but explores the possibility that it can lead our ethical evaluation astray. It is a film that elicits the disturbing ethical experience that there are moral situations in which conflicting impulses towards sympathy and condemnation, empathy and criticism, remain irreducibly at odds: situations of inherent moral ambivalence and emotional estrangement that cinema can simulate, that spectators can experience emotionally and aesthetically, but that also demand further critical reflection in order to be understood and evaluated.

Indeed, the 'moral lesson', so to speak, to be drawn from *Talk to Her* – one articulated experientially and aesthetically rather than abstractly or argumentatively – is that empathic verbal communication does not necessarily guarantee mutual acknowledgement or ethical understanding; that moral psychology is far more complex, in particular ethical situations, than we generally admit; and consequently, that moralizing judgment risks misunderstanding the complexity of meaning in moral situations where the intentions, motivations, and perspectives of individual agents remain opaque, deceptive, or ambiguous. The film thus tests our moral perceptions, strains our moral imaginations, forcing viewers to deal with ambivalent sympathetic and antipathetic responses – a case of moral cognitive dissonance, we might say – in their ethical and aesthetic evaluation of the stories of Benigno and Alicia, Marco and Lydia, as well as Marco and Benigno. As Carroll notes, '*Talk to Her* is an unsettling film because of the way in which it splits apart the tidy, co-ordinated, negative set of verdicts that we typically issue when condemning an act, its agent, and its consequences' (2009, 8). It forces us to deal with moral ambivalence, emotional ambiguity, and dissonant judgments; it prompts us to re-evaluate our initial responses to Benigno and his relationship with Alicia in light of a deeper understanding acquired through our difficult ethical experience of the film. This is an ethical experience of moral cognitive dissonance in which we are invited to inhabit and explore the perspective of an 'immoral' character who is nonetheless depicted sympathetically; a character whose capacity for moral self-deception renders his actions and motivations profoundly opaque, ambiguous, and confronting.

Indeed, one of the most striking features of *Talk to Her* is the manner in which it elicits emotional engagement and moral allegiance with Benigno, only to complicate this engagement and undermine this allegiance as the narrative unfolds. Our sympathetic engagement with Benigno is challenged once his crime is revealed, yet remains in force while being modified by an understanding of his situation; at the same time, any well-meaning attempts at understanding Benigno sympathetically are coupled with strong antipathetic responses to his deceptive violation of Alicia. This puts the viewer in the difficult ethical position of having to critically reflect on her initial evaluation of his character and actions: acknowledging Benigno's virtuous aspects, along with the complexity of his personal, psychological, and social situation, while at the same time having to reconcile this with the revelation of his rape of Alicia and deluded sense of being the victim of a tragically thwarted, *amour fou* romance. The tension that emerges in the film between verbal storytelling, what we are shown through (interrupted) flashbacks, and what is expressed through non-verbal, visual means, generates a complex, ambivalent range of moral responses (perceptually, emotionally, and intellectually) that demand further critical, indeed philosophical, reflection. Almodóvar's use of aesthetic elements (performance, gesture, colour, music, song, physical expressions of emotion, the allegorical use of film) in conjunction with verbal storytelling (dialogue, flashbacks, narrative exposition) establishes emotional rapport only to destabilize it, forcing us to revise our affective and emotional engagement while attempting to revise and comprehend our conflicted moralethical responses to what we have seen. This complex interplay of emotional engagement (or emotional estrangement) and critical re-evaluation is not just a means of eliciting abstract moral reflection. Rather, it is an experientially rich, aesthetically-mediated form of ethical understanding – one that emphasizes the opacity and ambiguity of moral situations, actions, and motivations, which we are nonetheless required to discern, understand, and critically re-evaluate – achieved through distinctively cinematic means.

***

In the next chapter, I explore this question further – how cinema can evoke an experience of ethical ambiguity or moral dissonance which more conventional forms of moral psychology would struggle to comprehend – by comparing two recent films combining melodrama and social realism (Iñárritu's *Biutiful* and the Dardenne brothers' *The Promise*). These two films, stylistically diverse but thematically close, explore how melodrama and realism might intersect or interact in dealing with difficult ethical problems (the ambivalence of moral choice) as well as social-political themes (illegal immigrants and social exploitation). All of these films I have discussed share a commitment to rendering problematic any unequivocal moral standpoint, engaging but also unsettling the viewer by immersing her in the experience of cognitive dissonance in relation to morally ambiguous situations: an experience of cinematic ethics that not only demands further critical reflection but reveals, through aesthetic experience, the complex worlds in which such confronting forms of moral ambiguity might begin to be understood.

Notes

1 Linda Williams has recently argued that the celebrated television serial *The Wire* can be understood as a case of 'institutional melodrama' (Williams 2014).

2 As Acevedo-Muñoz notes, the Hotel Youkali 'is also the name of a much-desired maternal estate in *Kika*'. The name is taken from a Kurt Weill piece, and 'is supposedly that of a utopian island paradise, but in both *Kika* and *Talk to Her*, it signifies the incestuous anxiety of a disturbed young man'. He also notes that the woman scientist's name, Amparo, 'is also a Spanish word for 'shelter'' (Acevedo-Muñoz 2007, 254).

3 This duality in Benigno's character, however, is arguably less sequential and opposed and more coeval and coexistent than Pippin's characterization would suggest.

4 As D'Lugo notes (2006, 106), Almodóvar modelled Benigno on a psychopathic character from a 1960 Patricia Highsmith novel (*This Sweet Sickness*): 'The protagonist is a man 'so obsessed with his ex-lover that he creates another identity ... through whom he feels able to satisfy his repressed desires and live out his dreams of domestic bliss with the fantasy image' (Wilson, 210)'. This suggests that readings of Benigno's character as a naïve innocent or moral exemplar are misguided (indeed that they have been misled by Benigno's charm).

5 As D'Lugo remarks, 'nonverbal communication between bodies' becomes an important means of expressing narrative meaning in the film and undermines Benigno's advice, 'Talk to her' 'as it suggests that images, especially those related to bodies, are more powerful than words' (2006, 113).

6 We should also note that Benigno, who unlike Marco, does not seem much moved by the dance, is attending such performances (along with silent movies at the *Cinematheque*), because Alicia told him, during their one brief conversation, that these are the two things she enjoys doing the most.

7 Acevedo-Muñoz also notes the allusions to Hitchcock's *Psycho*, comparing Norman Bates's mother to Benigno's mother, who is also 'immobile and in the background, yet no less repressive, no less damaging' (2007, 249).
8 The film appears to allude to Buñuel's *Viridiana* with its fantasy 'of the "raped" Sleeping Beauty mediated via the cinematic image' (Acevedo-Muñoz 2007, 240–241).

Bibliography

Acevedo-Muñoz, Ernesto R. *Pedro Almodóvar*. London: BFI Institute, 2007.

Brooks, Peter. *The Melodramatic Imagination: Balzac, Henry James, Melodrama and the Mode of Excess*. New Haven: Yale University Press, 1976.

Carroll, Noël. 'Talk to Them: An Introduction'. In A.W. Eaton (ed.) *Talk to Her* (Philosophers on Film), 1–10. Abingdon and New York: Routledge, 2009.

Cavell, Stanley. *Contesting Tears: The Hollywood Melodrama of the Unknown Woman*. Chicago: Chicago University Press, 1996.

Cavell, Stanley. *Cities of Words: Pedagogical Letters on a Register of Moral Life*. Cambridge, MA and London: Belknap Press of Harvard University Press, 2004.

del Rio, Elena. *Deleuze and the Cinemas of Performance: Powers of Affection*. Edinburgh: Edinburgh University Press, 2008.

D'Lugo, Marvin. *Pedro Almodóvar (Contemporary Film Directors)*. Urbana and Chicago: University of Illinois Press, 2006.

Eaton, A. W. 'Almodóvar's Immoralism'. In A. W. Eaton (ed.) *Talk to Her* (Philosophers on Film), 11–26. Abingdon and New York: Routledge, 2009.

Elsaesser, Thomas. 'Tales of Sound and Fury: Observations on the Family Melodrama'. In Christine Gledhill (ed.), *Home is Where the Heart Is: Studies in Melodrama and the Woman's Film*, 43–69. London: British Film Institute, 1987 [First published in *Monogram*, 4 (1972): 2–15].

Epps, Bradley S. and Kakoudaki, Despina. *All About Almodóvar: A Passion for Cinema*. Minneapolis: University of Minnesota Press, 2009.

Freeland, Cynthia. 'Nothing is Simple'. In A. W. Eaton (ed.) *Talk to Her* (Philosophers on Film), 69–83. Abingdon and New York: Routledge, 2009.

Gledhill, Christine. 'The Melodramatic Field: An Investigation'. In Christine Gledhill (ed.), *Home Is Where the Heart Is: Studies in Melodrama and the Woman's Film*, 5–39. London: BFI Books, 1987.

Mercer, John and Shingler, Martin. *Melodrama: Genre, Style, Sensibility*. London and New York: Wallflower Books, 2004.

Mulvey, Laura. *Fetishism and Curiosity*. London: BFI Books, 1996.

Nietzsche, Friedrich. *The Birth of Tragedy and The Case of Wagner*. Trans. Walter Kaufmann. New York: Vintage Books, 1967 [1872].

Pippin, Robert B. 'Devils and Angels in Almodovar's Talk to Her'. In A. W. Eaton (ed.), *Talk to Her* (Philosophers on Film), 27–44. Abingdon and New York: Routledge, 2009.

Williams, Linda. '"Something Else Besides a Woman": *Stella Dallas* and the Maternal Melodrama', *Cinema Journal*, 24.1 (Autumn 1984): 2–27.

Williams, Linda. 'Melodrama Revisited'. In Nick Browne (ed.), *Refiguring American Film Genres: History and Theory*, 42–88. Berkeley and Los Angeles: University of California Press, 1998.

Williams, Linda. *On The Wire*. Durham: Duke University Press, 2014.

Wilson, George W. 'Rapport, Rupture, and Rape: Reflections on *Talk to Her*'. In A. W. Eaton (ed.), *Talk to Her* (Philosophers on Film), 45–68. London, Abingdon and New York: Routledge, 2009.

Zarzosa, Augustin. *Refiguring Melodrama in Film and Television: Captive Affects, Elastic Sufferings, Vicarious Objects.* Lanham: Lexington Books, 2013.

Filmography

Adam's Rib. Dir. George Cukor (USA, 1949)
Ali: Fear Eats the Soul. Dir. Rainer Werner Fassbinder (Germany, 1974)
All That Heaven Allows. Dir. Douglas Sirk (USA, 1955)
The Awful Truth. Dir. Leo McCarey (USA, 1937)
The Bitter Tears of Petra von Kant. Dir. Rainer Werner Fassbinder (Germany, 1972)
Black Swan. Dir. Darren Aronofsky (USA, 2010)
Breaking the Waves. Dir. Lars von Trier (Denmark/Sweden/France/Netherlands/Norway/ Iceland/Spain, 1996)
Bringing Up Baby. Dir. Howard Hawks (USA, 1938)
Broken Embraces [*Los abrazos rotos*]. Dir. Pedro Almodóvar (Spain, 2009)
Eternal Sunshine of the Spotless Mind. Dir. Michel Gondry (USA, 2004)
Fight Club. Dir. David Fincher (USA/Germany, 1999)
Gaslight. Dir. George Cukor (USA, 1944)
His Girl Friday. Dir. Howard Hawks (USA, 1940)
It Happened One Night. Dir. Frank Capra (USA, 1934)
Johnny Guitar. Dir. Nicholas Ray (USA, 1954)
The Kingdom [*Riget*]. Dir. Lars von Trier (Denmark/Italy/Germany/France/Norway/ Sweden, 1994)
Kiss Me Deadly. Dir. Robert Aldrich (USA, 1955)
Law of Desire [*La ley del deseo*]. Dir. Pedro Almodóvar (Spain, 1987)
Letter from an Unknown Woman. Dir. Max Ophüls (USA, 1948)
Live Flesh [*Carne trémula*]. Dir. Pedro Almodóvar (Spain/France, 1997)
Mad Men [TV series]. Creator Matthew Weiner (USA, 2007–2015)
Now, Voyager. Dir. Irving Rapper (USA, 1942)
The Philadelphia Story. Dir. Howard Hawks (USA, 1940)
The Sopranos [TV series]. Creator David Chase (USA, 1999–2007)
Stella Dallas. Dir. King Vidor (USA, 1937)
Talk to Her [*Hable con ella*]. Dir. Pedro Almodóvar (Spain, 2002)
The Tree of Life. Dir. Terrence Malick (USA, 2011)
Twin Peaks [TV series]. Creators Mark Frost and David Lynch (USA, 1990–1991)
Viridiana. Dir. Luis Buñuel (Spain/Mexico, 1961)
The Wire [TV series]. Creator David Simon (USA, 2002–2008)

6   Melodrama, realism, and ethical experience (*Biutiful, The Promise*)

[E]thics is an optics.

Emmanuel Levinas (1991 [1961], 23)

This chapter explores cinematic ethics in both melodrama and social realism, suggesting that both genres can intersect, drawing elements from each for emotional, aesthetic, and ethical effect. Continuing the discussion of melodrama from the previous chapter, but extending it to explore its relationship with realism, I consider a recent moral-existential melodrama, Alejandro Iñárritu's *Biutiful* (2010), which includes elements of social realism inflected through a melodramatic perspective so as to articulate cinematically the clashing social and spiritual forces confronting a struggling family in the underclass of Barcelona. I then compare this with a case study by celebrated Belgian filmmaking duo, Jean-Pierre and Luc Dardenne, whose films have been acclaimed as social realist dramas with a strongly ethical orientation. Contrasting *Biutiful* with *The Promise* provides an illuminating way of bringing out the complementarities and conflicts between melodrama and social realism in the case of two films with similar narrative scenarios and thematic ethical concerns. At the same time, it will allow us to explore how generically distinct films can evoke emotional engagement and critical reflection by different aesthetic means in order to elicit distinctive kinds of ethical experience for the viewer. Like *Talk to Her*, both films, moreover, refuse to offer an unequivocal moral standpoint from which viewers would be tempted to 'judge' the characters or situations presented via the narrative. Rather, all three films render problematic this impulse to moralizing judgment, showing how the ostensibly moral (and immoral) actions of characters are embedded in a world that must be understood in its contradictory complexity in order to be able to evaluate more thoughtfully the events and actions depicted onscreen. The experience of ethical ambiguity here again invites, or even demands, further critical, philosophical reflection in order to work through the experience of moral uncertainty, suspension of judgment, or moral cognitive dissonance that such films can evoke. In this sense, these are powerful examples of films engaging in cinematic ethics that challenge, question, or render problematic some of our habitual attitudes, routine responses, and rigidified beliefs concerning poverty, morality, exploitation, and injustice.

Cinematic ethics as aesthetic understanding

As suggested throughout this book, the distinctive rhetorical power of cinema lies in its capacity to elicit affective and emotional forms of engagement that underlie our more reflective forms of moral judgment. Despite philosophers' traditional insistence on the dominance of reason over the passions, many theorists have argued that moral experience is as much affectively motivated and emotionally guided as it is intellectually tested and rationally grounded (Damasio 1994, De Sousa 2001, Nussbaum 2001). The enlightenment insistence on the intellectual and moral superiority of universal reason over the 'irrational' passions and emotions has been challenged by recent theoretical work in cognitive psychology and moral theory (Haidt 2001, Prinz 2009, 2004). Cognitive psychology as well as phenomenology and theories of embodiment argue that our cognitive engagement with the world spans the spectrum from affect, perception, and emotion to conceptual reflection and higher-order reasoning (Grodal 2009, Laine 2011, Plantinga 2009, Plantinga and Smith 1999, Prinz 2009, Robinson 2007, Stadler 2008). Our capacity for impartial rational judgment is less robust than we think; our propensity towards cognitive bias more pervasive than we assume. In ordinary moral experience, affective and emotional responses provide the experiential basis for our more reflective and conceptual normative judgments. Even the 'giving of reasons' so cherished by philosophers often appears as a specialized skill in justifying our unreflective convictions, a post-hoc rationalization supporting what may be our more emotionally-grounded moral appraisals. Hume's *aperçu*, in this respect, still rings true: 'Reason is, and ought only to be the slave of the passions' (1975 [1738], 415).

As I remarked previously, the recent theoretical focus on affective and emotional engagement has profound implications for cinema, from rethinking theories of spectatorship, analysing the workings of genre, to exploring the question of ethics. As Amy Coplan argues, phenomena such as 'emotional contagion' (the involuntary affective and emotional mimicry elicited in response to the perceived expressions, gestures, and actions of others) are particularly powerful in the cinema compared with the other arts (Coplan 2006). Compared with other art forms such as literature or theatre, this is one feature of cinema, and of cinematic experience, that appears distinctive: its power to elicit and direct, through visual, perceptive, and aesthetic means, powerful forms of affective engagement and emotional responsiveness. This observation is of great importance for thinking about morality and ethics in film. If moral judgment is grounded in affective and emotional responsiveness (what Jesse Prinz 2004 calls 'gut feelings'), with reflective judgment serving to clarify, organize, and rationalize our more emotively grounded appraisals (see Haidt 2001), then cinema's power to engage us affectively, emotionally, and reflectively at once means that it has a powerful ethical potential to move viewers towards distinctive patterns of moral allegiance.

Of course, it is also true that this potential for emotionally-driven persuasion can be used for the purposes of manipulation, mystification, or propaganda, as much film theory of the last century theorized at length. Challenging the manipulative character of the medium via aesthetic strategies of interruption, distantiation, critical self-reflexivity, and active spectatorship was thus at the core of the project of 'political modernism' in film theory and cinematic practice (see Rodowick 1994). Although this is one of the ways in which film can be used, it does not follow that cinema is an inherently manipulative or pernicious medium. On the contrary, it means that the question of the ethical use of the medium becomes more pressing and thus deserves further critical attention. For cinema has an exceptional and distinctive capacity for eliciting affective response and emotional engagement by aesthetic means; and the manner in which a film engages us within a fictional world – how that world is presented aesthetically and what its ontological features are – also carries moral-ethical significance, especially when we are dealing with conflictual experiences of, and ambiguous responses to, that world.

Biutiful

The cinema of Alejandro González Iñárritu is particularly apt for exploring this kind of ethical understanding, for his films elicit forms of affective and emotional engagement that often conflict with more 'rationalistic' moralizing judgments. Such films exercise our moral perception and ethical imagination, offering an 'aesthetic education' towards more perceptive, singular, and emotionally nuanced forms of moral receptivity (Schiller 2004 [1794]). At the same time, they disclose fictional worlds in which the failings and foibles of ethically imperfect characters in morally ambiguous situations serve to reveal the complex social and economic conditions that both motivate and undermine their social and moral agency. Films like *Amores Perros* and *21 Grams*, along with Iñárritu's better-known films *Babel* and *Biutiful*, are arresting examples of moral melodrama that elicit forms of emotional engagement to open up a space for moral questioning and critical reflection. While both *Babel* and *Biutiful* are expressions of the melodramatic mode, they differ in narrative style, the one being a complex network narrative, and the other a religiously-inflected character drama. Both narrative forms open up distinctive forms of ethical experience, albeit with different rhythms, emotional dynamics, and aesthetic intensities. The frenetic rhythms, dispersed engagement, coalescing events, and clashing storylines of the network narrative stand in marked contrast with the more focused narrative development, social realism, affective intensity, and dramatic continuity of the character-driven melodrama. Yet both films use melodrama, with its power of engaging viewers emotionally, as a way of evoking ethical experience: not by offering a didactic moral lesson but by revealing the alterity of a character's experience, opening up a space of imaginative engagement for the exploration of moral ambiguity and the experience of ethical dissonance. Both *Babel* and *Biutiful* thereby disclose, via cinematic means, the complexity of a conflictual world or milieu in ways that elicit sympathetic understanding, but also starkly expose, and thereby implicitly question, the characters' alienating conditions of social existence.

Biutiful *as Allegory*

A man dying of cancer assists his brother in brokering a deal with a Spanish construction company who want to hire illegal Chinese workers. Disturbed at the exploitative conditions they have to endure, the man purchases some cheap gas heaters to keep them warm at night as they sleep, under lock and key, in a warehouse basement. One morning the warehouse owner unlocks the door, as he does every morning, and finds all of the workers, including some of their children, dead from asphyxiation. The warehouse owners panic, wondering what to do with the bodies; later, one of the owners kills his business partner (and lover) and escapes, seemingly without punishment. The dying man who purchased the heaters is distraught, feels guilty for their deaths, although he does not go to the police. He experiences guilt, remorse, and remains haunted by the spirits of the dead, turning to his spiritual confidante for advice. He asks those who have died for their forgiveness, as he prepares himself and his broken family – his unstable, bipolar wife, his daughter and young son – for his own looming death from cancer. In death he is reunited with his own father, who died as a much younger man, fleeing from Franco's Spain to Mexico.

This scenario is taken from *Biutiful* (2010), a film by Mexican director Iñárritu, renowned for his engagement with the moral and political complexities of everyday life in multicultural societies. His films *Babel* (2006) and *Biutiful* present contrasting narratives that make explicit the challenges confronting marginalized subjects in a globalized world marked by pervasive social, religious, economic, and political conflicts. In this section, I explore Iñárritu's *Biutiful* as a moral melodrama that offers a case study in cinematic ethics: a film that uses elements of melodrama and realism in order to render the abstract forces of globalization through the story of a dying man's attempts to reconcile faith, family, and survival in the impoverished underclass of Barcelona. It is a film aiming to evoke a transformative ethical experience that resonates with the contemporary 'postsecular' turn in contemporary culture (see Sinnerbrink 2014).

In many ways, *Biutiful* is a retelling of Kurosawa's existential classic *Ikiru* [*To Live*] (1952), the moving story of an unremarkable civil servant dying of cancer who finds renewed existential meaning in life as he approaches death (see Cox and Levine 2011). Iñárritu, however, transposes Kurosawa's story of redemption through accepting mortality to the gritty underworld of social marginals struggling for survival in contemporary Barcelona. Kurosawa's civil servant is transformed into a lone father and marginalized street hustler; Kanji Watanabe's [Takashi Shimura] redemptive task of securing a children's playground is replaced by the dying Uxbal's [Javier Bardem] provisions to ensure his children have a chance at a meaningful future. Both characters, Watanabe and Uxbal, are forced to reckon with mortality, with their personal failures and disappointments; both undergo an experience of despair culminating in a sleazy nightclub with only alcohol and drugs to dull the pain of their dwindling existence. *Biutiful*, however, does not confine this existential drama to a lifeless bourgeois existence but transfers it to the socially marginalized underworld of a major European city.

Given its realism and poeticism, it is tempting to approach *Biutiful* as allegorical: as reflecting a Spain or Europe in a condition of (moral-spiritual) distress, or as suffering from a pervasive nihilism. From this perspective, *Biutiful* is a post-secular fable with moral-religious overtones responding to the aporias of globalization, a film that acts out the 'post-traumatic' effects of historical and political oppression (the references, for example, to Uxbal's father fleeing Franco's Spain for Mexico). Far from an ideological regression to mystificatory religiosity, it can be understood as exploring both the moral-spiritual and economic-social underworld of liberal democratic society (see Sinnerbrink 2014). An alternative, more critical reading would emphasize the film's competing impulses towards social realism and metaphysical spiritualism. Indeed, one could imagine an alternative version of the film rendered in a more 'realist' manner, exposing the interconnection between economic exploitation, social marginalization, and religion as an ambiguous source of hope. On this more 'secular' view, the main character's religiosity might well be portrayed as an expression of alienated self-consciousness, a mystification of the social and economic forces deciding his fate. The tragedy of Uxbal's precarious social existence would thereby serve as an allegory of the injustice pervading the larger social order. Such a realist-secularist approach would show the film as belonging to the tradition of critical exposés of class exploitation and bourgeois hypocrisy, demonstrating the social contradictions that become manifest in the alienation and despair afflicting characters all but crushed by oppressive social and economic circumstances.

These approaches, however, cannot be readily sustained in the case of *Biutiful*, for it is a film that refuses to present a harsh or disenchanted view of Uxbal's difficult world. It eschews depicting him and his family as alienated or passive victims of an unjust social and economic order. It confounds the demand for a purity of social realism, however stylized (compare the Dardenne brothers' work), with a spiritualist dimension that co-exists with social marginalization and economic struggle. Instead, *Biutiful* insists on humanizing Uxbal and his experience of social reality, however contradictory this may appear: it provokes moral sympathy for a character who participates in exploitative practices that lead to the death of many innocent people; it puts the spiritual and secular domains of experience on the same immanent plane as the social struggle for survival, and so on.

At the same time, it insists on the need to entertain a transcendent dimension if we are to acknowledge Uxbal's world, which is shaped by social struggle but also by religious faith. Indeed, the film's narrative is focalized by Uxbal's journey in preparing for death, chronicling the diminution of his vitality, the deterioration of his body, contrasted with his growing clarity of his vision and purpose as he approaches death.[1] It finds beauty in squalor, morality among the asocial, epiphany among the exploited. Tales of existential struggle and spiritual crises are usually reserved for 'bourgeois' characters of middle-class provenance (Tolstoy's 'The Death of Ivan Ilych', for example, or Kurosawa's *Ikiru*). *Biutiful*, however, finds its subject in the social underclass, whose own struggles, Iñárritu suggests, can be as tragic, moving, and dignified as those of anyone else. Critics might take this as ideological mystification; a reversion to religiosity that covers over the brutal reality of exploitation. Yet it is better taken as an argument to reconsider a purely secular understanding of globalization and the everyday struggles it engenders. For these remain abstract, lacking particularity, unless we can give sympathetic expression to the experiential perspective of the socially marginalized, which is precisely what *Biutiful*, as an ethically-engaged fiction, attempts to do.

It is for these reasons that I take *Biutiful* as a moral-existential melodrama that reveals the dignity of a compromised character undergoing a spiritual-social struggle in confronting death. It integrates a personalist-humanist perspective, acknowledging the religious or spiritual dimension of Uxbal's world, while maintaining a critical, broadly political perspective on the experience of social suffering generated by global capitalism. A purely 'moral' interpretation of the film, on the one hand, misses the social and economic background that conditions Uxbal's tragic story; a purely 'political' reading, on the other, misses the transcendent dimension of religiosity and belief that is essential to understanding his actions. It is this combination of moral-spiritual *and* political perspectives, I suggest, that makes *Biutiful* an instance of cinematic ethics: a poetic exploration of moral redemption compromised by the everyday struggles of a family caught within the social and economic vortices of a globalized world.

Magic social realism

We might call this combination of melodramatic, subjective, and realist elements a 'magic social realism'. The underworld of Barcelona, with its impoverished immigrants, its criminality and corruption, is rendered in sharp and gritty detail, using hand-held camera, natural light, and a grim urban colour palette (predominantly greys, blues, dull greens and browns). At the same time, Uxbal's perspective on this world, coloured by the knowledge that he is dying of cancer, is expressed lyrically and poetically. The film's opening scenes, for example, which return at the end of the film, are shot from Uxbal's perspective, with objects, spaces, and hands rendered in attentive close-up under muted light. The opening sequence of images accompanies what we later realize is Uxbal's final conversation with his daughter. He tells her the story of the ring given to him by his mother, which was given to her by his father before he fled from Spain as a young man, and then he drifts off, reminiscing about the radio programme he used to hear as a child, with its soothing sounds of wind and waves. As he slips peacefully into death, he finds himself in a winter forest deep in snow, where he sees a dead owl and meets a guarded young man, sharing with him a cigarette. The light is bright, the images sharp and crisp, the soundtrack now clear and spare. Snatches of conversation appear, which we will hear later in the film, the soundtrack of the radio program he heard as a child, phrases from his childhood, and a comforting silence, broken only by the muffled sound of boots in snow. All is illuminated; the images bright and luminous. The sequence concludes with the young man moving out of frame, Uxbal, after a moment, looking off-screen and asking, 'What's over there?' – cut to black.

This opening 'prelude' sets a mood of melancholy intimacy and existential reverie, slipping between the final moments of Uxbal's life and his death, between this world and another. It frames the movie as a study in mortality, opening and ending with death. Indeed, the entire film is an expression of Uxbal's life and death, animated by his mortality as immanent limit and unfathomable ground. The privileged perspective on the film's world, however, is a finite one, belonging to a dying man who does not yet fully accept, or exist authentically within, the temporal certainty of his own death. His vision encompasses both the living and the dead, yet he finds this vision hard to turn upon his own finite existence. It is only towards the end of his life that he accepts his mortality, which means the life that he has lived, such as it is (or was). The temporal horizon of the film is that limit between life and death ordinarily covered over in what Heidegger calls our everyday 'being-in-the-world': the absorbed busy-ness that propels us along the inexorable temporal track of our being-towards-death (Heidegger 2010 [1927]). Expressed differently, Uxbal's story takes place between two deaths: the death that was always within him as the finite ground of his existence, and the death to come that is only his own, his bodily demise. This is the death no one else can take over for him, and which gives the remainder of his life meaning and purpose. The entire film circles or cycles, radiates and returns, from this moment: the moment that gives significance to every moment he has lived. It is a meaning and purpose – of death in life and life in death – that had always been there, but which he had ignored, or recoiled from, as we all do.

Unlike an atheistic work of art, however, *Biutiful* does not shy away from the related question of faith, whether in God, in existence, or in the soul. It acknowledges Uxbal's spiritual experiences as pointing to a transcendent dimension that is immanent to his mundane existence. It finds ways to acknowledge the infinitude at the heart of our finitude, the co-existence of transcendent and immanent perspectives on the world. When Uxbal has visions of the dead, we bear witness as well; yet this is not simply a matter of subjective alignment with his point of view. In one sequence, for example, we glimpse a dead man in a mirror, a figure that Uxbal does not notice, thus underlining that the presence of the dead is a feature of this world, rather than of Uxbal's subjective perception, though his vision is not shared by others. One could call it a form of religious experience, or an existential awareness of mortality that is desirous of transcendence. Whatever we call it, the film develops its portrayal of Uxbal from the perspective of a radical finitude (his tangible mortality) that is mediated by a transcendent dimension (his communication with the dead) co-existing on the same plane as his mundane struggle for existence. This is one of the film's most daring moral propositions: to show everyday reality, with its social deprivation, its corruption and brutality, as enchanted by faith, limned by beauty, animated by belief.

For all the film's lyricism, however, *Biutiful* also retains an element of social realism. Uxbal and his family – his bipolar wife Marambra [Maricel Álvarez] their children Ana [Hanaa Bouchaib] and Mateo [Guillermo Estrella], and his brother, Tito [Eduard Fernández] – are embedded within the socio-economic underworld of Barcelona. Everyday life, for all its struggle and squalor, is also luminous and beautiful. Uxbal's world is portrayed as a social and spiritual reality that retains its share of pathos, tragedy, and dignity: it is social realism with a Levinasian face; moral melodrama in a lyrical, spiritual key.[2] Much like Deleuze and Guattari's 'minor literature' (1986), Iñárritu's 'minor cinema' takes a personal story of everyday suffering in a disenfranchised social milieu and uses these elements to disclose indirectly the dynamic social whole in which this story is embedded. These interconnecting forces are reflected in the melancholy melodrama of the dying man, his Stoic struggle to ensure a future for his children with the help of a Senegalese woman whose husband has been deported.

Biutiful *as post-secularist work*

Like a number of recent films that treat religious and spiritual themes, *Biutiful* received a mixed response from critics, in some cases bordering on the hostile.[3] What caused critical offence, I suggest, was less to do with the film's dramatic or aesthetic qualities than its undertone of spiritual transcendence: the metaphysical or supernaturalist dimensions that are rendered as realistically as the social drama with its global resonances.[4] *Biutiful* presents a world that shows morally ambiguous characters in a sympathetic light, along with religious or 'metaphysical' motifs – Uxbal's psychic ability to communicate with the dead, his afterlife encounter with a younger version of his father – presented on the same level as, indeed interwoven with, the realist depictions of everyday life in Barcelona's underclass.

This transgression of aesthetic and moral expectations has provoked various critics. One reaction to the film was to praise its cinematic accomplishments, notably Bardem's brilliant performance as Uxbal, while criticizing it for failing in its moral mission. Peter Bradshaw (2011), for example, complains that the film does not insist on a secular or legal remedy, but allows 'metaphysical' justice to take the place of police and the courts, representatives of the very institutions of power that the characters try to evade in their daily struggles. The critic adopts here the perspective of the law, morality, and the state: passing judgment on the moral culpability of the protagonist, and criticizing the film for failing to hold these marginal characters to account. Precisely this 'moralizing' perspective, however, is what the film challenges, questioning our blindness to the social and economic forces that constrain Uxbal's moral agency and hinder his capacity for social responsibility.

It is clear that for Bradshaw, as for other critics, the film fails to create moral 'allegiance' (Smith 1995) for Uxbal as a compromised character. What this approach misses, however, is that morally approving or disapproving the characters may not be as important as ethical acknowledgement of their experiential perspective – even if this means inhabiting a discomfiting, morally ambiguous point of view – leading to a deeper ethical understanding of how the exercise of moral agency might be undermined by the conflicting demands of their social situation. *Biutiful* prompts us to question the limits of morality in a state of scarcity, drawing attention to the complex social conditions required for moral autonomy (or legal justice) to flourish. 'Never trust a hungry man,' warns one of the characters in the film, a motto for what *Biutiful* sets out to dramatize through its depiction of Uxbal's world.

Instead of judging morally flawed characters (depicting them unsympathetically), their failures of judgment are presented as reflective of a complex social, economic, and political situation. This is one of the key features of the cinematic ethics at play in *Biutiful*: inviting the viewer to suspend temporarily the impulse towards 'moralizing' judgment, and exposing them to a discomfiting experience of moral dissonance or ambivalence, in order to open up a deeper understanding of the character's conduct in light of their particular social situation. This ambiguous ethical experience involves adopting a perspective that locates the moral-ethical wrong not just at the level of individual action, but in the characters' social reality and conditions of existence. The tragic deaths of the Chinese workers, for example, and Uxbal's moral-spiritual crisis in response, can be properly understood only in relation to the social and economic forces of globalization: 'invisible' suprapersonal forces that appear as 'irrational' fates afflicting individual characters in situations they can neither grasp nor control. To condemn the film for failing to satisfy secular morality and legal justice is to misunderstand the complex dialectical relationship between the characters' (limited) moral agency and the (complex) social forces constraining their exercise of moral agency.

The deeper ambiguity in the film, however, is that it both invites and undermines this kind of 'moralizing' judgment: it provokes the viewer to inhabit a morally ambivalent perspective, presents it sympathetically as shaped by the character's social reality, but at the same time invites further critical reflection in order to comprehend the ethical meaning of what we have seen. Who, or

Figure 6.1 Still from *Biutiful*, Dir. Alejandro González Iñárritu (2010)

what, for example, is responsible for the deaths of the Chinese workers tragically killed by the faulty gas heaters? Uxbal, who helped broker the deal – under pressure from his unscrupulous brother – to bring the Chinese onto a building site as illegal workers? Uxbal again, who bought the cheap gas heaters because he was disturbed by how the poor workers were being exploited? The Chinese factory owner Hai and his partner, who not only exploited the workers' labour but locked them (and their families) every night in the factory basement? Or the Spanish construction company manager 'Mendoza', who employed the illegal workers in order to circumvent the wages and conditions required for unionized Spanish workers? And let us not forget the well-heeled citizens and tourists who will buy and rent the attractive apartments built using such exploitative labour. Ultimately, the film suggests that it is the 'invisible' dynamics of the global economic system – within which all the characters in this harsh social and economic milieu are embedded – that lay behind the Chinese workers being imprisoned every night in the factory and thus ultimately led to their tragic deaths.

These intersecting lines of moral responsibility, economic exploitation, and social dependency profoundly shape Uxbal's fitful attempts at moral redemption. Insisting that Uxbal should have confessed to the police betrays the central moral argument of the film: that we cannot understand, let alone judge, the lives and actions of those existing within the social underclass in our midst unless we strive to imagine their experience and thus understand their situation, but also recognize our own involvement and complicity in the very system that exploits them. In depicting these harrowing deaths so vividly, as well as Uxbal's tragic role in what happens, *Biutiful* prompts us to reflect on the deeper systemic forces that shaped his fateful decision. This is an ethical experience inviting the viewer to reframe their emotional response so as to encompass the social, economic, and political realities in which the depicted characters vie for survival. Such ethical engagement thwarts the 'moralizing' judgment that would condemn Uxbal as 'immoral' while sparing the global system in which he and his family are caught. *Biutiful* thus attempts to evoke, through aesthetic means, a sense of ethical acknowledgement of the social suffering faced by the exploited, and of the dignity of those who struggle to find hope and meaning in the margins of our affluent but nihilistic consumer societies.

Ethical social realism: *The Promise* [*La promesse*]

A contrast between *Biutiful* and Jean-Pierre and Luc Dardenne's *The Promise* [*La promesse*] (1996) would be instructive at this point. This will allow us to examine how cinematic ethics might be explored in different genres while highlighting the differences between moral melodrama and social realism as alternative ways of exploring ethical experience through film. Whereas *Talk to Her* avoids social realism in favour of melodrama, *Biutiful* combines melodrama with elements of social realism (what I was calling 'magic social realism'). *The Promise*, by contrast, is a realist social drama, also portraying the social underworld of a contemporary European city (the Seraing/Liège region of French-speaking Wallonia in Belgium). Like *Biutiful*, it focuses on the struggles of socially marginalized characters (illegal immigrants and those who exploit them) and the morally compromising decisions they are forced to make given their difficult social, economic, and legal circumstances. All three films respond to ethical problems but do so by cinematic means, moving between melodrama and social realism to explore complex social situations generating a variety of moral (and amoral) responses that in turn pose questions about our understanding of social and moral agency as well as the compelling and constraining background forces of society, economics, and politics. At the same time, they elicit both emotional engagement and critical reflection, moving the viewer into a sympathetic understanding of the characters' perspectives while inviting critical reflection on the circumstances they confront within their social and cultural life-worlds. In a word, they invoke varieties of ethical experience via cinematic means.

The Dardenne brothers are among the most respected ethically- and politically-oriented filmmakers in the world today.[5] Coming from a background in documentary filmmaking, the Dardennes began making narrative films during the 1980s, and achieved critical success with their breakthrough film, *The Promise* (1996), followed by a series of highly acclaimed social realist dramas: *Rosetta* (1999), *The Son* [*Le fils*] (2002), *The Child* [*L'enfant*] (2005), *The Silence of Lorna* [*Le silence de Lorna*] (2008), *The Kid with a Bike* [*Le gamin au vélo*] (2011), and, most recently, *Two Days, One Night* [*Deux jours, une nuit*] (2014). Set in the economically-depressed, post-industrial town of Seraing (not far from Liège), *The Promise* focuses on the relationship between a father, Roger [Olivier Gourmet] and teenage son, Igor [Jérémie Renier]. There are, interestingly, a number of parallels here between *Biutiful* and *The Promise*: both films deal with the plight of socially marginalized characters and illegal immigrants living a precarious social existence in a major European city; both involve tragic deaths related to the exploitative work practices and conditions suffered by illegal immigrant workers; both centre on individuals confronting an unexpected situation involving a dying parent, promising the dying parent to look after their children after they are gone (Igor promising Amidou to look after his wife and child in the case of *The Promise,* and Ige promising Uxbal to look after his children in the case of *Biutiful*). Both films also use a familial story, emotional engagement, and aesthetic stylization to invoke an ethical experience of sympathetic understanding that prompts further ethico-political reflection. Where they differ most is in their cinematic and dramatic treatment of these comparable scenarios, and the degree to which they elicit emotional engagement and spectator 'identification'. On the one hand, this is in part due to their different genres and stylistic approaches (melodrama and social realism); on the other, it reflects different philosophical or ethical conceptions of how to treat their subjects and ethical subject-matter. Nonetheless, despite these differences, they can also be regarded as 'hybrid' forms of realism, *Biutiful* being a moral melodrama that draws on social realism, and *The Promise* a social realist drama drawing on melodrama as well as documentary.

The dramatic scenarios of *Biutiful* and *The Promise* both share a central concern with the plight of illegal immigrants. Like Uxbal in *Biutiful*, Roger, the overbearing (rather than sympathetic) father figure in *The Promise*, is involved in employing illegal immigrant workers in local building projects. Assisted by Igor, he organizes their travel, accommodation, and serves as their work manager and slum landlord. When immigration officials arrive for an inspection, the workers all scatter except for one, Amidou [Rasmane Ouedrago]. As he hastens to escape, Amidou falls off his scaffold and is seriously injured. Igor rushes to his aid, and seeing that he is dying, promises Amidou that he will look after Amidou's wife and child. When Roger arrives, Igor insists that Amidou must go to hospital, but his father decides this is too risky and refuses to help. Roger's decision to let Amidou die – removing a makeshift tourniquet Igor has fashioned, leaving the dying man hidden under a door and rubble, and lying to Amidou's wife Assita [Assita Ouedrago] – triggers a profound questioning in Igor, who until this point has reluctantly obeyed his father and helped him in his exploitative activities. As Assita continues to harbour suspicions over her husband's whereabouts, refusing offers to return her to her homeland, Roger conceives a plot to rid himself of the troubling tenant who makes it clear she will go to the police if foul play is involved in her husband's disappearance. Faced with a moral choice between helping his father lure Assita into what appears to be sexual slavery in Germany, Igor decides, impulsively, to escape with Assita and help her find safety with relatives in Italy. In a final confrontation with his father, Igor literally chains him up (turning the tables by 'enslaving' his overbearing father), fleeing again with Assita, their escape marking a definitive break with his father's authority as well as with the life of social exploitation in which Igor has been mired.[6] In a moment of moral reckoning, he confesses the truth to Assita that her husband has died; this revelation moves her to abandon her plans for escape, and return, crushed, to her life in the Belgian city. Once more on an impulse, Igor rushes to her side, again confirming his fidelity, honouring his promise to Amidou to stay with Assita and her child. The film concludes with a long, static shot of the unlikely couple, walking together away from our view, their future together open but uncertain.

A number of commentators have noted the moral-ethical dimensions of this film, citing co-director Luc Dardennes' comment that the film is an attempt to stage Levinas's 'face-to-face' encounter through cinema (Mosley 2012, 78). As Sarah Cooper notes, 'Luc Dardenne's diary *Au dos de nos images* (2005) documents their filmmaking from 1991 to 2005, and is interspersed with brief but erudite references to Levinas's work,' suggesting that Levinas remains 'a signal point of inspiration and ethical aspiration for their filmmaking' (2007, 66). For Cooper, the Dardenne Brothers' attempts to unsettle conventional film is bound up with their commitment to a Levinasian ethics emphasizing our responsibility to the Other (not just the other person but that transcendent dimension of 'alterity' – of infinite singularity or non-totalisable otherness – that cannot be reduced to what I know, represent, or comprehend about the Other, but towards which I have an absolute ethical responsibility) (see Levinas 1991, 194–219). This Levinasian inspiration is evident in the Dardennes' focus on the fundamental ethical question explored in their work: that of murder, whether to kill or not to kill another human being, posed as an ethical or metaphysical rather than a moral or psychological question. Indeed, this question lies at the heart of the 'mortal ethics' shaping their work, a cinematic attempt to see if art 'can institute the impossibility of killing the other crucial to Levinas's ethics' (Cooper 2007a, 67).

This task is pursued, moreover, by way of cinematic form: the Dardennes' remarkable exploration of a sensuous and affective 'proximity' to physically expressive characters without relying on a psychologically grounded sense of sympathetic or empathic involvement (see Cooper 2007a, Rushton 2014).[7] It is through the use of close-ups that eschew the face in favour of other parts of the body (the back, neck, and shoulders), coupled with a fragmentation of space that conceals the immediate environment but foregrounds the characters' gestures and actions, that an ethically significant proximity is afforded to the viewer which thwarts or blocks more conventional cinematic identification (Cooper 2007a, Dillet and Puri 2013).[8] Setting all of their films in the post-industrial region of Seraing, the Dardennes bring a strongly humanistic perspective to their filmmaking, emphasizing the socio-historical materiality of the characters' surroundings. They also give careful attention to the importance of things, material objects, and idiosyncratic inventions (in *The Promise*, for example, the ring given to Igor by his father, Igor's motor-scooter, and the go-kart he cobbles together with his friends) as expressions of a way of life as well as manifestations of an individual's singular existence.

As Cooper remarks (2007a, 67), drawing on the Dardennes' diary, the filmmakers attempt to use cinema as a way 'to look at what it means to be human today, not in general or abstract terms, but in the concrete and extreme situations constructed by a particular society (Dardenne 2005, 110)'. This practice is in keeping with their view of cinema's vocation as 'capturing the human gaze' (Cooper 2007a, 67), not in the abstract but in the ethical sense of revealing aspects of individuals' lives that would otherwise remain obscure or unintelligible. This task of capturing the human gaze, however, is ambiguous, encompassing both the murderous impulse at the heart of many of their stories, and the prohibition on murder that marks a fundamental ethical limit broached in their films. At the same time, and adhering to Levinas' scepticism towards the image – as potentially concealing, rather than revealing, the ethical alterity at the heart of each human being – their films need to find ways to show this alterity *indirectly* without reducing it to a generic representation or generalized abstraction, both of which would do 'violence' to this singular, transcendent dimension of the Other. Their films, in short, seek to render the relation between material and immaterial spheres of existence, but in a manner that invites an ethically-grounded rethinking of our received conceptions of mind and body (Cooper 2007a, 68).

This task becomes most acute in the case of filming the human face, the locus *par excellence* of emotion and feeling, yet where the ethical imperative not to kill becomes most demanding. The face-to-face encounter, through which I am exposed to the 'alterity' of the Other – that transcendent, infinite dimension of his or her existence that overflows my capacity to know or represent this singular individual – becomes ambiguous in the case of cinema, with its potential to evoke a sense of this transcendent encounter (via indirect means) but also to obscure, conceal, or distort it (via the 'psychologisation' of feeling and emotion). According to this Levinasian perspective, the challenge for cinema is to find a way to evoke indirectly this face-to-face encounter; a moment of ethical transcendence in which what is conveyed on screen overflows the narrative framework or the explicit representational content of the image. It is this moment of ethical transcendence, a transcendent experience of ethical responsibility towards the Other, that the Dardenne brothers seek to reveal, via indirect poetic means, in their cinematic work.

Although the 'Levinasian' approach to thinking through film and ethics has proven influential, especially with regard to the Dardennes, this position nonetheless faces certain difficulties. The first is how to deal with Levinas's own scepticism towards art and aesthetic experience, notably concerning the image. As Tanja Staehler notes, Levinas criticizes art in a number of his works, such as *Totality and Infinity* (1991 [1961]) and in his essay, 'Reality and its Shadow' (from 1948). In Levinas' words, art

> brings into the world the obscurity of fate, but it especially brings the irresponsibility that charms as lightness and as grace. It frees. To make or to appreciate a novel and a picture is to no longer to have to conceive, is to renounce the effort of science, philosophy and action. Do not speak, do not reflect, admire in silence and in peace – such are the counsels of wisdom satisfied before the beautiful. Magic recognized everywhere as the devil's, enjoys an incomprehensible tolerance in poetry.
>
> (Levinas 1989, 141)

To be sure, this strikingly Platonic dismissal of art as an enchanting, pleasurable distraction from reflection and action, as a seductive illusion cultivating moral irresponsibility, is tempered in Levinas's later thought, where poetry – at least in some cases – is valorized as contributing to our sense of ethical responsibility towards the alterity of the Other. Nonetheless, in this essay at least, Levinas criticizes art as lacking 'the immediacy of the ethical encounter with the Other': the sensuous character of art 'diverts us from our ethical responsibility, and by way of its multiple meanings and layers it provides a possibility for evasion' (Staehler 2010, 124). On the other hand, one can also find essays in his collection *Proper Names* (1996) where Levinas turns to certain kinds of literature (the poetry of Celan and the novels of Proust) to suggest a proximity to his own thought; in the case of visual art, as Staehler observes, 'Levinas singles out two artists, the abstract painter Jean Atlan and the sculptor Sacha Sosno, whom he takes to be part of an endeavour akin to his ethical philosophy' (2010, 124). From this perspective, it is through the possibility of an indirect evocation of what ordinarily remains 'invisible', unacknowledged or unknowable – the materiality of things but above all the alterity of individual human beings – that visual art might be regarded as ethical in this distinctively 'Levinasian' sense.

This ambiguity of art, as opening up our ethical experience of alterity but also as distracting us from it, remains a pressing question in philosophical explorations of Levinas and film (see Cooper 2006, Saxton 2008).[9] Indeed, there are passages where Levinas cites the cinema (the use of the close-up) as having the capacity to reveal the materiality of things outside of their context of instrumental use (see Schmiedgen 2002, 152).[10] And there are others where Levinas uses the dramatic and cinematic term *mise en scène* to describe the phenomenological method as well as how consciousness organizes its experience (see Girgus 2007, 90–91). In any event, as a number of critics have argued (Bruns 1996; Critchley 1997, 35–97; Hart 2005; Hart 1997), Levinas' later emphasis on the link between poetry and ethics, that is, how the poetic 'saying of language' – which refers to the expressive dimension of poetic disclosure rather than the representational content of linguistic utterances – can evoke an experience of alterity, suggests that a Levinasian approach to cinematic ethics should concern itself with the poetic potential of moving images.

The second issue arising for the Levinasian approach to the Dardenne brothers is how to reconcile this 'transcendent' ethical dimension with their political commitment to social injustice and the destruction of working-class solidarity following the economic collapse of urban industrial centres (such as Seraing). Ever since their early documentary films, the Dardenne brothers have maintained an ongoing political concern with the social impact of economic degradation on marginalized communities and alienated individuals. Their trajectory as filmmakers – from their documentaries to their social realist films – reflects an ongoing commitment to questions of social justice and exploring ethical resistance as a response to the collapse of socialist politics. This socio-political aspect, which does not sit comfortably with the individualist, transcendent, metaphysical tenor of Levinasian ethics, remains an essential feature of the Dardenne brothers' work (as is evident in *Two Days, One Night* (2014), their remarkable study of precarity in contemporary work and its impact on individuals and communities).

Critics, however, tend to foreground either the Levinasian ethical concern with moral responsibility (the cinematic quest for the face-to-face encounter with the Other) (Cooper, Saxton, and Girgus, for example), or else underline the Dardennes' post-Marxist concern with the effects of social and economic marginalization on the forgotten 'underclass' of post-industrial urban cities (Mosley).[11] The challenge, however, is to find a way to mediate between the Levinasian aspect of ethical alterity and the socio-political aspect that grounds these moral-existential dramas within the characters' material and social conditions of existence. In what follows, I draw on both aspects of these approaches to the Dardenne brothers in order to examine how *The Promise* explores the transcendent ethical encounter with the Other, while also revealing the socio-political conditions of these characters' world. It offers a remarkable case of cinematic ethics in its exploration of ethical resistance amidst social alienation, economic exploitation, and political disenfranchisement. Indeed, it reveals the possibility of an experience of ethical responsiveness to the Other, resonating with Levinas' idea of the transcendent face-to-face encounter. At the same time, it acknowledges the struggles of marginalized individuals in socially and economically depressed communities to find dignity through ethical resistance to the alienating and destructive forces of global capitalism.

As many commentators have noted, the Dardenne brothers' background in documentary informs their carefully composed and stylized version of social realism (see Mosley 2012, 39–62). The originality of their work lies in their cinematic exploration – combining realism, with elements of melodrama and documentary – of the moral ambiguity of singular characters set against the bleak social-economic background of a regional European city in decline. Indeed, both *Biutiful* and *The Promise* deal with the ethico-political aspects of contemporary urban life, yet *Biutiful* does so through melodrama and a concern with the spiritual dimension of Uxbal's experience, an element that is all but absent in *The Promise*, despite its attempts to evoke a sense of ethical transcendence (for example, in Igor's confession to Assita at the end of the film). As Mosley observes, however, one should be careful about taking the 'positive confrontation' between Assita and Igor at the end of the film as 'an attempt to illustrate the face-to-face encounter, for it remains a transcendent experience and is empirically unverifiable' (2012, 78). Nonetheless, instead of rejecting this possibility altogether, or proffering 'verifiable' evidence of its reality, I would suggest that the film leaves it open as a question, broaching a space for open-ended reflection concerning the nature of this ethical encounter. Ethics is indeed 'an optics' here (Levinas): offering a cinematic experience of transcendent moments of ethical experience that suggest the possibility of a 'face-to-face' encounter, without attempting, however, to fix the latter in a definite 'representation' (which would run counter to its meaning). In this respect, *Biutiful* and *The Promise* offer complementary, yet distinctive ethical presentations of social experience within contemporary European multicultural societies facing the challenges of rampant economic globalization.

At the same time, both films display a degree of crossover between melodrama and social realism that is worth exploring further. As remarked, *Biutiful* situates the moral melodrama of Uxbal's struggle to survive, ensure his children's future, and redeem himself before death, within the socially marginalized ethnic communities of Barcelona's urban underclass. *The Promise,* too, focuses on a father/son conflict against the backdrop of economic exploitation and social deprivation, with Igor achieving independence and ethical maturity by defying his father and honouring his promise to stand by Assita and her child. In this regard, as Mosley notes, the Dardennes follow the direction of other social realist filmmakers in focusing on interpersonal and familial dramas 'that are microcosmic versions of the agonies at large in the lower social strata' (2012, 12). This 'hybrid realism', as Mosley remarks, 'explores the intersection between realist aesthetics and the expectations of cinematic melodrama', while keeping faith with the conventions and concerns of social realism (2012, 12). *The Promise* offers a more explicitly social realist presentation of this urban underclass, but combines this with elements of melodrama, focusing on the father/son conflict between Roger and Igor, the moral choice facing Igor following his promise to the dying Amidou, and the unlikely formation of a new couple as Igor, Assita, and her child venture towards an alternative future. As Jacqueline Auberas remarks (2008, 13), the Dardennes venture into the territory of melodrama 'with all the emotion, surges, and narrative overload implied by this genre … but by shifting it, by writing it as if it were documentary' (quoted in Mosley 2012, 12). Expressed differently, the film explores an 'ethics in the ruin of politics', as O'Shaughnessy (2008) puts it, foregrounding an ethics of resistance in the absence of a collective politics; and it does so by combining social realism with elements of melodrama mediated through a naturalistic aesthetic and elements of documentary style.

Cinematic empathy versus ethical proximity

Despite their narrative and thematic affinities, the most significant difference between these films turns on their respective treatments of emotion. In *Biutiful* we find a more explicit elicitation of emotional engagement, the generation of cinematic empathy, encouraging subjective alignment with the focalizing character (Uxbal) but also inviting (and shifting) moral allegiances between character perspectives (chiefly Uxbal's, but also that of his wife Marambra). At the same time, there is an elicitation of ethical experience in the face of a morally devastating situation, profoundly ambiguous but also revealing of background social realities, one in which Uxbal's actions invite both sympathy and antipathy at once. In the case of *The Promise*, there is a subtle 'blocking' or thwarting of emotional identification: a refusal to present subjective character perspectives – through the avoidance of shot-reverse shot conventions, full-frontal close-ups, narrative exposition, a diminution of dialogue, the fragmentation of space, and a focus on gesture – thereby cultivating a sense of proximity with the character, of witnessing or acknowledging their plight, but without encouraging those forms of identificatory alignment or straightforward moral allegiance that would risk 'totalizing' the Other (taking over his or her perspective and assimilating it to one's own, thus subsuming their otherness to the realm of my own ego). This 'checking' of empathic emotional engagement in favour of a more diffuse, affective form of involvement opens up a different kind of ethical experience in the Dardenne brothers' film. Much like Bresson, the characters' moral sensibilities are depicted through gesture, physical expression, and action; the presentation of psychological motivation through subjective perspective-taking is minimalized, a strategy that renders the emotional interiority of characters opaque and ambiguous. The film offers less a case of cinematic empathy than one of *ethical proximity*: a sense of responsiveness to the Other, acknowledging their alterity, without seeking to 'judge' those who reveal themselves, however opaquely, through their gestures and actions, and without affording the viewer an unambiguous sense of moral allegiance that would risk subsuming the singularity of the Other under one's own conception of morality.

In both films, the moral-existential drama serves to reveal the social and economic complexities of the characters' life-world; at the same time, both films invite sympathetic engagement or ethical proximity while refusing to allow for simplistic moral judgment. Both films prompt the viewer to undergo an experience of moral uncertainty, indeed an experience of moral ambivalence combining sympathetic and antipathetic responses, a temporary suspension of ethical judgment, an openness towards these singular individuals and the complexities of their particular situation that invites further philosophical reflection, and much else besides. In this respect, they are both films that explore the possibility of film as a medium of ethical experience in ways that challenge, question, or extend more familiar conceptions of moral psychology and the manner in which philosophy seeks to persuade through moral argument.

Let us explore two important moments of philosophical, indeed 'Levinasian' ethical encounter between Igor and Assita, the first being Igor's break with his father's plan to sell Assita into sex slavery and to flee with her to safety, and the second being the culmination of their flight, which concludes with Igor telling Assita the truth about the death of her husband. In the first sequence, we see Igor looking on worriedly, as Roger leads Assita to his van, where she sits with her child, waiting to be driven to Cologne. In the scene preceding this one, set the night before, Igor learns that Roger plans to rid himself of Assita by luring her to Cologne on the pretext of meeting her husband (he arranges for her to receive a bogus telegram from Amidou telling her to meet him there). Igor asks what will happen to Assita once she realizes her husband is not there, and Roger answers, gruffly, that it's his problem to handle. Earlier that evening, before the bogus telegram arrives, Igor finds Amidou's battered radio (left behind after his accident), and feels compelled to return it to Assita, whose suspicions about her husband are again aroused. She kills one of her chickens and reads its entrails, declaring that her husband is not far away but somewhere nearby. A handheld camera witnesses the intimate but ambiguous encounter, revealing but at the same time concealing the true nature of this unanticipated, uncertain relationship. An uneasy bond has been established between them, with Assita unsure what to make of the young man but sensing that he is decent and knows more than he reveals, and with Igor's sense of responsibility, both for Amidou's death and for Assita's desire to know the truth, becoming more pressing – his agitation, uncertainty, and impulsive energy well captured by the kinetic, but also respectfully distant, camera.

To return to the scene in question, Igor helps Roger cart gas tanks from the van into the building, father and son passing each other in silence. As Igor returns to the van, we see him and Assita from inside it, Assita seated in the backseat and Igor standing behind her, outside the van, looking at her from behind and then turning away. As his father works away, Igor is shown in close shot, in profile, looking again at Assita's back, his eyes glancing downwards twice (as happens whenever he looks at her in the film). On an impulse, he jumps suddenly into his father's van, driving off with Assita and her child. After showing Roger racing out of the building, the camera remains inside the van and shows Assita, seated behind Igor, demanding to know what is happening. Igor is shown again in profile as he drives, the camera panning back to Assita seated behind him, as she interrogates him, holding a knife blade to his throat. He tells her that her husband is not in Cologne and that Roger was planning to 'sell her as a whore'. The camera remains focused on Assita's face as Igor answers, panning back to Igor after Assita tells him to drive to the police. He refuses, a little petulantly, admitting that his father is bad but that he (Igor) is no snitch, his response more like a protesting child than a defiant adult. The peculiar bond between Assita and Igor – combining elements of a mother/son relationship, a diffuse erotic fascination, and his implicit sense of moral responsibility – becomes more clearly manifest.

Despite his token protestations, the next scene finds them both in the police station reporting Amidou's disappearance, the camera showing Igor standing behind Assita, glancing at her more frequently, coming forward and explaining to the officer important details about Amidou's disappearance. Igor's break with his father and allegiance to Assita is thus made clear, but through gesture and action rather than dialogue or exposition. It is a solidarity expressed through an ethical being-with the other rather than through moral reflection or verbal affirmation.

In the film's climactic scene, Igor and Assita have taken shelter for the night in the garage where Igor had previously been employed as an apprentice mechanic. The sense of trust between them has grown after the ordeal of the previous days, which included taking her seriously feverish child to hospital, and receiving charitable help from a woman working there who also hails from Burkina Faso. She thanks Igor for all the help he has given her, extending her hand and touching him on the shoulder, the first physical gesture of affection and acknowledgement she has shown towards him. Igor, moved but unable to reply, looks at her with sympathy, but also with a note of anxiety, and withdraws to fix her broken statuette. While he is working, his father Roger suddenly enters the room and demands to know where Assita is; Igor, shocked, stares at him, warily, saying that they must tell her the truth. A chase and struggle ensues in the garage, interrupted by Assita hitting Roger on the head and knocking him out. In this final confrontation between Igor and Roger, Igor manages to chain up his father's leg, securing it with a padlock, effectively imprisoning him, and refusing Roger's pleas to be freed, his offers of money, and his promises that he will let Assita go. It is only when Roger says that he did everything for Igor, for their house, claiming Igor as his own ('You are my son!'), that Igor snaps and shouts at him, three times, to shut up. This moment of reckoning, with Igor refusing his father's paternal authority, marks the definitive break between them, the consolidation of Igor's commitment to Assita, and his desire to tell her the truth. Here again the ethical decision is enacted through gesture, expression, and action (Assita's gesture of thanks to Igor, his offer to fix her statuette, the violent physical struggle between Igor and Roger, and Igor's escape with Assita). This is a performative or enactive, rather than a reflective or contemplative, form of cinematic ethics.

In the film's final sequence, we see Assita and Igor walking together towards the railway station. They are shown in profile as they walk in silence, and then in profile as they approach the stairway leading up to the railway platform. Igor glances briefly at Assita as they round the corner before the stairway. As Assita mounts the stairs, the camera following her back, we hear Igor, off-screen, say quietly, 'Amidou is dead'. She stops, stands still, and listens, her back to Igor, as the camera pans back to him, his face looking up at Assita as he confesses the truth: 'He fell from a scaffold. I wanted to take him to hospital but

Figure 6.2 Still from *The Promise*, Dir. Jean-Pierre Dardenne and Luc Dardenne (1996)

my father wouldn't.' The camera then tilts up to Assita's back as he continues: 'To avoid problems. I obeyed him. We buried him behind the white house. In cement.' The camera tilts back to Igor, whose face is bowed, his eyes downcast, then back up to Assita, who removes her headscarf, turns around, and walks back down the stairs. Her face downcast, the camera following her, she passes Igor without looking at him, the camera now revealing both of them, side by side, but unable to face each other. Assita then stops and turns to face Igor, looking at him directly; he turns towards her, slowly, and faces her, his eyes still glancing downwards, but then holding her gaze more steadily. They look at each other, in silence, for several moments, before Assita turns away, her face again downcast, and walks off-screen. The camera holds on Igor's face for a few moments, his face is visible but opaque, his head tilted downwards but still gazing towards her, his expression conveying hints of shame, remorse, sorrow, relief. Another few moments pass before he jumps up and runs after her, joining her as they walk together away from the camera, Assita with her baby and Igor with her bag, the couple soon disappearing in the distance.

These two moments – Igor's impulsive decision to flee with Assita, and his confession of the truth about her husband's death – are remarkable instances of ethical transcendence that are psychologically opaque in terms of traditional moral psychology. We know that Igor realizes that Assita is being deceived, and that he feels on his conscience that he helped cover up Amadou's death; but the moment he decides to flee with her appears as an impulse rather than a reasoned decision. It does not seem to be the outcome of an exercise of practical reason, an act done in accordance with moral duty, a result of utilitarian calculation, or the expression of an ethical virtue or character trait. Rather, it appears as a spontaneous, 'ungrounded' moral action that arises out of a felt sense of ethical responsibility. The same can be said of the moment when he confesses the truth: we know he believes that she must be told the truth (as he tells his father), but the moment he decides to tell her, followed by the moment when he re-joins her, also seems impulsive or unmotivated in moral-psychological terms. In these moments of ethical transcendence, evident in many other Dardenne brothers' films, we experience another way of understanding ethics as an expression of an 'infinite' demand; not as a product of moral reasoning but as an ungrounded, yet compelling, expression of ethical responsiveness to the Other in their unknowable otherness and human vulnerability.

We might compare this with the exploration of Uxbal's subjectivity in *Biutiful*, the presentation of his moral-spiritual struggle as an existential challenge but also a subjectivist escape from an alienating world. This situation is reversed in *The Promise*, which describes an exploitative social world in which moments of ethical resistance are nonetheless possible. *The Promise* eschews direct representation of characters' subjectivity in favour of an ethical proximity coupled with empathic distance, one that maintains the material presence of the urban environment while revealing moments of ethical transcendence in the midst of social alienation. Moral psychology is reduced to a minimum in order to present a different conception of ethical agency, one predicated on a deeply felt, existentially binding, ineffable acknowledgement of responsibility for the Other. Indeed, these miraculous moments of ethical transcendence suggest a strong parallel with Levinas' 'existential' experience of ethics: the experience of an exposure to the Other that provokes an ethical response, a demand experienced as a responsibility irreducible to moral judgment, yet which remains binding on the individual's very being (Levinas 1991 [1961]). This is not a case of cinematic empathy (or cinempathy) but rather one of *ethical proximity*: an existential solidarity with, or responsibility towards, a vulnerable Other whose life is exposed within an indifferent community; an experience of proximity, combining intimacy without intrusion, solidarity without subsumption, conveyed through the Dardenne brothers' interruption of empathic alignment and emotional 'identification' in favour of a respectful being-with the Other.

Indeed, *The Promise* succeeds in showing an ethical situation in its infinite complexity rather than representing a moral example in its abstract simplicity. It reveals an individual being in a singular situation – a cinematic moral phenomenology rather than an application of phenomenology to cinematic narrative – such that the characters' actions, in all their ambiguity, become expressive and revelatory of the harsh and broken world in which they find themselves. The presentation of these moments, moreover, can be viewed as attempts to render the 'un-representable' dimension of ethical experience: that which 'overflows' or exceeds the determinate representation of an action by a rationally motivated agent. These moments gesture towards an ethical dimension that becomes manifest in the face-to-face encounter, one that is not depicted literally on screen (nor could be, according to Levinas) but is evoked indirectly via the gestures, actions, and bodies of diverse individuals in relation with each other. From this point of view, we could describe *The Promise* as a cinematic form of poetic social realism with a human (ethical) face.

The Levinasian approach to film as ethics, moreover, is not restricted to the face-to-face encounter. It is also concerned with exploring a phenomenology of ethical experience and its expression in action. The latter, however, is not presented as the rational outcome of a deliberative reflective process (as per Kantian morality or utilitarian ethics), nor as an expression of acquired moral virtues or settled ethical dispositions to act in accordance with reasoned judgment (Aristotelian *phronesis*). Rather, their films explore moments of 'ungrounded' moral action – centred on the question of killing or not killing – that appear spontaneous or impulsive, but which also express an existentially defining sense of responsibility towards the Other. The Dardennes thus offer a phenomenology of the incalculability of moral action, 'grounded' (though at the same time questioning the very notion of 'grounding') in a rich notion of ethical experience that emphasizes its ambiguity. Their cinema attempts to evoke this Levinasian experience of alterity: the poetic disclosure of that which over-flows the materiality of the world (or the narrative content of the image), yet in doing so offers a poetic sense of the transcendent alterity of the Other and the call to responsibility that he or she demands. The Dardennes achieve this singular ethical experience through the poetic disclosure of the ordinarily 'invisible' aspects of moral action, the transcendent alterity of vulnerable human beings in their unfathomable singularity – a cinematic experience of ethical transcendence within an indifferent and unjust world.

Notes

1 Iñárritu comments on the shift from handheld realist camera earlier in the film to the use of more composed shots, different lenses, and slower pacing, which brings objects and places into more focused relief as Uxbal's illness worsens and his insight deepens: 'The handheld camera becomes much more stable – the movement of the camera – and there's a moment when I thought that he would be seeing everything in much more of an expanded way. He would be much wiser, in a way. So I changed the format from 1:85 to 2:40. And then I changed it even to anamorphic. After that, everything became more relaxed. And every time there's a point-of-view shot, every time Uxbal looks at an object, I change the speed. Instead of shooting 24 frames per second, I shoot 27, so everything in the moment becomes a little bit slower. He observes things more clearly. It's very subtle. But I think it helps to navigate the emotional journey' (Iñárritu 2011).

2 The revelatory power of the face – Javier Bardem's/Uxbal's, but also those of his wife Marambra, his children Ana and Mateo, of those who have died, of Ige, the Senegalese woman, and of his dead father as a young man – is perhaps the most important aesthetic and ethical element of the film. I discuss the ethical question of the face, from a Levinasian perspective, in my discussion of *The Promise*.

3 See Bradshaw's (2011) ambivalent comments on *Biutiful* as oscillating between brilliant and bogus: 'Its attempt at a globalist, humanist aesthetic of compassion looks from certain angles thrillingly ambitious – and from others dreamy and self-congratulatory, like a Benetton ad from the 1990s, and verging on misery porn-chic'.

4 Cf. Malick's *The Tree of Life*, which also generated polarized responses, arguably because of its religiosity. See Sinnerbrink 2012.

5 They are among a select group of filmmakers who have won the Palme d'Or at Cannes twice (for *Rosetta* 1999 and *L'Enfant* [*The Child*] 2005).

6 See David Martin-Jones (2013) for a critical discussion, drawing on philosopher Enrique Dussel, of the post-colonialist aspects of *The Promise*, focusing on the question of Eurocentrism and the difficulty of avoiding it in (European) film. His reading of this scene explicitly emphasizes the allusions to slavery and colonialist history (references to the French colony of Burkina Faso and the literal 'enchainment' of Olivier by his son).

7 Cooper claims that the Dardennes avoid or block overt forms of emotional 'identification' in their films, whereas Rushton (2014) argues that they elicit a Cavellian 'empathic projection' that does not attempt to assume the perspective of the Other (which would be to assimilate it to one's self) but encourages us to 'imagine' their perspective in a manner that respects their singularity and difference.

8 As I discuss further below, Cooper (2007) offers a lucid analysis of the manner in which the Dardenne brothers' create a sense of proximity that thwarts conventional identification, whereas Dillet and Puri (2013) explore the Dardennes' use of space as a means of evoking an ethical sense of world, self, and the Other.

9 See also the special issue of *Film-Philosophy* (Cooper 2007b) devoted to this topic, 'The Occluded Relation: Levinas and Film'.

10 Cf. 'Effects of a similar kind are obtained In cinema with closeups. Their interest does not only lie in that they can show details; they stop the action in which a particular is bound up with a whole, and let it exist apart. They let it manifest its particular and absurd nature which the camera discovers in a normally unexpected perspective – in a shoulder line to which the close-up gives the hallucinatory dimensions, laying bare what the visible universe and the play of its normal proportions tone down and conceal' (Levinas 1978, 55).

11 Mosley mentions humanist Marxist Ernst Bloch as another philosopher whose work resonates strongly with the Dardennes' cinema (2012, 61–62).

Bibliography

Auberas, Jacqueline (ed.). *Jean-Pierre et Jean-Luc Dardennes.* Brussels: CGRI/CFWB, 2008.

Bradshaw, Peter. '*Biutiful* – review'. *The Guardian*, 27 Jan 2011. Available online at: www.guardian.co.uk/film/2011/jan/27/biutiful-review

Bruns, Gerald L. 'Blanchot/Levinas: Interruption (On the Conflict of Alterities)', *Research in Phenomenology*, 26.1 (1996): 132–154.

Cooper, Sarah. *Selfless Cinema? Ethics and French Documentary.* London: Legenda, 2006.

Cooper, Sarah. 'Mortal Ethics: Reading Levinas with the Dardenne Brothers', *Film-Philosophy*, 11.2 (2007a): 66–87. Available online at: www.film-philosophy.com/2007v11n2/cooper.pdf

Cooper, Sarah (ed.). 'The Occluded Relation: Levinas and Cinema', Special Issue of *Film-Philosophy*, 11.2 (2007b). Available online at: www.film-philosophy.com/index.php/f-p/issue/view/13

Coplan, Amy. 'Catching Characters' Emotions: Emotional Contagion Responses to Narrative Fiction Film', *Film Studies: An International Review*, 8 (2006): 26–38.

Cox, Damian and Levine, Michael P. *Thinking Through Film: Doing Philosophy, Watching Movies.* Malden, MA: Wiley-Blackwell, 2011.

Critchley, Simon. *Very Little … Almost Nothing: Death, Philosophy and Literature.* London and New York: Routledge, 1997.

Damasio, Antonio. *Descartes' Error: Emotion, Reason, and the Human Brain.* New York: Penguin, 1994.

Deleuze, Gilles and Guattari, Felix. *Kafka: Towards a Minor Literature.* Trans. Dana Polan. Minneapolis: University of Minnesota Press, 1986.

De Sousa, Ronald. 'Moral Emotions', *Ethical Theory and Moral Practice*, 4.2 (2001): 109–126.

Dillet, Benoît and Puri, Tara. 'Left-Over Spaces: The Cinema of the Dardenne Brothers', *Film-Philosophy*, 17.1 (2013): 367–382.

Girgus, Sam B. 'Beyond Ontology: Levinas and the Ethical Frame in Film', *Film-Philosophy*, 11.2 (2007): 88–107. Available online at: www.film-philosophy.com/2007v11n2/Girgus.pdf

Grodal, Torben. *Embodied Visions: Evolution, Emotion, Culture, and Film*. Oxford: Oxford University Press, 2009.

Haidt, Jonathan. 'The Emotional Dog and its Rational Tail: A Social-Intuitionist Approach to Moral Judgment', *Psychological Review*, 104.1 (2001): 814–834.

Hart, Kevin. 'Ethics of the Image'. In Jeffrey Bloechl and Jeffrey L. Kosky (eds), *Levinas Studies: An Annual Review*, Vol. 1. Pittsburgh: Duquesne University Press, 2005.

Heidegger, Martin. *Being and Time*. Trans. Joan Stambaugh. Albany: State University of New York Press, 2010 [1927].

Hume, David. *A Treatise on Human Nature*. L. A. Selby-Bigge (ed.), 2nd Edition revised by P. H. Nidditch. Oxford: Clarendon Press, 1975 [1738].

Iñárritu, Alejandro González. 'Art Should Provoke: Interview with Alejandro González Iñárritu', *Sounds and Colours*, July 11, 2011. Available online at: www.soundsandcolours.com/subjects/film/art-should-provoke-an-interview-with-alejandro-gonzalez-inarritu/

Laine, Tarja. *Feeling Cinema: Emotional Dynamics in Film*. London/New York: Continuum, 2011.

Levinas, Emmanuel. *Existence and Existents*. Trans. Alphonso Lingis. Dordrecht: Kluwer Academic Publishers. 1978 [1948].

Levinas, Emmanuel. 'Reality and its Shadow'. Trans. Alphonso Lingis. In Sean Hand (ed.), *The Levinas Reader*, 129–143. New York: Basil Blackwell, 1989.

Levinas, Emmanuel. *Totality and Infinity: An Essay on Exteriority*. Trans. Alphonso Lingis. Dordrecht: Kluwer Academic Publishers, 1991 [1961].

Levinas, Emmanuel. *Proper Names*. Trans. Michael B. Smith. Stanford: Stanford University Press, 1996 [1975].

Martin-Jones, D. 'The Dardenne Brothers Encounter Enrique Dussel: Ethics, Eurocentrism and a Philosophy for World Cinemas'. In M. Conceição Monteiro, G. Guicci, and N. Besner (eds), *Além dos Limites: Ensaios Para o Século XXI [Beyond the Limits: Essays for the XXI Century]*, 71–105. Rio de Janeiro: State University of Rio de Janeiro Press, 2013.

Mosley, Philip. *The Cinema of the Dardenne Brothers: Responsible Realism*. London and New York: Wallflower Press, 2012.

Nussbaum, Martha. *Upheavals of Thought: The Intelligence of Emotions*. Cambridge: Cambridge University Press, 2001.

O'Shaughnessy, Martin. 'Ethics in the Ruins of Politics: The Dardenne Brothers'. In Kate Ince (ed.), *Five Directors: Auteurism from Assayas to Ozon*, 59–83. Manchester: Manchester University Press, 2008.

Peters, Gary. 'The Rhythm of Alterity: Levinas and Aesthetics', *Radical Philosophy*, 82 (1997): 9–16.

Plantinga, Carl. *Moving Viewers: American Film and the Spectator's Experience*. Berkeley: University of California Press, 2009.

Plantinga, Carl and Smith, Greg (eds). *Passionate Views: Film, Cognition, and Emotion*. Baltimore: Johns Hopkins University Press, 1999.

Prinz, Jesse. *Gut Feelings: A Perceptual Theory of Emotion*. Oxford: Oxford University Press, 2004.

Prinz, Jesse. *The Emotional Construction of Morals*. Oxford: Oxford University Press, 2009.

Robinson, Jenefer. *Deeper than Reason: Emotion and its Role in Literature, Music, and Art*. Oxford: Oxford University Press, 2007.

Rodowick, D. N. *The Crisis of Political Modernism: Criticism and Ideology in Contemporary Film Theory*, 2nd Edition. Urbana: University of Illinois Press, 1994.

Rushton, Richard. 'Empathic Projection in the Films of the Dardenne Brothers', *Screen*, 55:3 (Autumn 2014): 303–316.

Saxton, Libby. *Haunted Images: Film, Ethics, Testimony, and the Holocaust*. London: Wallflower Press, 2008.

Schiller, Friedrich. *Letters on the Aesthetic Education of Man*. Trans. Reginald Snell. Dover Publications, 2004 [1794].

Schmiedgen, Peter. 'Art and Idolatry: Aesthetics and Alterity in Levinas', *Contretemps*, 3 (July 2002): 148–160.

Sinnerbrink, Robert. 'Cinematic Belief: Bazinian Cinephilia and Malick's *The Tree of Life*', *Angelaki*, 17.4 (2012): 95–117.

Sinnerbrink, Robert. 'Post-Secular Ethics: The Case of Iñárritu's *Biutiful*'. In Costica Bradatan and Camil Ungureanu (eds), *Religion in Contemporary European Cinema: The Postsecular Constellation*, 166–185. Abingdon and New York: Routledge, 2014.

Smith, Murray. *Engaging Characters: Fiction, Emotion, and the Cinema*. Cambridge: Cambridge University Press, 1995.

Stadler, Jane. *Pulling Focus: Intersubjective Experience, Narrative Film, and Ethics*. New York and London: Continuum Books, 2008.

Staehler, Tanja. 'Images and Shadows: Levinas and the Ambiguity of the Aesthetic', *Estetika: The Central European Journal of Aesthetics*, 47.2 (2010): 123–143.

Filmography

Amores Perros. Dir. Alejandro González Iñárritu (Mexico, 2000)
Babel. Dir. Alejandro González Iñárritu (France/USA/Mexico, 2006)
Biutiful. Dir. Alejandro González Iñárritu (Spain, 2005)
The Child [*L'enfant*]. Dir. Jean-Pierre and Luc Dardenne (Belgium, 2005)
Kika. Dir. Pedro Almodóvar (Spain/France, 1993)
Le gamin au velo [*The Kid with a Bike*]. Dir. Jean-Pierre and Luc Dardenne (Belgium, 2011)
The Promise [*La promesse*]. Dir. Jean-Pierre and Luc Dardenne (Belgium, 1996)
Rosetta. Dir. Jean-Pierre and Luc Dardenne (Belgium, 1999)
The Silence of Lorna [*Le silence de Lorna*]. Dir. Jean-Pierre and Luc Dardenne (Belgium, 2008)
The Son [*Le fils*]. Dir. Jean-Pierre and Luc Dardenne (Belgium, 2002)
Talk to Her [*Hable con ella*]. Dir. Pedro Almodóvar (Spain, 2002)
To Live [*Ikiru*]. Dir. Akira Kurosawa (Japan, 1952)
Two Days, One Night [*Deux jours, une nuit*]. Dir. Jean-Pierre and Luc Dardenne (Belgium, 2014)
21 Grams. Dir. Alejandro González Iñárritu (USA, 2003)

7 Gangster film

Cinematic ethics in *The Act of Killing*

> This is the true legacy of the dictatorship: the erasure of our ability to imagine anything other.
>
> Anonymous, co-director of *The Act of Killing*, Oppenheimer (2013)

My focus in this book thus far has been on fictional narrative film, spanning a number of genres and styles, from Hollywood melodrama to social realist drama. This focus on narrative film reflects much of the recent philosophical discussion of film and ethics within contemporary film theory, which has focused on popular and 'crossover' genre films, drawing on different cultural traditions of cinema, rather than 'art' films or documentary works, as was more common in earlier decades. No exploration of cinematic ethics, however, would be complete without considering non-fiction film. Indeed, the possibilities of cinema understood as a medium of ethical experience are richly evident in documentary, one of the most innovative areas in global cinema. Recent documentary theory, for example, has well highlighted the importance of ethics, subjectivity, reflexivity, fictional and aesthetic techniques in the production and reception of non-fictional film (Cooper 2006, Renov 2004, Saxton 2008, Winston 2000). Far from assuming a transparent or veridical relationship between cinematic image and documentary evidence, contemporary filmmakers – such as Werner Herzog, Michael Moore, and Errol Morris, for example – have explored the possibilities of non-fiction film to include fictional elements, to question the 'constructed' nature of images, and to explore the dialectic of complicity between filmmaker, subject, and spectator (see Williams 1993).

All of these elements are at play in one of the most confronting and original non-fiction films of recent years, *The Act of Killing* (2012), directed by Joshua Oppenheimer, Christine Cynn, and an Indonesian filmmaker (Anonymous). Emerging from a project dealing with the violent oppression of one of Indonesia's plantation unions, *The Act of Killing* explores the ongoing legacy of Indonesia's state-sanctioned death squads, who killed over a million alleged Communists and ethnic Chinese following the military coup of 1965. An extraordinary fusion of reflexive 'perpetrator documentary' (see Morag 2012) and cinematic investigation of the traumatic effects of political violence, *The Act of Killing* focuses on the perspectives of a number of 'gangster killers' involved in the 1965–1966 massacres, men who are not only treated as heroes by their community, freely boasting about their past, but are filmed making their own fictional movie re-enactments of their crimes. Its disturbing exploration of the traumatic intersection of cinema, violence, and politics makes Oppenheimer's metacinematic documentary a uniquely challenging case study in cinematic ethics.

'A documentary of the imagination'

The Act of Killing (*Jagal* [Butcher], 2012) is an astonishing and confronting non-fiction film.[1] Stunned by a viewing of Oppenheimer's early rushes in 2010, documentary master, Errol Morris, became an executive producer of the movie, comparing it to one of his favourite films, Kazuo Hara's *The Emperor's Naked Army Marches On* (1987). Legendary filmmaker Werner Herzog, who joined Morris as an executive producer after seeing a fine cut in early 2012, described it as the most 'powerful, surreal, and frightening' film he had seen in over a decade, one that was 'unprecedented in the history of cinema' (Oppenheimer 2013). Since screening at the Telluride (2012), Toronto (2012), and Berlin Film Festivals (2013), *The Act of Killing* has attracted widespread critical acclaim as well as pointed criticism, not only in Western countries but in Indonesia, where it remains a controversial cultural-political intervention (see Heryanto 2014).

Based on the 1965–1966 state-sanctioned massacres of over a million alleged 'communists', the film focuses on a small group of small-time 'movie-theatre gangsters' in the city of Medan (in Northern Sumatra), who scalped black market cinema tickets for a living before being recruited by the military to undertake covert acts of torture and murder. Anwar Congo, the charismatic central figure in the film, is today revered as a local 'war hero' and is one of the founding figures of the paramilitary organization Pancasila Youth (*Pemuda Pancasila*). The latter is now a politically powerful organization of self-styled 'gangsters' (*preman* or 'free men'), whose erstwhile members were used by the Suharto regime for the 'communist purge' that became a watershed event in Indonesia's political history. At once mythologized and disavowed, the massacres are passed over in official accounts of political history, which focus instead on the supposed 'communist threat' that was crushed by the Suharto regime.

The political turmoil erupted on 1 October, 1965, when a small group of Indonesian Armed Forces members calling themselves the 30th of September movement [*Gerakan 30 September* or G30S] attempted an abortive coup d'etat by assassinating six generals, declaring that they had seized control of media and communication apparatuses, and taking President Sukarno under their protection. The subsequent kidnapping and murder of the generals was used by General Suharto and the military to seize political control from Sukarno, and provided a pretext to blame the Communist Party of Indonesia (PKI) for having masterminded the failed G30S coup, and for planning a large-scale attempt to destabilize and take over the nation. As a consequence, the military-backed mass killing of up to a million alleged 'communists' was soon underway. Although mostly cloaked in secrecy, the massacres were carried out across the Indonesian archipelago, in some parts (like Northern Sumatra) by groups of military-recruited 'gangsters' who were permitted to kill with impunity. Instead of facing persecution or punishment, the perpetrators have been protected, even celebrated, for their key role in 'exterminating the communists'. Since the end of Suharto's regime in 1998, they have remained free men, intimidating their enemies, extorting bribes, engaging in criminal activities, exploiting political connections, and enjoying the fruits of their self--styled gangster / paramilitary hero way of life.

How did this extraordinary film come about? As Oppenheimer explains, he and his colleagues had originally planned to make a documentary dealing with the victims of the 1965–1966 massacres, but found many obstacles in their way: victims unwilling to speak about what happened, descendants of victims and perpetrators living side-by-side within the same neighbourhoods, hindrance of the project by local authorities, political interference, police harassment, and so on (Oppenheimer 2013). When it was suggested that Oppenheimer might find the perpetrators more willing to talk about their past, this turned out to be far more true than he could have imagined. In contrast with his earlier difficulties, after deciding to film the perpetrators he suddenly found 'all doors open', including support from police and government representatives. Thus a new project was born: a perpetrator documentary that not only focused on the movie gangsters' stories but invited them to put their recollections, thoughts, and feelings into images by creating movie scenes re-enacting their brutal acts of killing.

Framing *The Act of Killing*

The opening shots of *The Act of Killing* are extraordinary for their jarring combination of garish beauty, disturbing candour, and surreal strangeness. A statue of a fish, a giant carp, half-turning, its mouth open and fins erect, stands atop a ridge against a lush mountainous background with peaceful shimmering waters far below. A small raised track enters the fish from behind and exits from its mouth, covered in a bright red carpet. As a dreamy 'musical' number begins on the soundtrack, a line of dancing girls in hula skirts and pink tops emerge from the fish's mouth, swaying rhythmically in time with the music. The mood is dreamy, fantastical, but also peaceful and gentle; one isn't sure whether this is a dream, a fantasy, a surreal musical number, the images generating confusion as to the significance of the opening shots of this documentary on mass murder. As the dancing girls turn in unison, birdsong and water sounds can be heard as the music dies away.

The next shot is introduced by the sound of rushing water, filmed up close, gushing at the base of a magnificent waterfall. The camera pulls back to reveal two characters, one dressed in a sombre black robe, the other in garish blue satin drag. Surrounded by swaying dancing girls, sporting red tops and black feather headdresses, the figures both raise their arms towards the heavens, as we hear the voice of a 'director' offscreen issuing instructions via megaphone to the assembled actors: 'Peace! Happiness! Real joy and natural beauty! This is not fake!' A wide shot of the actors reveals the end of a movie take, as assistants enter the frame and provide cloaks for the actresses, soaked by the waterfall spray. The bizarre musical scene is revealed to be part of a documentary film within a film, reframing the opening shots by showing us the shooting of the scenes we have just witnessed. We are also obliquely introduced to the central 'protagonists' of *The Act of Killing* – Anwar Congo (dressed in an occult-like black robe) and Herman Koto (resplendent in drag) – as they project themselves in this fantasized movie version of the crimes. Indeed, this opening scene, as we discover at film's end, is a moment of fantasized forgiveness and redemption, all the more shocking and grotesque once we learn what Anwar and Herman have done and how their movie aims to portray their thoughts and feelings about their past atrocities.

The next shot stands in stark contrast: a dusty street at dusk, crumbling buildings with makeshift wires, TV antennae, sputtering motorbikes, old cars, a sense of desolate poverty. The film's title appears: *The Act of Killing*. A cut to a cityscape, another jarring contrast, this time a modern urban metropolis at dusk, with high-rise office blocks, neon signs, revolving advertisements, a McDonalds' sign prominent in the background: intertitles introduce the subject-matter of the film, the Indonesian government's state-sanctioned killings. We are told how, in 1965, the government of Indonesia was overthrown in a military coup; and how as a result of a failed assassination attempt, over a million alleged 'communists', intellectuals, ethnic Chinese, and other 'enemies' of the state, were murdered during 1965–1966 by government-recruited 'gangsters' in covert killing squads. Another contemporary shot of the city shows high-rises, neon signs, a plaza with skateboard and BMX ramps, as one might see in any Western metropolis. The intertitles reveal the core of the film:

> When we met the killers, they proudly told us what they did. To understand why, we asked them to create scenes about the killings in whatever ways they wished. This film follows that process, and documents its consequences.

A boy on a BMX bike shoots across screen, interrupting the melancholy urban scene. A typically realist 'documentary' shot follows, using handheld camera, introducing Anwar (an executioner in 1965) and Herman (gangster and paramilitary leader), clad in a sharp suit and paramilitary camouflage respectively. They walk down a street in Medan, Northern Sumatra, one of the largest cities in Indonesia, unlikely 'filmmakers' recruiting actors to play communist wives pleading for their lives before paramilitary 'gangsters' who threaten to burn down their houses. Herman acts out how he wants the scene to be played, using his megaphone to direct the action, while Anwar stands in the background, observing silently. Herman directs the rehearsal, his para-military comrades relishing the opportunity to display their rage against the 'communists', while the women and children scream and cry in a disturbing manner. At the end of a brief impromptu rehearsal, the actors and onlookers clap and cheer, everyone pleased with the realistic performances.

This short opening sequence condenses all of the important elements of this extraordinary film: the surreal movie sequences imagined and created by the killers as how they wanted their story portrayed; the juxtaposition between the gritty squalor of life for many, and the rapid transformation of Indonesia with its embrace of consumer capitalism; and the reflexive character of the documentary itself, which seeks to expose this suppressed historical episode of mass political violence, but does so by allowing the perpetrators to speak about – and indeed perform – their past crimes and present impunity. The film uses metacinematic framing in order to track the filmic and moral-ethical process by which Oppenheimer and his collaborators filmed fictional versions of the gangsters' crimes, using various cinematic genres and styles for the task (musical, cowboy film, war movie, and film noir). In the conversation between Anwar and Herman that follows the opening sequence, they discuss their hopes and ambitions for the movie they are making, how it needn't be a Hollywood blockbuster but could be a small film, which, step by step, will tell the untold story of the massacres – from the victors' point of view – thus narrating an important event in Indonesian history. Their disturbing candour and unembarrassed openness sets the tone for the rest of the film: a perpe-trator documentary in which the killers relish telling their stories, reflecting on the need to address this dark episode in Indonesia's past but desiring to do so via the medium of movies in a way that reflects their chosen self-image. On the one hand, cinema both enabled and inspired the killers to carry out their brutal deeds; on the other, as the film will show, it provides a medium that will expose their underlying fantasies and self-deceptions: the distorted ideological-moral imagination that made possible, sustained, and still celebrates, their brutal acts of violence.

Gangster film

It is cinema that provides the source of most Indonesians' understanding of this bloody episode in their political history. In 1984, a movie docudrama, *The Treachery of the September 30th Movement of the Indonesian Communist Party* [*Treachery of the G30S/PKI / Pengkhianatan G30S/PKI*] (directed by Arifin C. Noer), based on the 'official' version of the coup endorsed by Suharto's 'New Order' regime, was released with great popular commercial success.[2] The film became mandatory viewing on television and cinemas (until Suharto's resignation in 1998), with school students required to watch it every year when it was screened, on 30 September, to commemorate the crushing of the so-called coup. Depicting the assassination of the Generals as engineered by the PKI (Communist Party of Indonesia), who are presented as voluptuaries of violence relishing barbaric acts of torture, the propagandistic status of the film remained fixed in the Indonesian cultural-political imaginary. Since the end of the Suharto regime, it still remains a popular cinematic dramatization of the 'official' historical version of these events. Indeed, footage from the *Treachery of G30S/PKI* appears in *The Act of Killing*; as the gangster-perpetrators stage their disturbing re-enactments, it becomes clear that the film serves as an oblique source of images for their own cinematic efforts.[3] The direction of the 'treachery', however, is reversed in these bizarre re-enactments, with the gangster-torturers shown committing acts of cruelty against their helpless 'communist' victims. *The Act of Killing* is at once a deconstruction of the 'official' propagandistic version of events, and its perverse 'sequel' in that the perpetrators' re-enactments provide the 'missing' story of the massacres that followed the events upon which *Treachery of G30S/PKI* is based.

Why take such a controversial approach to this defining event in Indonesia's political history? Another powerful documentary, *40 Years of Silence: An Indonesian Tragedy* (2009), directed by anthropologist Robert Lemelson, is more conventional in style, combining historical-reconstruction with victim-testimonials, and concludes with a more hopeful vision of the ongoing reform process in Indonesia since the end of the Suharto regime. Why take the cinematic, ethical, and political risks that *The Act of Killing* takes? There are at least three reasons that Oppenheimer gives. First, there is the surprising fact that the gangster-killers Oppenheimer found in Medan were movie fans, who not only made their living scalping movie tickets but also modelled themselves – their fashion sense, personal style, even methods of killing – on their favourite movie stars and genres (Sidney Poitier, Al Pacino, John Wayne, Hollywood Westerns, film noirs, war movies, musicals, crime thrillers, and gangster films). This surprising conjunction between Hollywood movies and state-sanctioned mass murder surely invites further critical reflection.[4] Second, there is the disturbing fact that the killers have enjoyed impunity from the law for decades, and have gone on to flourish as revered (though still feared) members of the community with close ties to the powerful paramilitary organization, *Pemuda Pancasila* [Pancasila Youth]. Indeed, the film has been likened to one that might explore the legacy of Nazi war crimes, from the perspective of the perpetrators, had the Nazis been victorious and built their longed-for Third Reich.[5] This raised a number of important ethical and political questions for Oppenheimer and his collaborators. What are the nature and effects of this kind of impunity? How do the perpetrators of mass killings imagine that their image will be projected in history? What kind of 'imaginative procedures' make possible the sustaining of a society that is founded on acts of political violence? In exploring these questions, the film casts a disturbing yet revealing light on the deeper causes and traumatic effects of this suppressed history of violence.

The third reason to make the film in this style was to explore the peculiar nexus between cinema, subjectivity, and violence: to examine the 'imaginary economy of images' – the gangsters' own self-image, the image they wished to project historically, and the image their society projects of itself – that orders and maintains a community founded on acts of political violence; and to explore the possibility that this same medium – with its power to render narrative meaning and imaginative engagement through images – might nonetheless offer a means of effecting an ethical experience, however disorienting and confronting, leading to critical reflection on the causes and consequences of these crimes.

In short, Oppenheimer adopted this strategy of imaginative re-enactment in order to use cinema as a device for both projecting and revealing the minds of the killers, using dramatic performance and narrative reconstruction to explore how they imagined and experienced their actions. In this way, cinematic re-enactment could be used to materialize some of the ideological fantasies that underlay this particular history of traumatic violence – the most obvious manifestation of which is precisely the movie *Treachery of the G30S/PKI*, which remains a perverse palimpsest for *The Act of Killing*. In this respect, *The Act of Killing* can be regarded as a confronting ethical experiment in imaginative 'psychotherapy' using the cinematic reconstruction of traumatic events. It is this revealing conjunction between film, fantasy, and violence that motivates Oppenheimer's decision to avoid conventional forms of documentary presentation (historical contextualization, factual reconstruction, objective voiceover, victim testimonials, chronological order and narrative consistency) and to adopt instead a radically 'post-documentary' form of aesthetic presentation – one that uses 'non-documentary' techniques (Rosler 2004) to explore and reflect upon its subject-matter in a subjectively-inflected, generically hybrid, aesthetically challenging manner.

By using the metacinematic 'film within the film' device, for example, *The Act of Killing* aimed to create, as Oppenheimer puts it, a cinematic 'safe space' for the examination of the killers' imaginative and moral-psychological responses to their crimes. The movie scenes that Anwar Congo, Herman Koto, and their collaborators created – bizarre, brutal, and grotesque as they appear – provide an imaginative 'psychic topography': they represent a cinematic materialization of the economy of images underlying their acts of killing, and thus of the social-political imagination of violence that sustained them. Using elements from Hollywood genre movies and Indonesian propaganda film, and drawing on the ideological fantasy of 'communists' not only as deadly threats to the state but embodiments of sexual and moral perversity, the movie reconstructions provided an imaginative arena for staging and exploring the psychological-cultural sources and traumatic effects of the gangsters' actions on others (and on themselves). Instead of a factual-historical documentary explaining the causes and consequences of the massacres, *The Act of Killing* constitutes, rather, what Oppenheimer (2013) calls a *'documentary of the imagination'*: an exploration, through cinematic re-enactment, of the imaginative psychodynamics of traumatic political violence – traumatic effects that, for the perpetrators, remain suppressed by their intimidatory boasting, and, for the victims, remain an unacknowledged, debilitating reality of everyday life a generation later.

This becomes painfully evident in a remarkable sequence during the shooting of one of the re-enactment scenes. Anwar and another former executioner, Adi Zulkadry, are having movie make-up applied in order to look the part of tortured victims, even though they will be directing the scenes and acting as perpetrators at the same time.[6] During the course of the shooting, one of the 'extras' on set approaches the 'filmmakers' explaining that he has a 'true story' to relate. After all, he says, everything in this film should be true. He proceeds to tell the story of his step-father, a Chinese shopkeeper, who was kidnapped from the family home at 3 a.m. one morning and driven away by gangsters. Next morning, the man's son – the narrator, who was eleven or twelve at the time – and the boy's grandfather find the step-father's corpse by the side of the road, concealed under an oil drum that had been cut in half. The boy and his grandfather work hard to dig a grave, right there by the main road, where they buried the dead man 'like a goat'. All the Chinese families were then exiled, dumped in a shanty town by the edge of the city: 'That's why I've never been to school; I had to teach myself to read and write.' Suryono, the narrator, breaks off momentarily to exclaim, with a smile, 'Why should I hide this from you? We should also get to know each other, right?' Quickly wanting to reassure the gangsters that he does not mean to judge them, Suryono adds, smilingly, that he does not mean 'to criticise what we are doing here', but thought that his story would be useful for the film. Anwar, Herman, and Adi are nonplussed, unsure how to react to this revelation, especially given Suryono's friendly expression, even while relating the most painful details of his story. We already have too much material, they say, and anyway your story is too complicated to film, but perhaps we could use it for rehearsals, to put the actors in the mood. It would be difficult to imagine a more graphic illustration of how narratives of violence and suffering can be perverted into a means of distancing oneself from social and moral responsibility.

Suryono is next seen acting the role of a victim, a communist 'suspect' being questioned on his 'activities', then being offered a last cigarette before he is about to be killed. What follows is an extraordinary scene: the cinematic re-enactment of Suryono's stepfather's imagined interrogation, which involves the refusal of his final request to send a message to his family, culminating in an eruption of grief that is difficult to watch. Suryono breaks down, weeping in silence, tears and spittle dripping from his chin, his display of abject despair too intense to be simulated. The camera captures here a series of images of culturally repressed memories or a virtual experience of social suffering, one that would have otherwise remained suppressed by the propaganda celebrating the gangster/paramilitary defence of the nation against evil 'communist' threats, and by the social consensus of silence concerning the stories of the 'communist' victims of the massacres.

As a number of characters in the film remark, their movie is indeed all about 'image': the image that the gangsters project, the image portrayed by anti-communist propaganda, the image of contemporary Indonesia and its brutal political history, images that have distorted the moral perception and historical understanding of its citizens. It is also about the role of film, of moving images, not only as a means of suggesting violence but as an instrument of aesthetic 'shock therapy'; of imaginative psychological self-examination concerning the traumatic experience of political violence. For cinema itself plays a complex role in this story: as a medium implicated in the gangsters' acts of killing, in the state's attempt to manipulate the official political history of the nation, and in *The Act of Killing*'s attempts to expose the underlying imaginative economy of political violence. This remarkable ethico-political documentary thus aims to show, through the gangsters' re-enactments, the moral-psychological damage done to a society built on a disavowal of the violence at its heart.

Responses to the film

This audacious case of cinematic 'image therapy' has provoked intense critical debate. Not only in Indonesia, where the leading journal-magazine *Tempo* has published issues dedicated to the film, but also in Western film festival screenings, public forums, magazine interviews, and academic journals (a recent issue of *Critical Asian Studies*, for example). One aspect that most commentators mention, but neglect to explore, is the fascinating yet disturbing role of cinema in the killings. Film serves as both a mediating device enabling the killers to undertake and justify their actions, and as an imaginative instrument of self-examination, confronting the perpetrators with the effects of their actions. As Oppenheimer observes (2012, 301 ff.), cinema is a medium that enables a critical deconstruction of the ideological narrative versions of this historical event, exposing the failure of moral imagination coupled with the threat of political violence that maintains authoritarian rule in Indonesia. At the same time, cinema opens up the possibility of imagining and projecting an alternative history; one that acknowledges the violence and oppression of the past, and thereby provokes a more critical sense of the present as well as opening up possibilities for social transformation in the future. It is a medium that offers a cultural means of reinventing the damaged moral imagination of a society – indeed of any society, including one's own – that needs to acknowledge the traumatic violence in its past that still controls the present. In so doing, the film provokes a visceral form of moral self-examination that is not only a critique of Indonesia's past but a self-critique of our own complicity, as viewers, with this past and present state of denial. At once fascinated and appalled, 'Westerners' are called upon to participate in this critical self-examination, reflecting on the contributing role of our own governments in supporting these acts of killing, as well as the ongoing injustices that mark the histories of colonialism and the operations of global capitalism around the globe today.

The nexus between the Medan gangster killers and Western political responsibility is mediated by the pervasive image economy of (American) cinema. Indeed, it becomes apparent, early on in *The Act of Killing*, that cinematic imagery from Hollywood genre movies pervaded the minds of the gangsters as they tortured and killed their victims. In one scene, Anwar Congo explains how he would go to the local cinema, watch an upbeat, 'happy' film like an Elvis musical, and then dance across the road to the building that served as the paramilitary headquarters and perpetrate acts of violence and torture while enjoying his 'happy' movie mood. Hollywood movies served as an inspiration but also as a distancing device, a form of visually-mediated emotional distraction, from the brutal reality of their acts of killing. Oppenheimer's remarkable discovery, however, is that cinema was not only implicated in the perpetrators' violence but could also be used as an instrument of imaginative exploration and critical self-reflection. The invitation to imagine, perform, and re-enact their acts of killing for the camera served to expose, for both perpetrators and viewers, the falsity of the ideological fantasy that 'justified' the communist purge. It forced them, at least in some cases, to recognize, reflect upon, and begin to 'work through' the traumatic suffering they caused to others. From this point of view, *The Act of Killing* can be viewed as a perpetrator documentary that both questions and explores the nexus between cinema, subjectivity, and violence; one that opens up a cinematic space – an imaginative theatre of encounter – to excavate the imaginary foundations and explore the moral-psychological effects of the experience of political violence.

There are, however, a number of criticisms that have been levelled at the film. It has been challenged for lacking historical-political perspective, for a selective presentation of relevant facts, for its idiosyncratic and alienating mode of presentation, for glamorizing the perpetrators, even for propagating a perverse 'Orientalism' (see Cribb 2014). Others defend the film for its provocative intervention in Indonesian politics, for its ethically motivated examination of the link between atrocity and complicity, and for attempting to open up dialogue on the massacres both in Indonesia and internationally (Hearman 2014). Many of these criticisms return to the ethical and political questions raised by the film's 'post-documentary' non-fictional style, and its use of stylized re-enactments, starring the perpetrators themselves, in the film-within-the-film sections of the work. Let us summarize and respond to these in turn.

Lack of historical–political context

The film has been accused of omitting important elements of the historico-political context during the mid-1960s (the Cold War ideological background, the colonialist legacy in Indonesia, strong US and Western support for anti-communist paramilitary activities), which results in a distorted picture of the background, causes, and significance of the massacres within Indonesian political history (see Cribb 2014). In response, Oppenheimer concedes that his film does not focus on this historical background because its focus is on the imaginative conditions and ongoing effects of political violence, the simultaneous suppression and valorization of the massacres (and their perpetrators) in the present. It is a film that explores the ongoing social, cultural, and political effects of the massacres, and attempts to expose the distorted imaginative and moral horizons of the perpetrators. It explores the ideological economy of images that sustained their acts of killing – how the killers imagined themselves, how they wish to be viewed historically, and the image projected of them in society – thereby examining how a society founded on acts of political violence deals with the ongoing effects of this historical trauma.

Misleading view of the massacres

Some critics claim the film presents a misleading view of the massacres, whether over- or under-emphasizing the secrecy cloaking the killings, the degree to which they are celebrated publicly, regional differences in the extent of the violence, exaggerating the level of corruption in Indonesian society, and so on (see Cribb 2014). In response, Oppenheimer points out that the film presents a situated portrait of a select group of 'gangster-killers' (based in Medan in Northern Sumatra), who are celebrated as perpetrators of the 1965–1966 massacres. By foregrounding the perpetrators' perspectives, documenting the movie scenes depicting their acts of killing, the relationship between the 'gangsters', the military, the Indonesian government, and the media could be exposed and examined in ways that might have been impossible otherwise. The film thus aims to present an imaginative portrait of the ideological rewriting of history that helped to consolidate authoritarian social and political control in a society marked by a suppressed history of political violence.

Lack of victim perspective

Several critics have accused the film of silencing of victims of the massacres. In being absent from the centre of the film and thus unable to present their perspective, victims are marginalized in ways that reflect their 'official' silencing in Indonesian history and society (Dwyer 2014). In response, it is clear that the film was intended as a 'perpetrator documentary' that focuses on those who engaged in state-sanctioned violence, yet who today enjoy their power, status, and freedom with impunity from the law. Victims, however, are not entirely absent from the film. As remarked above, in one of its most powerful scenes, Anwar's neighbour, Suryono, an actor in one of the interrogation scenes, tells the gangsters the true story of how his step-father was kidnapped and murdered, and has what appears to be a nervous breakdown in playing a distraught victim who pleads to see his family again before he dies. This remarkable encounter between a descendant of one of the victims and those responsible for the killings is an example of how these cinematic re-enactments created, as Oppenheimer put it, a 'safe space' in which the perpetrators could be questioned, accounts of their crimes could be examined, and the consequences of their actions exposed to scrutiny.

Disconcerting, disturbing documentary style

Many critics of the film, while acknowledging its brilliance, have expressed unease with its unorthodox documentary style as misleading audiences as to the historical facts (Cribb 2014). Indeed, the use of fictional narrative and dramatic re-enactment is brought to bear on the perpetrators' experiences of torture and killing. This raises ethical questions, critics contend, about the morality of this mode of aesthetic presentation and the potentially misleading effects of using fictional narrative to depict acts of violence and the experience of suffering. Oppenheimer's response is that it is precisely the use of cinematic 'mediating' filters – different movie genres, dramatic re-enactment, exaggerated performances, and aesthetic stylization – that allowed the perpetrators to 'materialize' their experiences and begin to acknowledge their significance. The masking effects of cinematic narrative and powerful imagery enabled the perpetrators to imagine, model, and carry out their acts of violence, but also to distance themselves from these actions, to stylize, fictionalize, and thus abstract themselves from the brutal reality of the pain and suffering they caused. At the same time, however, the perpetrators are caught in the very medium they set out to manipulate: however much they think they are mastering the narrative, controlling the image, projecting their own self-chosen version of events, the more they are exposed, their ideological manipulation revealed, their brutality and moral indifference rendered visible, their self-justificatory narrative shown up as a morally empty, politically pernicious, illusion (see Oppenheimer 2012 on the 'Snake River project' which preceded the making of *The Act of Killing*).

One powerful example of this process is the gangsters' conversation concerning historical truth versus ideological mystification. During the filming of some of the torture scenes, one of the executioners, Adi Zulkadry, points out that their film is reversing the 'official' history of events (as presented in *Treachery of the G30S/PKI*) by depicting the gangsters as cruel, sadistic killers and the communists as innocent, suffering victims: 'It will disprove the propaganda,' he remarks, 'and prove that we were the cruel ones.' The point here, Adi notes, is that how they are represented is not about fear, 'but about image'. 'But why should we hide from our history,' Herman responds, 'if that's the truth?' Adi replies that the consequence will be that everything he and Anwar have said about the massacres in the past will be proven false; it's not the communists but we who were really the cruel ones. 'That's true,' Anwar answers. 'I'm absolutely aware that we were cruel, but not everything true should be presented to the public' (Anwar thus offering a rough version of the 'noble lie' necessary to maintain authoritarian democracy, an idea found in Plato but also, more recently, in neo-conservative ideology). A close shot of victim-descendant Suryono, privy to this confronting 'philosophical' debate, shows him choking back tears.

The sequence following features a bored-looking Adi, strolling with his wife and daughter through a soulless shopping mall, and then debating moral relativism with Oppenheimer as they drive together in his car. When asked whether he fears being charged with war crimes at The Hague, Adi laughs and replies that, when George Bush was in power, detention at Guantanamo Bay was deemed right and just, but now it is regarded as wrong: what counts as a 'war crime' is defined by the victors; we are the victors, so we get to define what war crimes are. The Geneva conventions, for example, might be replaced by the 'Jakarta Conventions', he quips, which he assures Oppenheimer would be defined very differently. On the question of there being some truths that are harmful for a society, Adi suggests – obviously thinking of the film – that 're-opening this case' (concerning the 1965–1966 massacres) is a case in point; but what of the victims' families, Oppenheimer asks, surely acknowledging what happened will be good for them? Murder has always existed, he replies, and historically there have always been massacres – Adi cites Cain and Abel and the near-extermination of the Native American Indians – but in the end, he claims, 'might makes right'. These revealing debates concerning historical and moral relativism, the need for 'noble lies' to maintain order in a democracy, and how rewriting history would destabilize society, encapsulate some of the most important ethical and political stakes of *The Act of Killing*. The film explores these, however, in a manner tied to the role of the image: how the perpetrators wish to see their actions projected into the narrative of Indonesian history, the self-image of a society founded on repressed political violence, and the effects of confronting the truth of this historical narrative for perpetrators, victims, and for their shared social-political community.

Unethical aspects of the documentary process

Some critics have maintained that the film panders to a perverse Western 'Orientalism' (making the Indonesians seem like barbaric, exotic, 'killers'), while downplaying the key role of the military and of anti-communist Western political powers who supported the Indonesian 'communist purge' (Cribb 2014). In response, we should note that the film avoids imposing any narrative or ideological framework upon the protagonists (apart from the collaborative staging of the 'gangster film' movie scenes); nor does it avoid pointing to the role of the military, the media, and the government – both in the past and, shockingly, in the present – in the perpetration and justification of these crimes. Indeed, the link between the paramilitary groups, military forces, media, and corrupt politicians, is all too plainly evident in the film: we see Chinese shopkeepers being extorted by gangsters for 'protection' money, Pancasila youth leaders and prominent politicians candidly outlining the illegal activities they are involved in, Herman running for parliament with the sole aim of being in a position to extort bribes from his community, and media proprietors boasting of their key role in ordering the killings (ridiculing foot soldiers like Anwar for thinking that they were important), and a serving government minister visiting one of the movie re-enactment shoots, offering the paramilitaries a rousing motivational speech, and then personally whipping the Pancasila cadres into a frenzy of murderous anti-communist hatred.

The Indonesian protagonists, moreover, are as much filmmakers as subjects of the film, which cuts against the charge of a cynical Western attempt to portray Indonesians as barbarian 'Others'. Indeed, an Indonesian filmmaker (Anonymous) was central to its making (most of the crew, also listed as 'Anonymous', were forced to hide their identities). The film also responds to the propaganda version of events surrounding the 'Killing of the Generals' and subsequent mass killings, and offers an alternative version of this propaganda narrative based upon the perpetrators' re-enactments of what they did to their victims – victims whose absence (with a notable exception) are testimony to the silencing of their social suffering.

Moreover, although the film does not foreground the role of Western powers in the 'communist purge', the key allegorical role played by American movies – the Hollywood cinematic imaginary standing in for a generalized Western presence – cannot be ignored. As Oppenheimer remarks (2013), 'that Anwar and his friends so admired American movies, American music, American clothing – all of this made the echoes more difficult to ignore, transforming what I was filming into a nightmarish allegory'. This subtle allegorical evocation of the 'cultural imperialist' background to the state-sanctioned killings – mediated by Hollywood cinema and the moviegoers' ideological fantasies – adds layers of cultural and political background that makes charges of Western 'Orientalism' hard to sustain. Because of its exploration of the effects of suppressed political violence, and the role of images in mediating and managing moral and political perceptions of such actions, *The Act of Killing* is better regarded as a 'global' story that happens to be set in Indonesia, one that continues to have ethical-political relevance across national borders, whether we live in Jakarta or Johannesburg, Medan or Manchester, Bali or Boston, Sumatra or Sydney.

Manipulation of the documentary 'subjects'

One of the more unusual criticisms of the film is that Oppenheimer manipulated and deceived his central documentary 'subjects', the two gangster paramilitary leaders Anwar Congo and Herman Koto. The latter, some critics claim, were surely unaware of the agenda behind the re-enactment process, or thought that they were making a mainstream movie actually intended for general release (a 'family movie', as Anwar muses at one point), or that Oppenheimer manipulated the footage he captured of them in order to present them in the most grotesque light possible. In response, Oppenheimer claims that his subjects were well-informed throughout the filmmaking process that he was only filming the 'making of' their imagined movie, rather than producing a 'real' movie intended for general release; he therefore incorporated scenes of the gangsters watching and commenting on rushes of the film scenes that he had just shot, which in turn became part of the film that we see (as do the responses of the gangster filmmakers to the rushes of their own movie, which in turn informs how they wish it to be seen). Moreover, Oppenheimer continued to maintain contact with the gangsters during the post-production process, and claims that Anwar Congo, in particular, was satisfied with the final cut of *The Act of Killing* (a claim that some critics have since disputed). One could argue, however, that even if there is a degree of deception or manipulation involved (and arguably any documentary, particularly one dealing with such a controversial issue in such an unorthodox way, would inevitably involve complex negotiations that could be described as 'manipulative'), such deception or manipulation could be readily justified. When asked whether he was troubled by not having 'sincerely' presented Anwar and Herman's vision of the killings, Oppenheimer answered that, given that their vision of mass murder was exculpatory and celebratory, there is no way he could have agreed to present such a vision in an unchallenged or unquestioned manner. Indeed, the moral demand on the filmmaker in this instance is to expose the perpetrators and the kind of society to which their acts has given rise. Given the ethical-political aims of the film, and the historical stakes of bringing the perpetrators to the screen, some degree of 'manipulation' seems morally justifiable, despite the claim that the film is a genuinely collaborative work.

A related criticism concerns Oppenheimer's manipulation of the film footage in order to present a more redemptive narrative arc to the film. The *Act of Killing*'s concluding sequence features a subdued Anwar returning to the scene of his crimes, but, unlike earlier in the film, we now witness him break down and retch uncontrollably, a belated moment of moral recognition, visceral and traumatic, concerning the reality of his violence and cruelty. Some critics claim that this scene was filmed quite early in the filmmaking process, yet it appears at the end of the film, thus suggesting that Anwar's moral insight arrives at the end of the traumatic re-enactment process. From this perspective, the sequence thus suggests a redemptive concluding note to the film, in which Anwar's experience of moral insight is shown to be the dramatic and ethical conclusion of the filmmaking process. It is difficult to determine whether this is the case; yet the fact that we see Anwar at night, now visibly aged, his hair turned white, retching violently as he recounts his acts of killing, suggests that the footage was shot late in the process, even though it is difficult to say whether it preceded or followed the 'earlier' sequence of Anwar on the rooftop, dancing the cha-cha after demonstrating his strangulation-by-wire technique. Yet even if this is true, it does not mean that showing Anwar's moment of moral reckoning at the conclusion of *The Act of Killing* is unjustified. The final scene is an allegory of what Oppenheimer and his collaborators hope will be a national process of 'moral retching'; a forced 'regurgitation' of the undigested, unacknowledged violence of the past that still haunts the present. The appalling, gut-wrenching spectacle of Anwar's visceral moral disgust in recognition of his crimes does not simply document one individual's personal or moral experience; it evokes a culturally, ethically, and politically significant moment of rupture with his society's shared historical narrative, its cultural-imaginational enslavement to the powerfully pernicious ideological conviction, clearly evident in the killers as still 'justifying' their barbarous actions, that the acts of killing they performed were a moral-political duty to protect the nation.

Indeed, Anwar, according to Oppenheimer, does undergo, unlike some of his comrades, a moral conversion during the re-enactment process; he experiences, during one of the re-enacted torture scenes, a moment of empathic involvement that seems to open up for him the perspective of those he killed in a manner that had not been possible before. After visibly breaking down during the re-enactment of a torture scene, filmed in a film-noir/gangster film style, Anwar sits in his chair, limp and inert, unable to move, the will and energy drained from his body; he says, weakly, that he cannot go through this again. Later, while watching the scene on a video monitor, he explains to Oppenheimer that at that moment he felt his dignity had been broken and replaced by an intense fear; at that moment, he wonders, did he feel what his victims must have felt? Could they have felt this way too? No, Oppenheimer replies, in their case it was much worse: you knew that this was a movie, but they knew that they were going to die. Anwar seems stunned by this remark, unable to process what he has done, and then is overcome by remorse – 'But Joshua, I did this to so many people!' Anwar's extraordinary belated moment of insight and

Figure 7.1 Still from *The Act of Killing*, Dir. Joshua Oppenheimer, Christine Cynn and Anonymous (2012)

recognition, staggering in its delayed emergence and apparent sincerity, is testimony to the imaginative power of the cinematic re-enactments and their power to exercise the perpetrators' – and viewers' – moral imaginations and perceptions. Anwar appears genuinely remorseful acknowledging what he has done, a recognition that, as he readily admits, he has suppressed for most of his life. That is why the spirits of the tortured and the dead, who come at night to haunt him, gaze at him, troubling Anwar's dreams, appear so frequently in the film – dreams that are not merely personal but belong to the nightmare of history.

Conclusion

One can address these concerns by taking note of Oppenheimer's ambiguous strategy: using cinema to both expose and to question the distorted imagination, circulation of images, and ideological narratives that shaped these acts of killing. Such images contributed to establishing a repressive social consensus – using demonstrations of impunity to instil a sense of fear and to silence dissent (see Anderson 2012) – on the basis of a traumatic history of political violence. It is a metacinematic documentary that deconstructs itself in exploring the ambivalent role of cinema as providing a fantasy frame through which the perpetrators were able to commit mass murder; but also a forensic mirror that confronts them – via cinematic re-enactment – with the traumatic effects of their socially-sanctioned image as feared and revered gangster 'heroes'. Their naïve attempts to control the projected image of themselves through film are undone by public exposure, which suggests that they might have to acknowledge, finally, the devastating moral and political consequences of the brutal ideological fantasy in which they played a starring role.

***

The Act of Killing, for all its controversial features, is a remarkable case study in cinematic ethics, showing how moving images can serve as a medium of ethical experience. The film opens an ethico-aesthetic space of engagement that allows the perpetrators, through cinematic re-enactments, to 'materialize' elements of the imaginative economy of images that continues to sustain a history of political repression. Indeed, the film exploits, in an extraordinary manner, what we might call the paradox of 'camera candour': the manner in which the camera reveals far more than what its subjects intend, capturing a dimension of truth or unintended meaning that eludes or remains inaccessible to the documentary subjects being filmed. This is a phenomenon, distinctive to cinema, that is well known to filmmakers like Errol Morris, who has explored it in relation to criminality and the law, institutional violence, global geopolitics, and the psychology of power (see *The Thin Blue Line* (1988), *Standard Operating Procedure* (2008) on the Abu Ghraib photographs, and *The Unknown Known* (2013) on Donald Rumsfeld and the so-called 'War on

Terror'). In *The Act of Killing*, Oppenheimer applies it to his collaborative project with Anwar and Herman and the shocking 'gangster film' they, with their collaborators, collectively create. What is revealed is something more than an exercise in ideological manipulation, cinematic propaganda, or psychological pathology. It is an ethical experiment in seeing how the use of a camera to film imaginative re-enactments of traumatic acts reveals the underlying imaginary elements, condensed into images, that not only helped shape the minds of the killers but propagated the social meaning of their crimes. Oppenheimer's collaborative experiment thus aims to document the moral confusion, ideological distortion, and imaginary distanciation that allowed 'ordinary' people to commit mass murder. It confronts the viewer with a harrowing demonstration of how moral atrocity can be narrated, imagined, and lived as political salvation. The confronting final sequence of the film – showing Anwar, retching in disgust, walking slowly down a staircase, a shattered man; and a return of the mysterious fish and dancing girls, a musical fantasy masking violence and brutality – leaves one hoping that this traumatic process of historical recognition, indeed of moral 'retching', will continue, enabling the victims' generation to begin finally to tell their stories,[7] thus creating a common space in which historically traumatized individuals and communities are once again able to imagine something other.

Notes

1 The difference between the Indonesian and English-language titles is intriguing, suggesting a more lurid, brutal sense in the original than the more pathos-laden phrase used for the Anglophone release.

2 As Oppenheimer remarks, 'These thousands of screenings surely constitute the most potent performance of the official history of 1965–66. As such, *G30S* is marked by (or marks) the generic imperatives, stylistic tendencies and performative routines and effects of the New Order history' (Oppenheimer 2012, 288–289).

3 The film can be viewed on YouTube (without subtitles): https://www.youtube.com/watch?v= ywrZ642HDTI

4 Indeed it is a connection almost entirely ignored by most critics who have commented on the film regarding its ethical and political dimensions.

5 Oppenheimer (2013) also remarks that it was the circulation of the photographs from Abu Ghraib prison that suggested further parallels with the situation regarding the gangster-killers in Medan.

6 Interestingly, one can observe in the foreground a small photograph of a torture victim taken from *Treachery of G30S/PKI* that is being used as a model by the make-up artists. In many ways Anwar and Adi embody the figure of the 'empathic torturer', who 'empathizes' with his victims in order to gauge, adjust, and intensify how his actions are harming the other (although in a later scene, as I discuss below, Anwar will experience a moment of empathic involvement with the suffering of his victims).

7 Hence Oppenheimer's sequel, *The Look of Silence* (2014) – focusing on the victim/survivor perspective – which documents the brother of a victim of the Indonesian massacres confronting his sibling's killer.

Bibliography

Anderson, Benedict. 'Impunity'. In Joram Ten Brink and Joshua Oppenheimer (eds), *Killer Images: Documentary Film, Memory, and the Performance of Violence*, 268–286. New York: Columbia University Press, 2012.

Cooper, Sarah. *Selfless Cinema? Ethics and French Documentary.* Oxford: Legenda, 2006.

Cooper, Sarah. 'Mortal Ethics: Reading Levinas with the Dardenne Brothers', *Film-Philosophy*, 11.2 (2007): 66–87. Available online at: www.film-philosophy.com/2007v11n2/cooper.pdf

Cribb, Robert. '"The Act of Killing", *Critical Asian Studies*, 46.1 (2014): 147–149.

Dwyer, Leslie K. 'Picturing Violence: Anti-Politics and *The Act of Killing*', *Critical Asian Studies*, 46.1 (2014): 183–188.

Hearman, Vannessa. '"Missing Victims" of the 1965–1966 Violence In Indonesia: Representing Impunity On-Screen in *The Act of Killing*', *Critical Asian Studies*, 46.1 (2014): 171–175.

Heryanto, Ariel. 'Great and Misplaced Expectations', *Critical Asian Studies*, 46.1 (2014): 162–166.

McGregor, Katharine. 'Inside the Minds of Executioners: Reimagining the Loss of Life in the 1965 Indonesian Killings', *Critical Asian Studies*, 46.1 (2014): 189–194.

Morag, Raya. *Waltzing with Bashir: Perpetrator Trauma and Cinema.* London and New York: I.B. Tauris, 2012.

Oppenheimer, Joshua. 'Show of Force: A Cinema-Séance of Power and Violence in Sumatra's Plantation Belt'. In Joram Ten Brink and Joshua Oppenheimer, *Killer Images: Documentary Film, Memory and the Performance of Violence,* 287–310. London and New York: Wallflower Press, 2012.

Oppenheimer, Joshua. *The Act of Killing Press Notes.* Berlin: Wolf, 2013. Available online at: http://ff.hrw.org/sites/default/files/THE%20ACT%20OF%20KILLING%20press%20notes.pdf

Renov, Michael. *The Subject of Documentary.* Minneapolis: University of Minnesota Press, 2004.

Rosler, Martha. 'Post-Documentary, Post-Photography?' In Martha Rosler, *Decoys and Disruptions: Selected Writings, 1975–2001,* 207–244. Cambridge, MA: The MIT Press, 2004.

Saxton, Libby. *Haunted Images: Film, Testimony, Ethics, and the Holocaust.* London: Wallflower Press, 2008.

Sears, Laurie J. 'Heroes as Killers or Killers as Heroes?' *Critical Asian Studies*, 46.1 (2014): 204–207.

van Klinken, Gerry. 'No, The Act Of Killing Is Not Unethical', *Critical Asian Studies*, 46.1 (2014): 176–178.

Wieringa, Saskia E. 'Sexual Politics as a Justification for Mass Murder in *The Act Of Killing*', *Critical Asian Studies*, 46.1 (2014): 195–199.

Williams, Linda. 'Mirrors without Memories: Truth, History, and the New Documentary', *Film Quarterly*, 46.3 (1993): 9–21.

Winston, Brian. *Lies, Damn Lies and Documentary.* London: BFI Books, 2000.

Filmography

The Act of Killing [Jagal]. Dir. Joshua Oppenheimer, Christine Cynn, and Anonymous (Denmark/Norway/UK, 2012)

The Emperor's Naked Army Marches On [Yuki Yukite shingun]. Dir. Kazuo Hara (Japan, 1987)

The Look of Silence. Dir. Joshua Oppenheimer (Denmark/Finland/Indonesia/Norway/UK, 2014)

Standard Operating Procedure. Dir. Errol Morris (USA, 2008)

The Thin Blue Line. Dir. Errol Morris (USA, 1988)

The Treachery of the September 30th Movement of the Indonesian Communist Party [*Treachery of the G30S/PKI / Pengkhianatan G30S/PKI*]. Dir. Arifin C. Noer (Indonesia, 1984)

The Unknown Known. Dir. Errol Morris (USA, 2013)

40 Years of Silence: An Indonesian Tragedy. Dir. Robert Lemelson (USA, 2009)

Conclusion

Is it possible to once more become innocent and political?

Thomas Elsaesser (2005, 40)

The argument of this book can be summarized succinctly: cinema has the potential to be understood as a medium of ethical experience, and this ethical potential is important to recognize if we are to appreciate why cinema matters today. Indeed, philosophical film theory should reclaim ethics as central to what matters in the film-philosophy relationship, for cinema offers an experientially rich way of attuning us to ethical questions and political problems. It is a medium with the aesthetic power to evoke ethical experience – through affective response, emotional engagement, and cognitive understanding – that invites, indeed in some cases demands, critical and philosophical reflection. Cinematic ethics, we might say, is thus extended and elaborated via philosophical conversation, which in turn opens up new ways of thinking about the ethical significance of particular films, and about cinema's ethical potential as a medium more generally. In this way, cinema and philosophy can work together as equal partners in exploring ethical experience, exercising our moral perceptions and ethical imaginations while provoking our critical engagement and philosophical understanding. Cinema, moreover, can be an aesthetic means of imaginative transformation that can reveal obscured, marginalized, or dissonant elements of a world or the unexpected ethical complexities of a moral-ethical or social-political situation. It might even have the capacity, in some cases, to effect an ethical conversion, altering our horizon of understanding and transforming how we think, feel, and conduct ourselves in the world.

In Part I, I explored the 'ethical turn' in film-philosophy, suggesting that this signalled a retrieval of the idea that film can contribute to ethical understanding via cinematic means rather than merely manipulating spectator subjectivity or promulgating ideology. In Part II, I examined some of the key contemporary philosophical approaches to cinematic ethics: namely, Cavellian moral perfectionism in response to cultural and moral scepticism; the Deleuzian ethics of cinematic belief and minor politics as a response to nihilism; and phenomenological and cognitivist approaches to emotion, empathy/sympathy, and the ethical evaluation of narrative film. Cavellian cinematic ethics foregrounds moral perfectionism as an alternative way of conceiving ethical understanding, and explores this possibility in relation to the subgenres of remarriage comedy and the melodrama of the unknown woman; yet Cavell's individualist approach is constrained, especially with regard to melodrama, when it comes to acknowledging the social-cultural and political conditions that both enable and sometimes prevent an individual's perfectionist quest to 'become who one is'.

Deleuze's cinematic ethics emphasizes the role of cinema in fostering 'belief in this world' as a response to cultural nihilism, the loss of belief in prevailing narrative and normative frameworks essential for orienting ourselves in social-historical reality. Deleuze also offers a non-teleological way of exploring how cinema, especially within marginalized, colonized, or subaltern traditions, can construct a creative form of cinematic politics in the absence of a pre-existing 'people' as the subject of history. Yet Deleuze's ethics of belief and political conception of a minor cinema do not really explain how this kind of ethico-political engagement is possible. Indeed, Deleuze draws upon a hybrid philosophico-historical account of the post-war 'crisis of the action-image' to explain the shift towards time-image cinema in response to the post-war condition of nihilism or collapse of belief in received narrative frameworks of meaning and value; but he does not explain how a non-subjective, transpersonal concept of 'affect' (rather than emotion) can play a motivating, action-directing role in 'classical' narrative film (let alone ideology), given that these are both supposed to be structured by the 'sensory-motor action schema'.

Consequently, I turned to phenomenological and cognitivist accounts of affective, emotional, and evaluative responses to narrative cinema, arguing that the 'thick' descriptive approach of phenomenology should be supplemented by the causal-explanatory approach of cognitivist theories. This would provide a synthesis of 'subjective' and 'objective' perspectives on emotional and cognitive engagement that better accounts for the most salient experiential aspects of our ethical experience of film. I explored this thesis with reference to empathy/sympathy, suggesting that cinema excels in encouraging both empathic and sympathetic engagement, modulating emotional involvement and moral allegiance across diverse character points of view (cinempathy), demonstrating this claim via a close analysis of a key sequence from Asghar Farhadi's Iranian domestic drama, *A Separation*.

In Part III I turned to analysing select case studies across different genres (melodrama, realism, and documentary), showcasing how cinematic ethics works in more vivid and concrete detail. This more 'performative' part of the book began with the moral melodrama, engaging critically with Cavell's moral perfectionist reading of *Stella Dallas*, arguing that the film is as much about the social constraints and emotionally conflictual dimensions of the desire for 'class' as it is about the question of gender, the conflicting roles of 'mother' and 'woman', or the moral perfectionist task of a woman's self-education and personal transformation. In Chapter 6, I analysed a contemporary moral-existential melodrama (*Biutiful*) in conjunction with a celebrated social realist drama (*The Promise*), suggesting that both genres can complement each other, but also offer different ways of engaging in cinematic ethics (*The Promise*'s minimalization of cinematic empathy, for example, in favour of an ethical proximity that respects the 'alterity' of the Other, compared with *Biutiful*'s meshing of social realism with metaphysically-oriented religious experience as a response to social alienation). Both melodrama and social realism, however, offer complementary ways of bringing ethical experience and political reflection together by aesthetic means. They confront the viewer with morally ambiguous actions and normatively conflicted situations – in short with experiences of moral cognitive dissonance – that demand further critical reflection, thus demonstrating the philosophical potential of cinema understood as a medium of ethical experience.

Finally, I considered the possibilities for cinematic ethics afforded by non-fictional film, taking as my case study the confronting metacinematic documentary, *The Act of Killing*. The latter stages a risky form of cinematic ethics involving the imagined filmic re-enactment of perpetrators' acts of violence as part of an experiment in exploring – psychologically, cinematically, and philosophically – the suppressed history of political violence in contemporary Indonesia. This provocative film-philosophical experiment showed how cinema could be both a mediating and distancing device that enabled the perpetrators in question to execute their crimes. At the same time, it revealed how cinema could expose the underlying economy of images that made possible, and continues to legitimate, the social and ideological meaning of the perpetrators' acts of violence, which still require the mediation of (cinematic) images in order to shore up social domination and facilitate political control. The meta-cinematic character of the film, with its confronting film-within-a-film featuring the perpetrators' cinematic re-enactments of their crimes, explores the ideological imagination that facilitated their acts of violence. It also confronts viewers with their own complicity in relation to this disturbing nexus between cinema, imagination, violence, and politics. The Janus-faced nature of cinema, as politically manipulative on the one hand, and ethically emancipatory on the other, is thus demonstrated in a confronting manner.

I conclude with a brief reflection, gesturing towards future inquiry, on the 'fourth dimension' of cinematic ethics; namely, how aesthetic form can be understood as a means of evoking ethical experience. Here I suggest that the recent resurgence of interest in cinephilia offers a rich vein of inquiry relevant to both film-philosophy and cinematic ethics. On the one hand, the resurgence of interest in cinephilia expresses a desire for more affective, affirmative, and aesthetic forms of engagement with cinematic works; on the other, it bespeaks a desire to retrieve the implicit ethical potential of an impassioned, involved, and interested engagement (as distinct from Kantian 'disinterested' pleasure) with cinematic art. Indeed, cinephilia is not simply reducible to an aestheticist pose or fetishizing of connoisseurship; nor is it merely an attempt to revivify stylized or experimental forms of creative theorization (as practised by the romantics, for example). Rather, it can be understood philosophically as a way of articulating the intimate and expressive nexus between aesthetics and ethics in the art of film.

To wax speculative for a moment, we might think of cinephilia as a cinematic version of the ancient (but also romantic, existentialist, and perfectionist) idea of 'philosophy as a way of life' (Hadot 2005). Instead of taking its place as just another 'professional', academic discipline within the humanities pursuing technical knowledge and institutional recognition, film-philosophy also has the potential to become a richly experiential mode of shaping our existence ethically and aesthetically through the thoughtful engagement with film. It can become a form of cultural practice defined by a love of cinema (and of philosophy), but also by a commitment to the idea that cinema can reveal the world anew, disclosing the everyday in unexpected ways, bringing it to our attention under different aspects, or wiping away, as Bazin once wrote, 'that spiritual dust and grime with which my eyes have covered it' (1967, 15). By depicting virtual worlds, cinema opens up an aesthetically intensified experience of reality, expressing a love of the world and a care for being, whether for human beings or non-human beings, for nature or spirit, or for whatever exceeds our habitual ways of knowing. It could provide a way of bringing philosophy and cinema together as complementary ways of understanding ourselves in response to the virtual worlds that cinema reveals. Philosophical cinephilia, understood as a practice of cinematic ethics, indeed as a way of life, could open up new ways of thinking, new modes of being, sensuously revealed through images of life and love.

Bibliography

Bazin, André. *What is Cinema? Volume I*. Trans. Hugh Gray. Berkeley/Los Angeles/ London: University of California Press, 1967.

Elsaesser, Thomas. 'Cinephilia or the Uses of Disenchantment'. In Marijke de Valck and Malte Hagener (eds), *Cinephilia: Movies, Love and Memory*, 27–43. Amsterdam: University of Amsterdam Press, 2005.

Hadot, Pierre. 'There are Nowadays Professors of Philosophy but no Philosophers'. Trans. J. Aaron Simmons. *Journal of Speculative Realism*, 19.3 (2005): 229–237.

Appendix 1: Bibliography – further readings on cinematic ethics

The following is a (briefly) annotated bibliography of readings that would be of interest to pursue in relation to each chapter in this book. I have included the key texts that I have cited, as well as some additional texts that would repay further study in regard to cinema and ethics.

Chapter 1 Cinematic ethics: film as a medium of ethical experience (and for whole book)

Andersen, Nathan. *Shadow Philosophy: Plato's Cave and Cinema.* London: Routledge, 2014.

An engaging and articulate introduction to philosophical thinking on film, centred on a detailed engagement with Kubrick's classic, *A Clockwork Orange*, emphasizing many of the film's ethical and cinematic complexities.

Badiou, Alain. *Cinema.* Trans. Susan Spritzer. Cambridge and Malden, MA: Polity Press, 2013 [2010].

An absorbing collection of the controversial French philosopher's writings on film (plus interviews), including Badiou's intriguing discussion of ethics as one of the key ways of thinking philosophically about cinema.

Choi, Jinhee and Frey, Mattias (eds). *Cine-Ethics: Ethical Dimensions of Film Theory, Practice, and Spectatorship.* Abingdon and New York: Routledge, 2014.

Excellent edited collection of essays focusing on various aspects of the cinema/ethics relationship from diverse philosophical and film-theoretical perspectives, exploring a wide range of genres, styles, and traditions. See the helpful Introduction by the editors plus the chapters by Rodowick, Stadler, Carroll, King, Frey, Ponech, Hjort, and Erickson.

Cooper, Sarah. *Selfless Cinema? Ethics and French Documentary.* London: Legenda, 2006.

A finely written and nuanced study of the ethics of documentary film, focusing on filmmakers such as Jean Rouch, Chris Marker and Agnès Varda from an explicitly Levinasian perspective (one of the first studies to bring Levinas to film-philosophy).

Cox, Damian and Levine, Michael P. *Thinking Through Film: Doing Philosophy, Watching Movies*. Malden, MA: Wiley-Blackwell, 2011.

Invigorating introduction to the idea of film as philosophy, arguing, from an analytical perspective, that film can not only supplement philosophy but can in some cases surpass it. Includes detailed case study chapters on moral philosophy in film (*Crimes and Misdemeanours, The Lives of Others, The Dark Knight*, and *La Promesse*).

Downing, Lisa and Saxton, Libby. *Film and Ethics: Foreclosed Encounters*. Abingdon and New York: Routledge, 2010.

Innovative, co-authored exploration of the relationship between film and ethics that inter-cuts Levinasian (Saxton) and Foucaultian/Queer/psychoanalytic (Downing) perspectives in a striking and thought-provoking manner.

Jones, Ward E. and Vice, Samantha. *Ethics at the Cinema*. Oxford: Oxford University Press, 2011.

A fine co-edited collection of essays by noted scholars exploring a wide range of issues pertinent to the cinema/ethics relationship. Includes a section on film and ethics with three chapters investigating Reed's *The Third Man*.

Kowalski, Dean. A. *Moral Theory at the Movies: An Introduction to Ethics*. Lanham: Rowman and Littlefield Publishers, 2012.

Lively, user-friendly introduction to ethics through examination of a range of popular films. A useful pedagogical text for teaching film and philosophy courses.

Kupfer, Joseph H. *Visions of Virtue in Popular Film*. Boulder, CO: Westview Press, 1999.

One of the earlier Anglophone books dealing with film and ethics, focusing on updated Aristotelian virtues (the virtuous individual, romantic friendship, and the co-operative community, as well as disruptions of these) as articulated in popular cinematic works.

Litch, Mary M. *Philosophy through Film*. 2nd Edition. Abingdon and New York: Routledge, 2010.

Another good pedagogical text for teaching philosophy through film, including a section on ethics, free will and moral responsibility dealing with *Crimes and Misdemeanours, Gattaca,* and *Memento*.

Mulhall, Stephen. *On Film*. 2nd Edition. Abingdon and New York: Routledge, 2008.

A 'classic' text in the field of film and philosophy with some discussion of ethical aspects in films such as *Blade Runner* (Nietzsche and Heidegger), the *Alien* quadrilogy, *Minority Report*, and the *Mission: Impossible* trilogy.

Nagib, Lúcia. *World Cinema and the Ethics of Realism*. New York and London: Continuum Books, 2011.

A timely and original study that renews Bazinian realism, emphasising the filmmaker's desire for truth and the image's material link with reality, exploring an ethics of realism within four 'waves' of diverse 'world cinemas'.

Pippin, Robert B. *Hollywood Westerns and American Myth: The Importance of Howard Hawks and John Ford for Political Philosophy.* New Haven and London: Yale University Press, 2010.

Pippin, Robert B. *Fatalism in American Film Noir: Some Cinematic Philosophy.* Charlottesville: University of Virginia Press, 2012.

Two enlightening philosophical studies of genre that explore ethical dimensions of these films – including their contribution to theorizing moral agency and understanding the role of political mythology – within a distinctively American context.

Rancière, Jacques. *Film Fables.* Trans. Emiliano Battista. Oxford and New York: Berg Books, 2006.

An important text by an increasingly influential French philosopher featuring a critique of Deleuze's philosophy of cinema and detailed readings of Rossellini's works offered as critical responses to Deleuze's account.

Read, Rupert and Goodenough, Jerry (eds). *Film as Philosophy: Essays on Cinema After Wittgenstein and Cavell.* Basingstoke: Palgrave Macmillan, 2005.

Interesting and influential collection of essays on film as philosophy from, broadly speaking, a variety of Wittgensteinian and Cavellian perspectives. See in particular the essays by Mulhall and Critchley.

Rodowick, D. N. *The Virtual Life of Film.* Cambridge, MA and London: Harvard University Press, 2007.

Rodowick's first volume on the fate of film theory following the digital revolution and the retreat from 'Grand Theory' which includes important chapter sections on cinematic ethics in both Cavell and Deleuze.

Rodowick, D. N. *Philosophy's Artful Conversation.* Cambridge, MA and London: Harvard University Press, 2015.

A significant intervention in contemporary film theory defending the ethical value of the humanistic study of film and of 'Continental' approaches to philosophical film theory, focusing on Cavell's and Deleuze's philosophical explorations of worlds, time, and belief.

Rodowick, D. N. (n.d.). 'Ethics in film philosophy (Cavell, Deleuze, Levinas)', unpublished text. Available online at: http://isites.harvard.edu/fs/docs/icb.topic242308.files/Rodowick ETHICSweb.pdf

One of the few texts dealing specifically with 'Continental' ethics in film philosophy, drawing out implicit connections between Cavell on scepticism and Deleuze on belief in contrast with Levinas's ethics of the Other.

Rushton, Richard. *The Politics of Hollywood Cinema: Popular Film and Contemporary Political Theory.* Basingstoke: Palgrave Macmillan, 2013.

A refreshingly clear and insightful discussion of the philosophical potential of Hollywood genre movies, demonstrating how such films engage in ethically and politically significant forms of cultural-philosophical reflection.

Shaw, Dan. *Morality and the Movies: Reading Ethics through Film.* London and New York: Continuum, 2012.

A fine introduction to ethics and moral philosophy by one of the pioneers in the film and philosophy field (and editor of the influential journal *Film and Philosophy*).

Stadler, Jane. *Pulling Focus: Intersubjective Experience, Narrative Film, and Ethics.* New York and London: Continuum, 2008.

Excellent interdisciplinary study of ethics in film drawing on phenomenological, cognitivist, and narrative ethics perspectives, and including detailed readings of a variety of ethically challenging and generically diverse films.

Tersman, Folke. 'Ethics'. In Paisley Livingston and Carl Plantinga (eds), *The Routledge Companion to Philosophy and Film*, 111–120. Abingdon and New York: Routledge, 2009.

A clear, concise, and helpful overview of key issues in theorizing ethics in relation to film, focusing principally on analytic approaches to philosophical film theory.

Wartenberg, Thomas. E. *Thinking on Screen: Film as Philosophy.* Abingdon and New York: Routledge, 2007.

Another 'classic' text in the film and philosophy field, which makes a strong case for the philosophical contribution of cinema. Includes two chapters on film ethics (*Eternal Sunshine of the Spotless Mind* as a counter-example to utilitarianism and *The Third Man* as a study in the limits of moral intelligence and ethical responsibilities of friendship).

Wheatley, Catherine. *Michael Haneke's Cinema: The Ethic of the Image.* New York and Oxford: Berghahn Books, 2009.

Fascinating and insightful study of Haneke's 'ethical cinema', drawing on Kant's moral philosophy and Cavell's philosophy of film, focusing on theorizing the experience of spectatorship in different phases of Haneke's work.

Chapter 2 From scepticism to moral perfectionism (Cavell)

Cavell, Stanley. *Pursuits of Happiness: The Hollywood Comedy of Remarriage.* Cambridge, MA and London: Harvard University Press, 1981.
Cavell, Stanley. *Contesting Tears: The Hollywood Melodrama of the Unknown Woman.* Chicago and London: University of Chicago Press, 1996.

Cavell's two classic texts on these two significant subgenres of melodrama and romantic comedy read as philosophical explorations of an Emersonian ethic of self-transformation.

Cavell, Stanley. *Cities of Words: Pedagogical Letters on a Register of Moral Life.* Cambridge, MA and London: Belknap Press of Harvard University Press, 2004.

Based on Cavell's Harvard Lecture Courses on Moral Reasoning, this volume presents much of the later Cavell's thinking on cinema and ethics, focusing on Emersonian moral perfectionism but also dealing with questions of scepticism, politics, and democracy.

Cavell, Stanley. 'The Good of Film'. In William Rothman (ed.), *Cavell on Film*, 333–348. Albany: State University of New York Press, 2005a.
Cavell, Stanley. 'Moral Reasoning: Teaching from the Core'. In William Rothman (ed.), *Cavell on Film*, 349–359. Albany: State University of New York Press, 2005b.

Two short but illuminating texts from the wonderful *Cavell on Film* collection dealing specifically with ethics, cinema, and philosophical pedagogy (although most of the texts in this volume will be relevant for the study of cinematic ethics).

Eldridge, Richard (ed.). *Stanley Cavell.* Cambridge: Cambridge University Press, 2003.

Illuminating collection of essays by internationally recognized scholars exploring various aspects of Cavell's work. Includes chapters on Cavell on ethics (Bates), aesthetics (Bernstein), romanticism (Desmond), and Cavell on film, television, and opera (Rothman).

Goodman, Russell (ed.). *Contending with Stanley Cavell.* Oxford: Oxford University Press, 2005.

An earlier collection of essays aiming to explicate Cavell's work but also focusing on the question of Cavell's 'difficulty' as a philosopher (in relation to his style of writing). Includes thoughtful chapters by Mulhall and Critchley, and a fine discussion of Cavell and film by Klevan, acknowledging the link between Cavell's aesthetics and ethics.

Hammer, Espen. *Stanley Cavell: Skepticism, Subjectivity and the Ordinary.* Cambridge and Oxford: Polity Press, 2002.
Mulhall, Stephen. *Stanley Cavell: Philosophy's Recounting of the Ordinary.* Oxford: Oxford University Press, 1994.

Two of the best studies of Cavell's work as a whole, integrating Cavell's philosophical background in Wittgenstein and ordinary language philosophy (Austin) with his interests in scepticism, romanticism, Emersonian perfectionism, and philosophy of culture (literature, aesthetics, and film).

Chapter 3 From cinematic belief to ethics and politics (Deleuze)

Barker, Joseph. 'Visions of the Intolerable: Deleuze on Ethical Images', *Cinema: Journal of Philosophy and the Moving Image*, 6, Susana Viegas (ed.), 'Deleuze and Moving Images' (2014): 122–136.

An interesting discussion of Deleuze's ethics of the image, arguing that it is in theorizing our response to the 'intolerable' that we find the core of Deleuze's cinematic ethics.

Bernstein, J. M. '"Movement! Action! Belief?" Notes for a Critique of Deleuze's Cinema Philosophy', *Angelaki: Journal of the Theoretical Humanities,* 17.4 (2012): 77–93.

Acute and incisive critique of Deleuze's account of the role of belief and its relationship to time and memory in post-war cinema, focusing on a close critical reading of Resnais' *Hiroshima mon amour.*

Bogue, Ronald. 'To Choose to Choose – to Believe in this World'. In D. N. Rodowick (ed.), *Afterimages of Gilles Deleuze's Film Philosophy,* 115–134. Minneapolis: University of Minnesota Press, 2010.

Insightful discussion of Deleuze's 'existentialist' ethics focusing on the Pascalian-Kierkegaardian ethic of 'choosing to choose' and 'faith of belief in this world' in relation to Deleuze's account of post-war auteurs such as Dreyer and Bresson.

Boljkovac, Nadine. *Untimely Affects: Gilles Deleuze and an Ethics of Cinema.* Edinburgh: Edinburgh University Press, 2013.

An engaging, performative study focusing on the works of Chris Marker and Alain Resnais, arguing in relation to these films that Deleuze's cinematic ethics involves an affective, transformative response to images oriented towards a creation of 'the ever new'.

Deleuze, Gilles. *Cinema 1: The Movement-Image.* Trans. Hugh Tomlinson and Barbara Habberjam. Minneapolis: University of Minnesota Press, 1986 [1983].
Deleuze, Gilles. *Cinema 2: The Time-Image.* Trans. Hugh Tomlinson and Robert Galatea. Minneapolis: University of Minnesota Press, 1989 [1985].

Deleuze's famous two volumes on cinema, which draw heavily on his previous philosophical work, offering a typology of varieties of movement-image and time-image and an ontology of cinematic images as immanent expressions of movement, time, affect, and thought. The most relevant sections for our purposes are Deleuze's accounts of the 'crisis of the action-image' and transition to 'time-image cinema' at the end of *Cinema 1* and beginning of *Cinema 2*, along with Chapter 8 (in Cinema 2) on 'Cinema, the Body and Brain, and Thought'.

Flaxman, Gregory (ed.). *The Brain is the Screen: Deleuze and the Philosophy of Cinema.* Minneapolis: University of Minnesota Press, 2000.

One of the earliest (and best) edited collections specifically devoted to Deleuze's cinematic philosophy with a helpful Introduction by the editor, enlightening chapters by noted Deleuze scholars (including one on Deleuze's ethics of immanence), and a famous interview with Deleuze, 'The Brain is the Screen'.

King, Alisdair. 'Fault Lines: Deleuze, Cinema, and the Ethical Landscape'. In Jinhee Choi and Mattias Frey (eds), *Cine-Ethics: Ethical Dimensions of Film Theory, Practice, and Spectatorship,* 57–75. London and New York: Routledge, 2014.

An illuminating discussion of Deleuze's cinematic ethics, focusing on the relationship between expressions of the body and belief in this world (a philosophical 'ethology'), explored through the 'ethical landscape' in Christian Petzold's German film, *Wolfsburg* (2003).

Marrati, Paola. *Gilles Deleuze: Cinema and Philosophy*. Trans. Alisa Hartz. Baltimore: The Johns Hopkins University Press, 2006.

One of the best studies of Deleuze's cinematic philosophy, which ably defends Deleuze against Rancière's critique (see below), and includes a brief exploration of the relationship between Cavell and Deleuze.

Martin-Jones, David. *Deleuze and World Cinemas*. London and New York: Continuum, 2011.

Excellent study offering a critique of Deleuze's 'Eurocentrism' in the *Cinema* books, while also extending Deleuze's key theses on ethics and politics in cinema to a variety of case studies in contemporary 'World Cinemas'.

Pisters, Patricia. *The Neuro-Image: A Deleuzian Film-Philosophy of Digital Screen Culture*. Stanford: Stanford University Press, 2012.

Influential interpretation of Deleuze's *Cinema* books in relation to the 'neuro-image' as a significant new cinematic form; includes exploration of the crossover between Deleuze's interest in the brain/body in cinema and contemporary neuro-scientific theory applied to film.

Rancière, Jacques. *Film Fables*. Trans. Emiliano Battista. Oxford and New York: Berg Books, 2006.

One of the most significant recent books published in contemporary 'Continental' film-philosophy; includes important critique of the 'two ages' of cinema in Deleuze's *Cinema* books and close analyses of Bresson's films in response to Deleuze's claims concerning time-image cinema.

Rodowick, D. N. 'The World, Time'. In D.N. Rodowick (ed.), *Afterimages of Gilles Deleuze's Film Philosophy*, 97–114. Minneapolis: University of Minnesota Press, 2010.

Rodowick's most explicit engagement with Deleuze's cinematic ethics, exploring the relationship between Cavell and Deleuze on cinema and ethics. Focuses on the Nietzschean aspects (Welles) of Deleuze's cinematic ethics, and the crisis of belief in the world and the need to affirm this belief through images that inaugurates post-war cinema (Dreyer, Bresson).

Rodowick, D. N. *Gilles Deleuze's Time Machine*. Durham and London: Duke University Press, 1997.

One of the earliest (and most enlightening) studies of Deleuze's cinematic philosophy covering the most important philosophical background (Bergson, Peirce, Nietzsche) to the *Cinema* books and offering detailed exegeses of Deleuze's key cinematic concepts.

Chapter 4 Cinempathy: phenomenology, cognitivism, and moving images

Allen, Richard and Smith, Murray (eds). *Film Theory and Philosophy*. Oxford: Oxford University Press, 1997.

A landmark collection of essays marking the analytic-cognitivist turn in film theory. Includes three chapters focusing on issues on ideology and ethics (on feminism, ideology, and race) and four chapters on emotional response (see Plantinga's chapter on 'Spectator Emotion and Ideological Criticism', and M. Smith's chapter on 'Imagining from the Inside').

Barker, Jennifer M. *The Tactile Eye: Touch and the Cinematic Experience*. Berkeley: University of California Press, 2009.

A good example of the 'strong' version of phenomenological 'tactile' or haptic affect theory approaches in film studies, including a number of contemporary film analyses.

Bordwell, David and Carroll, Noël (eds). *Post-Theory: Reconstructing Film Studies*. Madison: University of Wisconsin Press, 1996.

Bordwell and Carroll's noted collection announced the analytic-cognitivist turn in film theory and launched a polemical critique of so-called 'Grand Theory'. Surprisingly little attention, however, is given to emotion or ethics (excepting Neill's chapter on 'Empathy and (Film) Fiction').

Clark, Andy. *Supersizing the Mind: Embodiment, Action, and Cognitive Extension*. Oxford: Oxford University Press, 2008.

Clear, engaging, and enlightening introduction to embodied/extended mind theories of cognition by one of the leaders in the field.

Coplan, Amy and Goldie, Peter (eds). *Empathy: Philosophical and Psychological Perspectives*, IX-XLVII. Oxford: Oxford University Press, 2011.

Excellent co-edited collection of essays with helpful Introduction by the editors. See in particular Coplan's chapter 'Understanding Empathy', Currie's on 'Empathy for Objects', M. Smith's on 'Empathy and the Extended Mind', and Carroll's discussion of empathy and spectator engagement. See also the concluding part (six chapters) on empathy and morality.

Currie, Gregory. *Image and Mind. Film, Philosophy, and Cognitive Science*. New York: Cambridge University Press, 1995.

Important and rigorous early monograph on cognitivist approaches to theorizing film and our cognitive experience of it.

Damasio, Antonio. *Descartes' Error: Emotion, Reason, and the Human Brain*. New York: Penguin, 1994.

Damasio, Antonio. *The Feeling of What Happens: Body and Emotion in the Making of Consciousness*. Newcourt: Harcourt Brace, 1999.

Two engaging and highly readable accounts of neurophysiological theories of emotion and the role of emotion in the development and functioning of consciousness.

de Sousa, Ronald. *The Rationality of Emotion*. Cambridge, MA: The MIT Press, 1987.

De Sousa's major work on the emotions, arguing for their vital role in cognitive experience and key contribution to our capacity for reasoning, both moral and practical.

de Sousa, Ronald. 'Moral Emotions', *Ethical Theory and Moral Practice*, 4.2 (2001): 109–126.

A succinct and articulate account of de Sousa's influential work on moral emotions.

Goldie, Peter. *The Emotions: A Philosophical Investigation*. Oxford and New York: Oxford University Press, 2002.

Important and enlightening philosophical study of the emotions by one of the leading philosophers in this field of inquiry; see in particular the chapters on emotion and mood, emotional contagion, empathy and sympathy.

Grodal, Torben. *Embodied Visions: Evolution, Emotion, Culture, and Film*. Oxford: Oxford University Press, 2009.

A 'strong' version of the neuro-cognitivist, evolutionary bio-culturalist approach to film theory (see the chapters on the 'PECMA flow model' (perception-emotion-cognition-motor action)). Despite certain reductivist tendencies there are intriguing parallels with Deleuze's 'sensory-motor action schema' and the (cognitive-aesthetic) effects of its breakdown.

Hanich, Julian. *Cinematic Emotion in Horror Films and Thrillers: The Aesthetic Paradox of Pleasurable Fear*. New York: Routledge, 2010.

Interesting account of the 'paradox of pleasurable fear' in movies drawing on phenomenology and cognitivist theory; argues that the pleasure we take in fear – of five types relating to bodily, temporal, and social experience – has implications for understanding modernity.

Laine, Tarja. *Feeling Cinema: Emotional Dynamics in Film Studies*. New York and London: Continuum, 2011.

Engaging and thoughtful study of emotional dynamics in film experience, emphasizing not only spectator response but the ethical interplay between spectator and film in our emotional, aesthetic, and affective involvement in movies. Focuses on a key film for each major emotion.

Marks, Laura U. *The Skin of the Film: Intercultural Cinema, Embodiment, and the Senses*. Durham: Duke University Press, 2000.

Marks, Laura U. *Touch: Sensuous Theory and Multisensory Media*. Minneapolis: University of Minnesota Press, 2002.

Two highly influential texts on Deleuzian 'haptic' theory emphasizing the importance of multi-sensorial engagement/the tactile image, while underlining the centrality of embodiment and cultural difference to our film experience (using 'intercultural cinema' examples).

Menary, Richard. *Cognitive Integration: Mind and Cognition Unbounded*, Basingstoke: Palgrave Macmillan, 2007.
Menary, Richard (ed.). *The Extended Mind*. Cambridge, MA: The MIT Press, 2010.

Two excellent, informative philosophical studies of the 'extended mind' approach to cognition that are both accessible and philosophically sophisticated.

Nannicelli, Ted and Taberham, Paul (eds). *Cognitive Media Theory*. Abingdon and New York: Routledge, 2014.

Path-breaking new volume on cognitivist approaches to film/media studies showcasing the breadth and depth of contemporary inquiries in cognitivist theory; see in particular the chapters by M. Smith, Ed Tan, Carl Plantinga, and Torben Grodal.

Nussbaum, Martha. C. *Love's Knowledge: Essays on Philosophy and Literature*. Oxford: Oxford University Press, 1992.
Nussbaum, Martha. C. *Upheavals of Thought: The Intelligence of Emotions*. Cambridge: University of Cambridge, 2001.

Two of Nussbaum's most eloquent and influential texts dealing with the relationship between philosophy and art and the vital role of aesthetic experience in ethics and moral imagination.

Plantinga, Carl and Smith, Greg (eds). *Passionate Views: Film, Cognition, and Emotion*. Baltimore: Johns Hopkins University Press, 1999.

Important and influential 'early' collection of essays on cognitivist approaches to emotion, narrative, and spectator engagement in film; see in particular the chapters by Carroll, Cynthia Freeland, Greg M. Smith, Berys Gaut, M. Smith, and Plantinga.

Prinz, Jesse. *Gut Reaction: A Perceptual Theory of Emotion*. Oxford: Oxford University Press, 2004.
Prinz, Jesse. *The Emotional Construction of Morals*. Oxford: Oxford University Press, 2009.

Two fascinating texts on the role of emotion in morality and Prinz's perceptual account of emotions and 'gut feelings' (embodied appraisals) as affective/emotional guides to social cognition and moral evaluation.

Robinson, Jenefer. *Deeper than Reason: Emotion and its Role in Literature, Music, and Art*. Oxford: Oxford University Press, 2007.

An excellent study of the role of emotion in art, culture, and human cognition more generally, arguing that emotional expression and response are key to literature, music, and the arts.

Sinnerbrink, Robert. '*Stimmung*: Exploring the Aesthetics of Mood', *Screen*, 53.2 (Summer 2012): 148–163.

My contribution to theorizing mood in cinema as a neglected but essential aspect of emotional engagement in movies; moods are world-building/world-revealing ways of situating us within a plausible cinematic world in order to facilitate emotional responsiveness.

Smith, Greg M. *Film Structure and the Emotion System*. Cambridge: Cambridge University Press, 2003.

One of the few dedicated studies on the topic of mood in film, arguing for its importance for emotional involvement in film and analysing the manner in which moods are cued by various cinematic devices and directorial strategies.

Smith, Murray. *Engaging Characters: Fiction, Emotion, and the Cinema*. Oxford: Oxford University Press, 1995.

A 'classic' text in the study of cinema and emotion, which introduced Smith's highly influential model of emotional engagement with its three aspects of recognition, alignment, and (moral) allegiance in response to fictional characters in movies.

Sobchack, Vivian. *The Address of the Eye: A Phenomenology of Film Experience*. Princeton: Princeton University Press, 1992.
Sobchack, Vivian. *Carnal Thoughts: Embodiment and Moving Image Culture*. Berkeley: University of California Press, 2004.

Two key texts in the phenomenological turn in film theory, the former introducing (Husserlian and Merleau-Pontian) phenomenological analysis to film theory, and the latter exploring diverse aspects of embodiment in our experience of moving images.

Stadler, Jane. *Pulling Focus: Intersubjective Experience, Narrative Film, and Ethics*. New York and London: Continuum, 2008.
Stadler, Jane. 'Affectless Empathy, Embodied Imagination and *The Killer Inside Me*', *Screening the Past*, 37 (2013). Available online at: www.screeningthepast.com/2013/10/affectless-empathy-embodied-imagination-and-the-killer-inside-me/#_edn3
Stadler, Jane. 'Cinema's Compassionate Gaze: Empathy, Affect, and Aesthetics in *The Diving Bell and the Butterfly*'. In Choi and Frey (eds), *Cine-Ethics: Ethical Dimension of Film Theory, Practice, and Spectatorship*, 27–42. New York and London: Routledge, 2014.

Illuminating pieces that explore affect, emotion, and embodied imagination in recent cinema; Stadler's monograph, moreover, is an excellent example of how phenomenological and cognitivist perspectives can provide a rich interdisciplinary matrix for theorizing affect, emotion, and ethics in narrative film.

Yacavone, Daniel. *Film Worlds: A Philosophical Aesthetics of Cinema*. New York: Columbia University Press, 2015.

Ambitious and perspicuous philosophical study of film worlds, drawing on Nelson Goodman's constructivist aesthetics, Dufrenne's phenomenology, and Gadamer's hermeneutics to argue for the centrality of film worlds in our aesthetic experience of film.

Chapter 5 The moral melodrama (*Stella Dallas, Talk to Her*)

Berlant, Lauren. *The Female Complaint: The Unfinished Business of Sentimentality in American Culture*. Durham: Duke University Press, 2008.

Fascinating study of the formation of 'women's culture' – focusing considerably on filmic melodrama – and its role in the 'sentimentality' informing American culture and politics.

Brooks, Peter. *The Melodramatic Imagination: Balzac, Henry James, Melodrama and the Mode of Excess*. New Haven: Yale University Press, 1976.

Very influential study of the melodramatic imagination as a cultural 'mode' that has been widely applied to cinema; introduces the idea of melodrama as cultural inheritor of tragedy in a post-sacred world, the locus of a suppressed 'moral occult' or cryptic source of value that provides evidence of 'moral legibility' in the absence of universalist normative foundations.

Cavell, Stanley. *Contesting Tears: The Hollywood Melodrama of the Unknown Woman*. Chicago: Chicago University Press, 1996.
Cavell, Stanley. *Cities of Words: Pedagogical Letters on a Register of Moral Life*. Cambridge, MA and London: Belknap Press of the Harvard University Press, 2004.

The texts of Cavell's that engage most explicitly with melodrama, in particular the melodrama of the unknown woman, as a cinematic response to moral/other minds scepticism, with *Cities of Words* focusing on the Emersonian moral perfectionist aspects of these films.

D'Lugo, Marvin. *Pedro Almodóvar (Contemporary Film Directors)*. Urbana and Chicago: University of Illinois Press, 2006.

Fine, succinct study of Almodóvar's work providing useful cultural context and insightful critical discussions of individual films in his *oeuvre* (but only up to 2006).

Eaton, A.W. (ed.) *Talk to Her* (Philosophers on Film), 11–26. Abingdon and New York: Routledge, 2009.

Excellent volume in the 'Philosophers on Film' series focusing on Almodóvar's *Talk to Her* with a useful Introduction by Noël Carroll, and featuring philosophical essays on the film by A.W. Eaton, Cynthia Freeland, Robert Pippin, and George Wilson.

Elsaesser, Thomas. 'Tales of Sound and Fury: Observations on the Family Melodrama'. In Christine Gledhill (ed.), *Home is Where the Heart Is: Studies in Melodrama and the Woman's Film*, 43–69. London: British Film Institute, 1987 [First published in *Monograms*, 4, 1972: 2–15].

One of Elsaesser's most influential pieces, this erudite study of melodrama provides a rich framework for exploring the interrelated cultural, ethical, and aesthetic dimensions of cinematic melodrama in historical perspective.

Gledhill, Christine. 'The Melodramatic Field: An Investigation'. In Christine Gledhill (ed.), *Home Is Where the Heart Is: Studies in Melodrama and the Woman's Film*, 5–39. London: BFI Books, 1987.

Another highly influential study of melodrama in film promoting the idea of melodrama as a 'mode' of cultural experience; Gledhill argues that the construction of the 'family melodrama' obscured the many kinds of 'melodramatic rhetoric' to be found in both melodramatic and realist forms of popular movie narrative.

Goss, Brian Michael. *Global Auteurs: Politics in the Films of Almodóvar, von Trier, and Winterbottom*. New York: Peter Lang, 2009.

Auteur study of three said filmmakers emphasizing the international, historical, and production context of their work, and using this background in order to explore the political significance (institutional rather than cultural-political) of their films.

Mercer, John and Shingler, Martin. *Melodrama: Genre, Style, Sensibility*. London and New York: Wallflower Books, 2004.

A highly readable and insightful overview of the history of differing schools of theoretical work on melodrama within film studies, including helpful discussions of individual films.

Williams, Linda. 'Melodrama Revisited'. In Nick Browne (ed.), *Refiguring American Film Genres: History and Theory*, 42–88. Berkeley and Los Angeles: University of California Press, 1998.
Williams, Linda. '"Something Else Besides a Woman": *Stella Dallas* and the Maternal Melodrama', *Cinema Journal*, 24.1 (Autumn 1984): 2–27.

Two key pieces on melodrama by Williams, the latter being one to which Cavell responds in his reading of *Stella Dallas*, and the former developing further the idea of melodrama as a mode, now taken as definitive of American popular narrative cinema *tout court*.

Chapter 6 Melodrama, realism, and ethical experience (*Biutiful, The Promise*)

Cooper, Sarah. *Selfless Cinema? Ethics and French Documentary*. London: Legenda, 2006.
Cooper, Sarah. 'Mortal Ethics: Reading Levinas with the Dardenne Brothers', *Film-Philosophy*, 11.2 (2007): 66–87. Available online at: www.film-philosophy.com/2007v11n2/cooper.pdf
Cooper, Sarah. (ed.). 'The Occluded Relation: Levinas and Cinema', Special Issue of *Film-Philosophy*, 11.2 (2007). Available online at: www.film-philosophy.com/index.php/f-p/issue/view/13

Cooper's path-breaking work on Levinas and film is essential reading, balancing philosophical interpretation with cinematic engagement; her edited special issue of *Film-Philosophy* on 'Levinas and Cinema' remains a landmark contribution. As mentioned, her book on French documentary demonstrates the richness of a Levinasian cinematic ethics.

Mai, Joseph. *Jean-Pierre and Luc Dardenne*. Urbana: University of Illinois Press, 2010.
Mai, Joseph. 'Lorna's Silence and Levinas's Ethical Alternative: Form and Viewer in the Dardenne Brothers', *New Review of Film and Television Studies*, 9:4 (2011): 435–453.

Mai's article and book offer detailed readings of the Dardenne brothers' work from a Levinasian perspective, emphasizing the relationship between aesthetic and ethical dimensions of their films.

Mosley, Philip. *The Cinema of the Dardenne Brothers: Responsible Realism*. London and New York: Wallflower Press, 2012.

An enlightening and articulate critical account of the Dardenne brothers' films, exploring their cultural-political background, documentary work, and ongoing political commitment to an ethically and socially responsible form of cinematic realism.

Rushton, Richard. 'Empathic Projection in the Films of the Dardenne Brothers', *Screen*, 55:3 (Autumn 2014): 303–316.

Lucid and insightful discussion of the Dardenne brothers' films, arguing that they are not only ethical but political, and exploring the role of 'empathic projection' (imaginative proximity without intrusive instrumentalization) as evinced in their work.

Saxton, Libby. *Haunted Images: Film, Ethics, Testimony, and the Holocaust*. London: Wallflower Press, 2008.

An excellent film-philosophical study of the ethics of documentary filmmaking focusing on the question of testimony, trauma, and memorialization in respect of the 'unrepresentable' character of the Holocaust. Relevant not only for this chapter but for the next as well.

Sinnerbrink, Robert. 'Post-Secular Ethics: The Case of Iñárritu's *Biutiful*'. In Costica Bradatan and Camil Ungureanu (eds), *Religion in Contemporary European Cinema: The Postsecular Constellation*, 166–185. Abingdon and New York: Routledge, 2014.

A longer discussion of Iñárritu's *Biutiful* as a case of 'post-secular cinematic ethics', linking the film with recent explorations of the relationship between film, philosophy, social-historical experience, and religion.

Staehler, Tanja. 'Images and shadows: Levinas and the ambiguity of the aesthetic', *Estetika: The Central European Journal of Aesthetics*, 47.2 (2010): 123–143.

A helpful discussion of the vexed issue of Levinas, art, and aesthetics in relation to his ethics.

Chapter 7 Gangster film: cinematic ethics in *The Act of Killing*

Anderson, Benedict. 'Impunity'. In Joram Ten Brink and Joshua Oppenheimer (eds), *Killer Images: Documentary Film, Memory, and the Performance of Violence*, 268–286. New York: Columbia University Press, 2012.

The volume edited by Oppenheimer and Ten Brink has fascinating explorations of the ethics of cinema in relation to social domination and political violence; Anderson's chapter on *The Act of Killing* argues that the perpetrators' boasting about their crimes has the performative effect of demonstrating impunity and thus ensuring social control and silencing of dissent.

Cribb, Robert. 'The Act of Killing', *Critical Asian Studies*, 46.1 (2014): 147–149.

Dwyer, Leslie K. 'Picturing Violence: Anti-Politics and *The Act of Killing*', *Critical Asian Studies*, 46.1 (2014): 183–188.

Hearman, Vannessa. '"Missing Victims" of The 1965–66 Violence In Indonesia: Representing Impunity On-Screen in *The Act of Killing*', *Critical Asian Studies*, 46.1 (2014): 171–175.

Heryanto, Ariel. 'Great and Misplaced Expectations', *Critical Asian Studies*, 46.1 (2014): 162–166.

McGregor, Katharine. 'Inside the Minds of Executioners: Reimagining the Loss of Life in the 1965 Indonesian Killings', *Critical Asian Studies*, 46.1 (2014): 189–194.

All of the above articles offer brief, penetrating analyses of *The Act of Killing* by scholars with expertise in the areas of Indonesian studies, anthropology, and political studies. They provide important context for my discussion of the film as a case study in cinematic ethics.

Morag, Raya. *Waltzing with Bashir: Perpetrator Trauma and Cinema*. London and New York: I.B. Tauris, 2012.

Fascinating exploration of the idea of 'perpetrator documentary' in relation to recent Israeli documentary film with significant theoretical relevance for understanding *The Act of Killing*.

Oppenheimer, Joshua. 'Show of Force: A Cinema-Séance of Power and Violence in Sumatra's Plantation Belt'. In J. Ten Brink and J. Oppenheimer, *Killer Images: Documentary Film, Memory and the Performance of Violence,* 287–310. London and New York: Wallflower Press, 2012.

Oppenheimer, Joshua. The Act of Killing *Press Notes*. Berlin: Wolf, 2013. Available online at: http://ff.hrw.org/sites/default/files/THE%20ACT%20OF%20KILLING%20press%20notes.pdf

Oppenheimer's chapter is essential reading in order to understand why he adopted the 'cinematic re-enactment' strategy in collaboration with the perpetrators. It also provides important background for Oppenheimer's follow-up film, *The Look of Silence* (2015), which focuses on the brother of one of the victims confronting the killers today.

Renov, Michael. *The Subject of Documentary*. Minneapolis: University of Minnesota Press, 2004.

Important study of the 'new documentary' exploring the adoption of 'post-documentary', fictional techniques of narrative film and foregrounding of subjectivity in creating works that blur received distinctions between fictional and non-fictional film.

Saxton, Libby. *Haunted Images: Film, Testimony, Ethics, and the Holocaust*. London: Wallflower Press, 2008.

An excellent film-philosophical study of the ethics of documentary filmmaking focusing on the question of testimony, trauma, and memorialization in respect of the 'unrepresentable' character of the Holocaust. Relevant not only for this chapter but for the previous one as well.

Sears, Laurie J. 'Heroes as Killers or Killers as Heroes?' *Critical Asian Studies*, 46.1 (2014): 204–207.
Van Klinken, Gerry. 'No, The Act Of Killing Is Not Unethical', *Critical Asian Studies*, 46.1 (2014): 176–178.
Wieringa, Saskia E. 'Sexual Politics as a Justification for Mass Murder in *The Act Of Killing*', *Critical Asian Studies*, 46.1 (2014): 195–199.

See my comments above about this special issue of *Critical Asian Studies* dedicated to Oppenheimer's *The Act of Killing*.

Winston, Brian. *Lies, Damn Lies and Documentary*. London: BFI Books, 2000.

Another key study exploring the epistemic, ethical, and political questions raised by the blurring of the fiction/non-fiction, truth/illusion, objectivity/subjectivity distinctions within contemporary forms of documentary.

Conclusion

Hadot, Pierre. *Philosophy as a Way of Life: Spiritual Exercises from Socrates to Foucault*. Arnold Davidson (ed.). Trans. Michael Chase. Oxford: Basil Blackwell, 1995.
Hadot, Pierre. 'There are Nowadays Professors of Philosophy but no Philosophers'. Trans. J. Aaron Simmons. *Journal of Speculative Realism*, 19.3 (2005): 229–237.

Fascinating discussions of the ancient Greek idea of philosophy as a way of life. Hadot's article is particularly interesting given that it explores the link between Cavell, Emerson, and an ethos of a life devoted to philosophical inquiry, self-transformation, and ethical conduct.

Sinnerbrink, Robert. 'Cinematic Belief: Bazinian Cinephilia and Malick's *The Tree of Life*', *Angelaki*, 17.4 (2012): 95–117.

A discussion of Malick's *The Tree of Life*, linking it to Bazinian realism but also to the idea of an ethical account of cinephilia as an aesthetic expression of the 'love of the world'.

Appendix 2: Filmography for teaching and research

What follows is a filmography of movies that would be useful or relevant for teaching and researching topics related to cinematic ethics. These are movies mentioned in the book, and related ones that would be worth considering; some are frequently discussed in the literature, others are less well-known but thought-provoking, but of course any such list will inevitably be contingent, subjective, or partial, and could never pretend to be exhaustive or definitive. I hope, nonetheless, that it provides some helpful suggestions for further study and research.

21 Grams. Dir. Alejandro González Iñárritu (USA, 2003)
2001: A Space Odyssey. Dir. Stanley Kubrick (USA/UK, 1968)
A Clockwork Orange. Dir. Stanley Kubrick (UK/USA, 1971)
A.I. Artificial Intelligence. Dir. Steven Spielberg (USA, 2001)
A Man Escaped [*Un condamné à mort s'est échappé ou Le vent souffle où il veut*]. Dir. Robert Bresson (France, 1956)
A Separation [*Jodaeiye Nader az Simin*]. Dir. Asghar Farhadi (Iran, 2011)
A Short Film about Killing [*Krótki film o zabijaniu*]. Dir. Krzysztof Kieslowski (Poland, 1988)
The Act of Killing [*Jagal*]. Dir. Joshua Oppenheimer, Christine Cynn, and Anonymous (Denmark/Norway/UK, 2012)
Adam's Rib. Dir. George Cukor (USA, 1949)
Ali: Fear Eats the Soul. Dir. Rainer Werner Fassbinder (Germany, 1974)
Alien. Dir. Ridley Scott (USA, 1979)
All About My Mother [*Todo sobre mi madre*]. Dir. Pedro Almodóvar (Spain/France, 1999)
All That Heaven Allows. Dir. Douglas Sirk (USA, 1955)
American Sniper. Dir. Clint Eastwood (USA, 2014)
Amores Perros. Dir. Alejandro González Iñárritu (Mexico, 2000)
Amour. Dir. Michael Haneke (France/Germany/Austria, 2012)
Argo. Dir. Ben Affleck (USA, 2012)
Au hasard Balthazar. Dir. Robert Bresson (France/Sweden, 1966)
Avatar. Dir. James Cameron (USA/UK, 2013)
L'Avventura. Dir. Michelangelo Antonioni (France/Italy, 1960)
The Awful Truth. Dir. Leo McCarey (USA, 1937)
Babel. Dir. Alejandro González Iñárritu (France/USA/Mexico, 2006)
Badlands. Dir. Terrence Malick (USA, 1973)
Batman Begins. Dir. Christopher Nolan (USA, 2005)

The Battle of Algiers [*La battaglia di Algeri*]. Dir. Gillo Pontecorvo (Italy/Algiers, 1966)
Benny's Video. Dir. Michael Haneke (Austria/Switzerland, 1992)
Bicycle Thieves [*Ladri di biciclette*]. Dir. Vittorio De Sica (Italy, 1948)
The Bitter Tears of Petra von Kant. Dir. Rainer Werner Fassbinder (Germany, 1972)
Biutiful. Dir. Alejandro González Iñárritu (Spain, 2005)
Black Swan. Dir. Darren Aronofsky (USA, 2010)
Blade Runner. Dir. Ridley Scott (USA/Hong Kong/UK, 1982)
Breaking Bad [TV Series]. Creator Vince Gilligan (USA, 2008–2013)
Breaking the Waves. Dir. Lars von Trier (Denmark/Sweden/France/Netherlands/Norway/
    Iceland/Spain, 1996)
Bringing Up Baby. Dir. Howard Hawks (USA, 1938)
Brokeback Mountain. Dir. Ang Lee (USA/Canada, 2005)
Broken Embraces [*Los abrazos rotos*]. Dir. Pedro Almodóvar (Spain, 2009)
Caché [*Hidden*]. Dir. Michael Haneke (France/Austria/Germany/Italy, 2005)
Cave of Forgotten Dreams. Dir. Werner Herzog (Canada/USA/France/Germany/UK, 2010)
The Child [*L'enfant*]. Dir. Jean-Pierre and Luc Dardenne (Belgium, 2005)
Children of Men. Dir. Alfonso Cuarón (USA/UK, 2006)
Chinatown. Dir. Roman Polanski (USA, 1974)
Cinema Paradiso [*Nuovo Cinema Paradiso*]. Dir. Giuseppe Tornatore (Italy/France, 1988)
City of God [*Cidade de deus*]. Dir. Fernando Meirelles, Kátia Lund (Brazil/France, 2002)
City Lights. Dir. Charles Chaplin (USA, 1931)
Code Unknown [*Code inconnu: Récit incomplet de divers voyages*]. Dir. Michael Haneke
    (France/Germany/Romania, 2000)
Crash. Dir. Paul Haggis (Germany/USA, 2004)
Crimes and Misdemeanors. Dir. Woody Allen (USA, 1989)
The Dark Knight. Dir. Christopher Nolan (UK/USA, 2008)
The Dark Knight Rises. Dir. Christopher Nolan (UK/USA, 2012)
Day of Wrath [*Vredens dag*]. Dir. Carl Theodor Dreyer (Denmark, 1943)
Diary of a Country Priest [*Journal d'un curé de campagne*]. Dir. Robert Bresson (France, 1951)
District 9. Dir. Neill Blomkamp (USA/New Zealand/ Canada/South Africa, 2009)
The Diving Bell and the Butterfly [*Le scaphandre et le papillon*]. Dir. Julian Schnabel
    (France/USA, 2007)
Do the Right Thing. Dir. Spike Lee (USA, 1989)
Dogville. Dir. Lars von Trier (Denmark/UK/Sweden/France, 2003)
The Double Life of Veronique [*La double vie de Véronique*]. Dir. Krzysztof Kieslowski
    (France/Poland/Norway, 1991)
East of Eden. Dir. Elia Kazan (USA, 1955)
Easy Rider. Dir. Dennis Hopper (USA, 1969)
An Education. Dir. Lone Scherfig (UK/USA, 2009)
Elephant. Dir. Gus van Sant (USA, 2003)
The Emperor's Naked Army Marches On [*Yuki Yukite shingun*]. Dir. Kazuo Hara (Japan,
    1987).
Eternal Sunshine of the Spotless Mind. Dir. Michel Gondry (USA, 2004)
Europe '51 [*Europa '51*]. Dir. Roberto Rossellini (Italy, 1952)
Far From Heaven. Dir. Todd Haynes (USA/France, 2002)
Fat Girl [*À ma soeur!*]. Dir. Catherine Breillat (France/Italy, 2001)
Festen [*The Celebration*]. Dir. Thomas Vinterberg (Denmark, 1998)
Fight Club. Dir. David Fincher (USA/Germany, 1999)
The Five Obstructions. Dir. Jorgen Leth/Lars von Trier (Denmark/Switzerland/Belgium/
    France, 2003)

The 400 Blows [*Les quatre cent coups*]. Dir. François Truffaut (France, 1959)
40 Years of Silence: An Indonesian Tragedy. Dir. Robert Lemelson (USA, 2009)
Full Metal Jacket. Dir. Stanley Kubrick (USA/UK, 1987)
Funny Games. Dir. Michael Haneke (USA/France/UK/Austria/Germany/Italy, 2007)
Gallipoli. Dir. Peter Weir (Australia, 1981)
Game of Thrones [TV Series]. Creators David Benioff, D.B. Weiss (UK/USA, 2011–)
Le gamin au vélo [*The Kid with a Bike*]. Dir. Jean-Pierre and Luc Dardenne (Belgium, 2011)
Gaslight. Dir. George Cukor (USA, 1944)
Gattaca. Dir. Andrew Niccol (USA, 1997)
Germany Year Zero [*Germania, anno zero*]. Dir. Roberto Rossellini (Italy, 1948)
Getrud. Dir. Carl Theodor Dreyer (Denmark, 1964)
Gone Baby Gone. Dir. Ben Affleck (USA, 2007)
Grizzly Man. Dir. Werner Herzog (USA, 2005)
Groundhog Day. Dir. Harold Ramis (USA, 1993)
Hiroshima mon amour. Dir. Alain Resnais (France/Japan, 1959)
His Girl Friday. Dir. Howard Hawks (USA, 1940)
The Hunt [*Jagten*]. Dir. Thomas Vinterberg (Denmark/Sweden, 2012)
The Hurt Locker. Dir. Kathryn Bigelow (USA, 2008)
I Confess. Dir. Alfred Hitchcock (UK, 1953)
The Ice Storm. Dir. Ang Lee (USA/France, 1997)
The Idiots [*Idioterne*]. Dir. Lars von Trier (Denmark/Spain/Sweden/France/Netherlands/
    Italy, 1998)
Incendies. Dir. Denis Villeneuve (Canada/France, 2010)
In the Mood for Love [*Fa yeung nin wa*]. Dir. Kar-Wai Wong (Hong Kong/China, 2000)
Into the Abyss. Dir. Werner Herzog (USA/UK/Germany, 2011)
It Happened One Night. Dir. Frank Capra (USA, 1934)
It's a Wonderful Life. Dir. Frank Capra (USA, 1946)
Jaws. Dir. Steven Spielberg (USA, 1975)
Johnny Guitar. Dir. Nicholas Ray (USA, 1954)
Journey to Italy [*Viaggio in Italia*]. Dir. Roberto Rossellini (Italy/France, 1954)
Jules et Jim. Dir. François Truffaut (France, 1962)
Kika. Dir. Pedro Almodóvar (Spain/France, 1993)
The Kingdom [*Riget*]. Dir. Lars von Trier (Denmark/Italy/Germany/France/Norway/
    Sweden, 1994)
Kiss Me Deadly. Dir. Robert Aldrich (USA, 1955)
La grande illusion. Dir. Jean Renoir (France, 1937)
Law of Desire [*La ley del deseo*]. Dir. Pedro Almodóvar (Spain, 1987)
Le Havre. Dir. Aki Kaurismäki (Finland/France/Germany, 2011)
Letter from an Unknown Woman. Dir. Max Ophüls (USA, 1948)
Life of Pi. Dir. Ang Lee (USA/Taiwan/UK/Canada/France, 2012)
Lili Marleen. Dir. Rainer Werner Fassbinder (West Germany, 1981)
Live Flesh [*Carne trémula*]. Dir. Pedro Almodóvar (Spain/France, 1997)
To Live [*Ikiru*]. Dir. Akira Kurosawa (Japan, 1952)
Lolita. Dir. Stanley Kubrick (UK/USA, 1962)
The Look of Silence. Dir. Joshua Oppenheimer (Denmark/Finland/Indonesia/Norway/UK,
    2014)
Los Olvidados. Dir. Luis Buñuel (Mexico, 1950)
Lost in Translation. Dir. Sofia Coppola (USA/Japan, 2003)
M. Dir. Fritz Lang (Germany, 1931)
Mad Men [TV series]. Creator Matthew Weiner (USA, 2007–2015)

The Man Who Shot Liberty Valance. Dir. John Ford (USA, 1962)
Melancholia. Dir. Lars von Trier (Denmark/Sweden/France/Germany, 2011)
Metropolis. Dir. Fritz Lang (Germany, 1927)
Mr. Deeds Goes to Town. Dir. Frank Capra (USA, 1936)
Monster's Ball. Dir. Marc Forster (USA, 2001)
Mouchette. Dir. Robert Bresson (France, 1967)
Muriel, or The Time of Return [*Muriel ou Le temps d'un retour*]. Dir. Alain Resnais
    (France/Italy, 1963)
Night and Fog [*Nuit et brouillard*]. Dir. Alain Resnais (France, 1955)
No Country for Old Men. Dir. Ethan Cohen, Joel Cohen (USA, 2007)
Now, Voyager. Dir. Irving Rapper (USA, 1942)
Ordet. Dir. Carl Theodor Dreyer (Denmark, 1955)
Paisan [*Paisà*]. Dir. Roberto Rossellini (Italy, 1946)
The Passion of Joan of Arc [*La passion de Jeanne d'Arc*]. Dir. Carl Theodor Dreyer
    (France, 1928)
The Past [*Le passé*]. Dir. Asghar Farhadi (France/Italy/Iran, 2013)
Paths of Glory. Dir. Stanley Kubrick (USA, 1957)
Peeping Tom. Dir. Michael Powell (UK, 1960)
Persona. Dir. Ingmar Bergman (Sweden, 1966)
The Philadelphia Story. Dir. George Cukor (USA, 1940)
Pickpocket. Dir. Robert Bresson (France, 1959)
The Promise [*La promesse*]. Dir. Jean-Pierre and Luc Dardenne (Belgium, 1996)
Psycho. Dir. Alfred Hitchcock (USA, 1960)
Rabbit-Proof Fence. Dir. Phillip Noyce (Australia, 2002)
Rashomon. Dir. Akira Kurosawa (Japan, 1950)
Rebecca. Dir. Alfred Hitchcock (USA, 1940)
Redacted. Dir. Brian de Palma (USA/Canada, 2006)
Rome, Open City [*Roma, città aperta*]. Dir. Roberto Rossellini (Italy, 1945)
Rosetta. Dir. Jean-Pierre and Luc Dardenne (Belgium, 1999)
The Rules of the Game [*La règle du jeu*]. Dir. Jean Renoir (France, 1939)
Safe. Dir. Todd Haynes (UK/USA, 1995)
Samson and Delilah. Dir. Warwick Thornton (Australia, 2009)
The Sea Inside [*Mar adrento*]. Dir. Alejandro Amenábar (Spain/France/Italy, 2004)
The Searchers. Dir. John Ford (USA, 1956)
Shoah. Dir. Claude Lanzmann (France/UK, 1985)
The Silence [*Tystnaden*]. Dir. Ingmar Bergman (Sweden, 1963)
The Silence of Lorna [*Le silence de Lorna*]. Dir. Jean-Pierre and Luc Dardenne (Belgium,
    2008)
The Snowtown Murders [*Snowtown*]. Dir. Justin Kurzel (Australia, 2011)
The Son [*Le fils*]. Dir. Jean-Pierre and Luc Dardenne (Belgium, 2002)
The Sopranos [TV series]. Creator David Chase (USA 1999–2007)
Standard Operating Procedure. Dir. Errol Morris (USA, 2008)
Stella Dallas. Dir. King Vidor (USA, 1937)
Stromboli. Dir. Roberto Rossellini (Italy/USA, 1950)
Talk to Her [*Hable con ella*]. Dir. Pedro Almodóvar (Spain, 2002)
Taste of Cherry [*Ta'm e guilass*]. Dir. Abbas Kiarostami (Iran/France, 1997)
Taxi Driver. Dir. Martin Scorsese (USA, 1976)
Tehran Taxi. Dir. Jafar Panahi (Iran, 2015)
Ten Canoes. Dir. Rolf de Heer and Peter Djigirr (Australia, 2006)
The Thin Blue Line. Dir. Errol Morris (USA, 1988)

The Thin Red Line. Dir. Terrence Malick (USA, 1998)

The Third Man. Dir. Carol Reed (UK, 1949)

This is Not a Film [In film nist]. Dir. Mojtaba Mirtahmasb, Jafar Panahi (Iran, 2011)

Three Colours: Blue [Trois couleurs: Bleu]. Dir. Krzysztof Kieslowski (France/Poland/ Switzerland, 1993)

To the Wonder. Dir. Terrence Malick (USA, 2012)

Tokyo Story [Tokyo monogatari]. Dir. Yasujiro Ozu (Japan, 1953)

Total Recall. Dir. Paul Verhoeven (USA, 1990)

The Treachery of the September 30th Movement of the Indonesian Communist Party [Treachery of the G30S/PKI / Pengkhianatan G30S/PKI]. Dir. Arifin C. Noer (Indonesia, 1984)

The Tree of Life. Dir. Terrence Malick (USA, 2011)

True Detective [TV series]. Creator Nic Pizzolatto (USA, 2014–)

Twin Peaks [TV series]. Creators Mark Frost and David Lynch (USA, 1990–1991)

Two Days, One Night [Deux jours, une nuit]. Dir. Jean-Pierre and Luc Dardenne (Belgium, 2014)

Ulysses' Gaze [To vlemma tou Odyssea]. Dir. Theo Angelopolos. (Greece/France/Italy/Germany/UK/Federal Republic of Yugoslavia/Bosnia and Herzegovina/Albania/Romania, 1995)

Umberto D. Dir. Vittorio De Sica (Italy, 1952)

Unforgiven. Dir. Clint Eastwood (USA, 1992)

The Unknown. Dir. Tod Browning (USA, 1927)

The Unknown Known. Dir. Errol Morris (USA, 2013)

Upstream Color. Dir. Shane Carruth (USA, 2013)

The Virgin Suicides. Dir. Sofia Coppola (USA, 1999)

Viridiana. Dir. Luis Buñuel (Spain/Mexico, 1961)

Waltz with Bashir [Vals Im Bashir]. Dir. Ari Folman (Israel/France/Germany/USA/Finland, 2008)

The White Ribbon [Das weiße Band – Eine deutsche Kindergeschichte]. Dir. Michael Haneke (Germany/Austria/France/Italy, 2009)

The Wind Will Carry Us [Bad ma ra khahad bord]. Dir. Abbas Kiarostami (Iran/France, 1999)

The Wire [TV series]. Creator David Simon (USA, 2002–2008)

Young Adult. Dir. Jason Reitman (USA, 2011)

Zero Dark Thirty. Dir. Kathryn Bigelow (USA, 2012)

Index